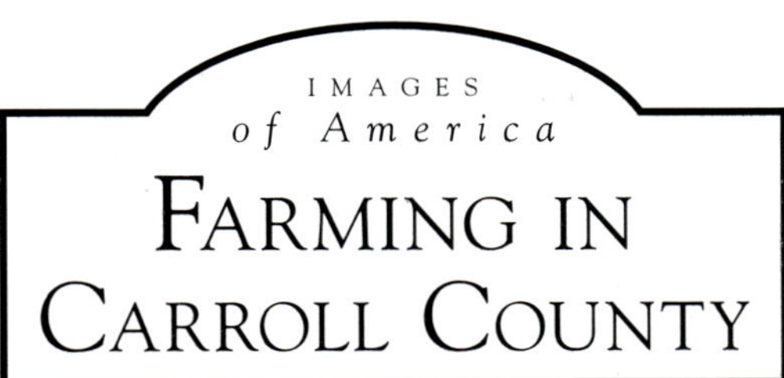

From Earl

Christmas 2010

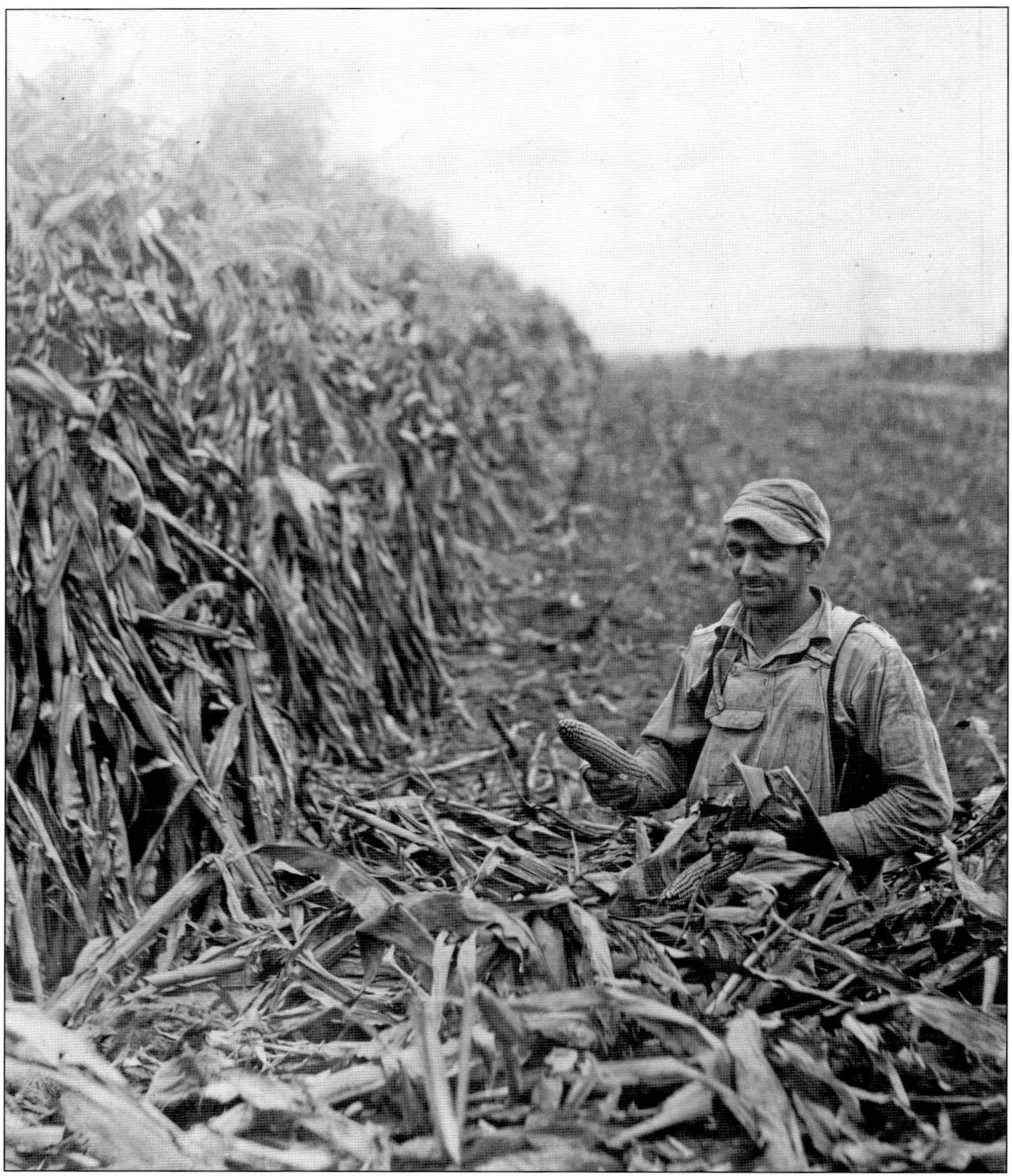

Hubert Jacob Null of Taneytown is husking corn in the late 1940s. According to the U.S. Census in 1950, the county agent's report noted that there were 2,766 farms, averaging 91.3 acres, with a value of produce of $4,134 per farm. Carroll County led the 23 counties in Maryland in the production of corn, barley, peas, mature chickens, and eggs. Ninety-three percent of the farms had electricity. (Courtesy of the Null family.)

On the Cover: These farmers are baling hay on the Hoke farm in Bachman Valley. The tractor driver is Grace Hoke, and from left to right are Fannie Mae Hoke, Ethel Ward (standing), Florence Hoke Wolfe, and S. L. Hoke Sr. in 1942. (Courtesy of the University of Maryland Extension Service, Carroll County.)

IMAGES
of America

FARMING IN CARROLL COUNTY

Lyndi McNulty

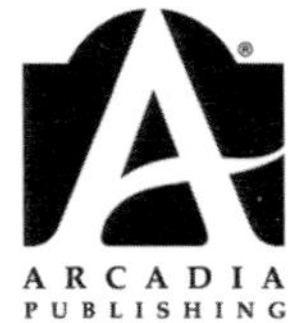

ISBN 978-0-7385-6833-3

Published by Arcadia Publishing
Charleston SC, Chicago IL, Portsmouth NH, San Francisco CA

Printed in the United States of America

Library of Congress Control Number: 2008937256

For all general information contact Arcadia Publishing at:
Telephone 843-853-2070
Fax 843-853-0044
E-mail sales@arcadiapublishing.com
For customer service and orders:
Toll-Free 1-888-313-2665

Visit us on the Internet at www.arcadiapublishing.com

In memory of Betty Stevenson McNulty.

Contents

Acknowledgments

A country drive through Carroll County today will reward one with views of landscapes filled with pristine farms, cows leisurely grazing in the field, and fields of corn as far as the eye can see. A stop for homemade ice cream is a must.

My family has been here since the early 1700s. My great-grandfather owned seven farms in the county, and my grandfather grew up on a farm just on the outskirts of Westminster. Attending farm auctions with my mother, Betty Stevenson McNulty, when I grew up, I found a love of old farm implements that led me to become a farm museum curator and design farm exhibits for Carroll County, Baltimore County, and Frederick County Museums.

This book began as a history of farming in Carroll County, but after visiting farm families throughout the county, convincing them to pull their old photographs from albums, walls, and attics, the book became about them. This book is a tribute to the farm families of Carroll County. Royalties from this book will be donated to the historical societies of Carroll County and local farm-related groups.

A special thank-you goes to James C. Voter, U.S. Navy (Retired), who spent hundreds of hours with me researching, interviewing farm families, compiling 2,600 photographs, and supplying technical support. Voter spent 24 years in the U.S. Navy and during his career was captain of the USS *Von Steuben* submarine. His family roots are in Maine, where he worked in the summers on Voter Hill farm. The farm was passed down through five generations to his great-uncle. In high school, he worked on the Kuerner farm, of Andrew Wyeth fame, that was the property next to his home in Chadds Ford, Pennsylvania. Today he is a resident of Carroll County.

Others who must be thanked include Cathy Baty (curator of the Historical Society of Carroll County), Brian Butler (University of Maryland Cooperative Extension, Carroll County), Nancy Eyler (Taneytown History Museum), Kari Greenwalt and Erroll Smith (director and curator of the Sykesville Gatehouse Museum, respectively), Mike Eacho (Historical Society of Mount Airy), Bryce Workman (New Windsor Heritage Committee), Julia Berwager (Manchester Historical Center), and the farm families of Carroll County.

Introduction

Roadside farm stands in August boast large, ripe tomatoes, squash, and cucumbers grown on local farms. Here and there, a produce stand is just a table with a cardboard box for money, a traditional honor system in Carroll County for purchasing extra vegetables from small local farms. Traditions live on in Carroll County, where often things are still done the old way, as neighbors stop by Grace Weant's farm in Harney to leave their money on her porch for her brown eggs, recycling their egg boxes.

Carroll County boasts many achievements in farming history. One of the most important was the invention of the first self-raking reaper by Jacob R. Thomas in Union Bridge, demonstrated in 1811.

Carroll County was the home of the first complete county Rural Free Delivery Service in the United States in 1899.

R. Wyndham Walden moved to Middleburg in 1872 and established one of the top Thoroughbred horse farms in the late 19th century in America at Bowlingbrook. Horses he bred and trained won more than 1,000 races. Walden was inducted into the National Racing Hall of Fame.

Carroll County produced the world supply of wormseed oil, used as a hookworm remedy and wood preservative.

After World War II, the farm of W. Roger and Olive V. Roop on Middleburg Road in Union Bridge was the gathering place for the international Heifer Project.

In the early days, farms in Carroll County were sustenance farms. Farmers were able to raise enough to feed their families and, sometimes, a little money for needed supplies. Working long hours in snow and rain, and with sheer determination, they raised crops and farm animals. With technological advances, improved farm practices, the use of fertilizers and insecticides, and the construction of local canning factories, the farm business grew and prospered. Farmers had successes working in co-ops and organizations with other farmers. As a result, Carroll County farms supplied milk, produce, beef, and eggs to nearby cities.

In 1941, the county agent reported that Carroll County ranked first in the state in eggs produced, first in the number of chickens, first in the production of corn, and third in the amount of milk produced. Eighty-five percent of the wealth in the county was in agriculture, and 93 percent of the land was in farms.

This book illustrates, with photographs and personal stories, the journey of Carroll County farm families throughout the last century. These families loved farming, its hard work, and its triumphs. As you peruse the photographs in this book, you will see firsthand the faces of the farmers who contributed to Carroll's farming heritage.

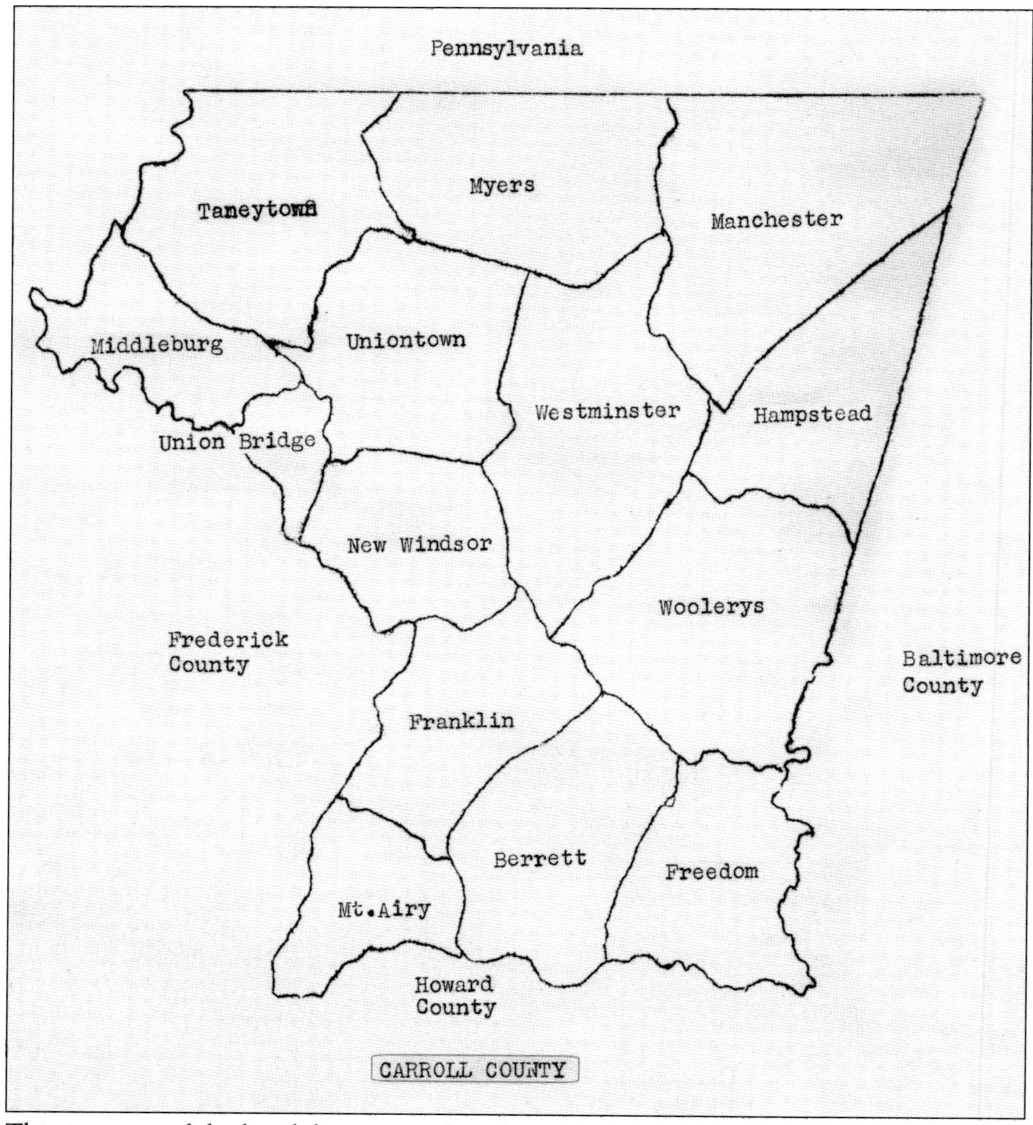

This is a copy of the hand-drawn map that the county extension agent used to illustrate his annual report starting in 1932. (Courtesy of the University of Maryland Cooperative Extension, Carroll County.)

One

The Family Farm

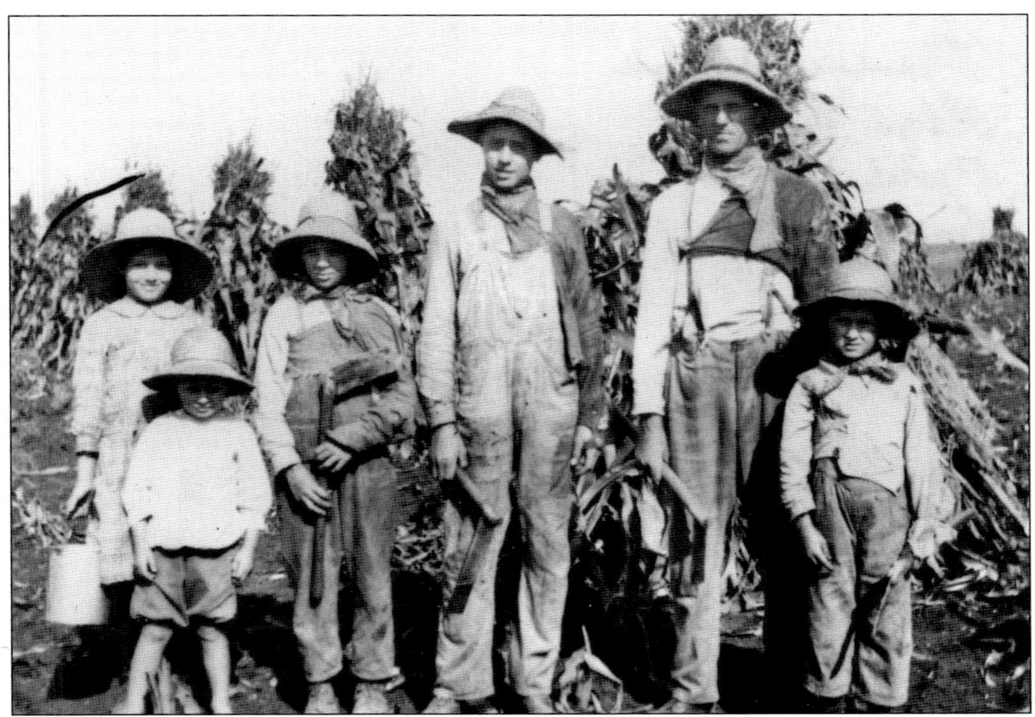

In 1918, on Thanksgiving Day, when the children were home from school, the Wilhide family of Keysville harvested corn. An old pants leg, slipped over their shoulders, protected their clothing from the sharp stalks and kept dirt from going down their necks. They held 20 pounds of stalks in their left arm while cutting it with a corn chopper with their other hand. Big hats kept the corn from cutting their faces. Their mother, May Wilhide, brought their fried chicken dinner to the field. Pictured, from left to right, are children Louise, Clyde, Mehrle, Lloyd, and Maurice with their father, Carroll Wilhide (second from right). (Courtesy of the Wilhide family.)

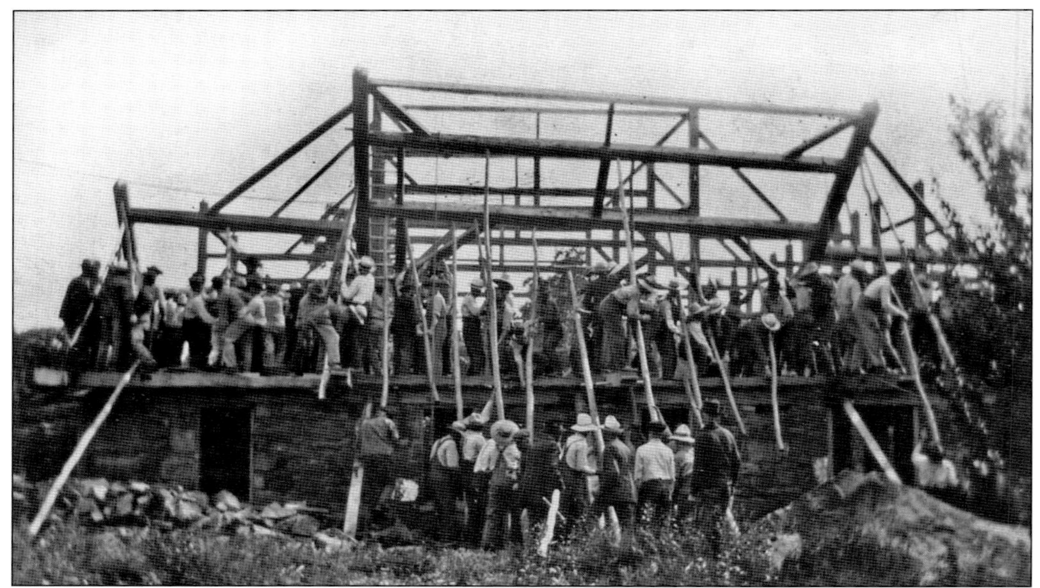

Men are raising Peter Wilhide's barn in Keysville around 1925. It was common for neighbors and relatives to help raise the barn. Farm women had special recipes to feed so many people. (Courtesy of Mildred Stine.)

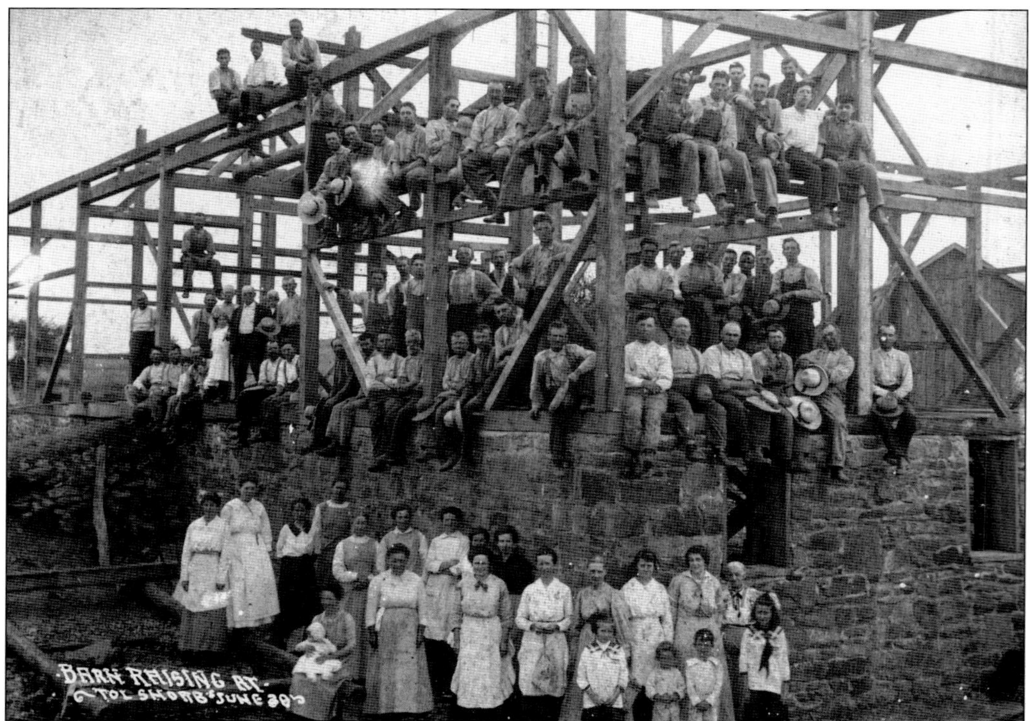

James Tolbert Garfield Shorb built this barn on his farm near Piney Creek in 1916. The barn is still standing between Keysville and Taneytown off Roop Road. Shorb is standing dead center in this photograph. (Courtesy of the Steffen family.)

Hubert Null is pictured on the Jacob Null farm riding a draft horse around 1914 in Taneytown. This is a Century Farm in Carroll County, a farm owned by the same family for at least 100 years that is still being farmed. The original 50 acres were purchased by Michael Null for 150£ from Daniel Brown. (Courtesy of the Null family.)

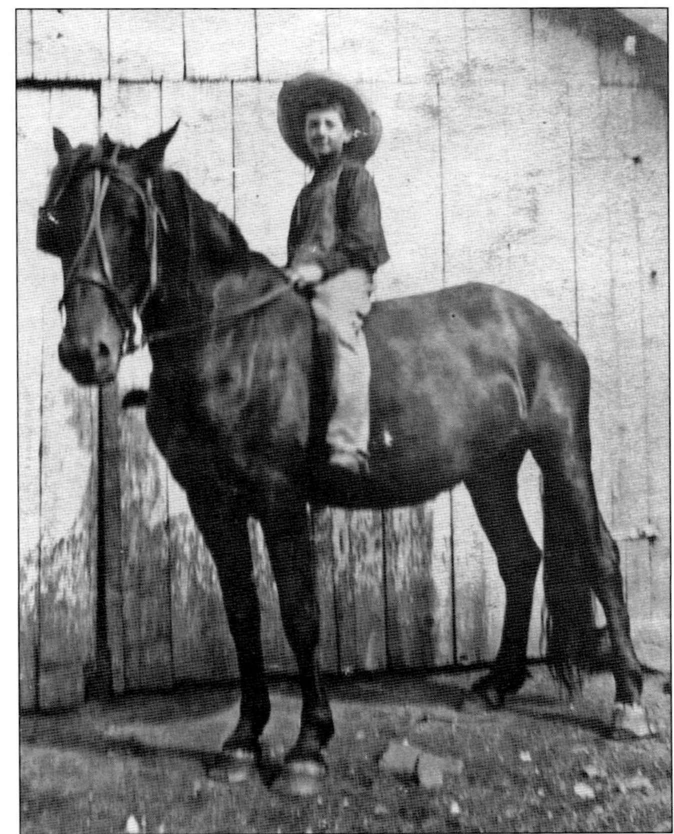

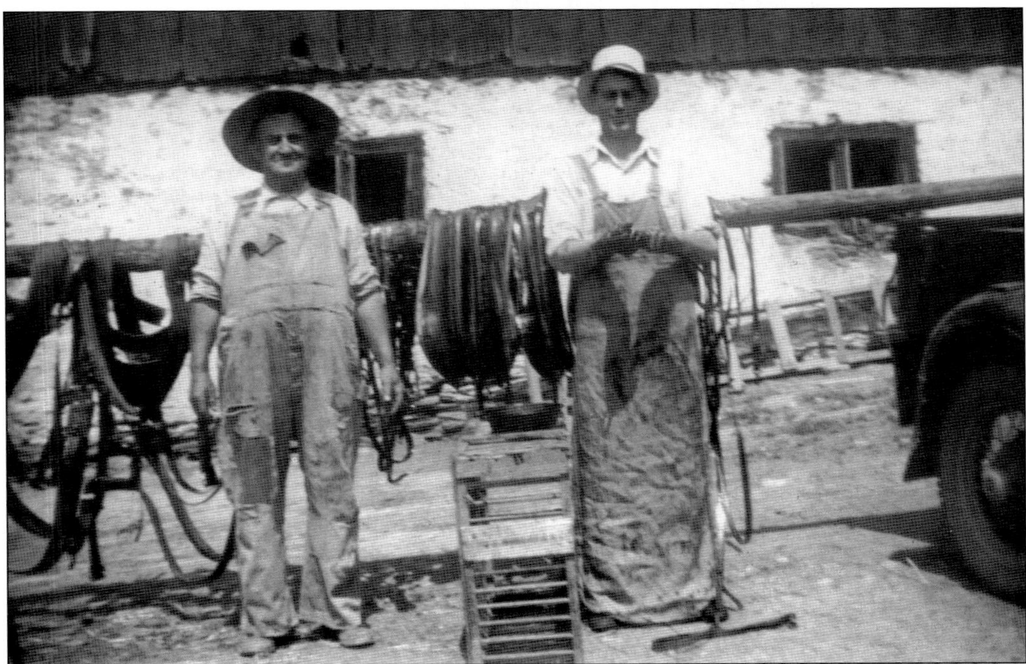

Francis Hoff and his son Herman Hoff are pictured greasing harnesses around 1940 in Gamber. (Courtesy of the Hoff family.)

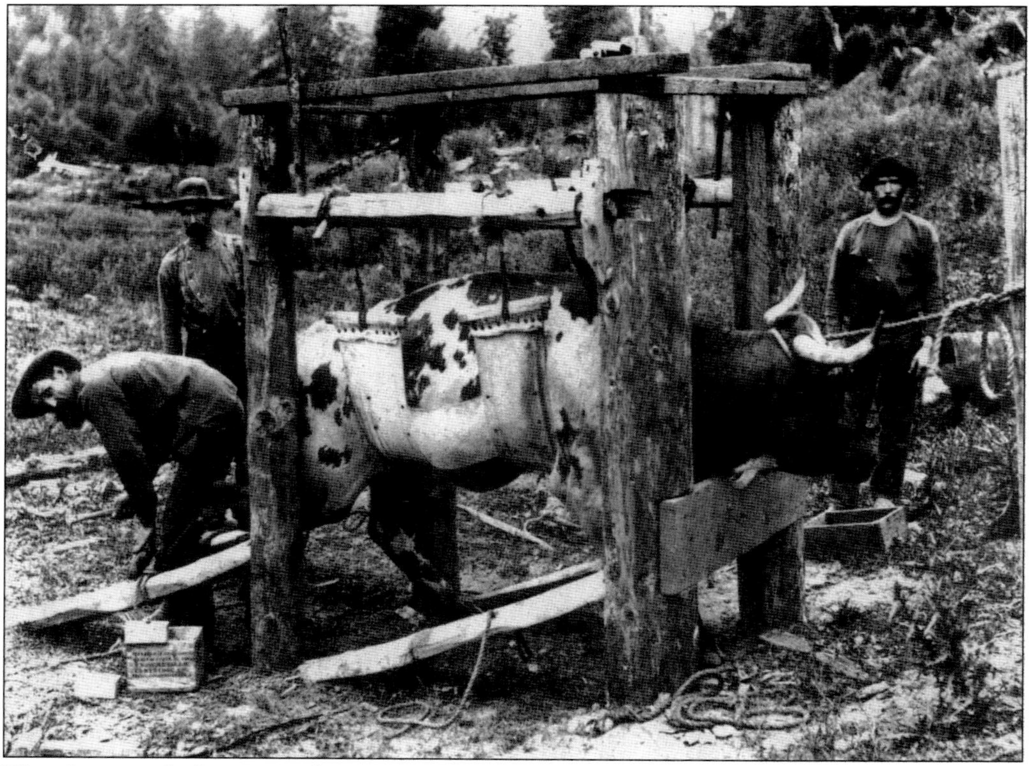

This photograph shows men shoeing an ox in the 19th-century Sykesville area. It was not an easy task. (Courtesy of the Sykesville Gate House Museum.)

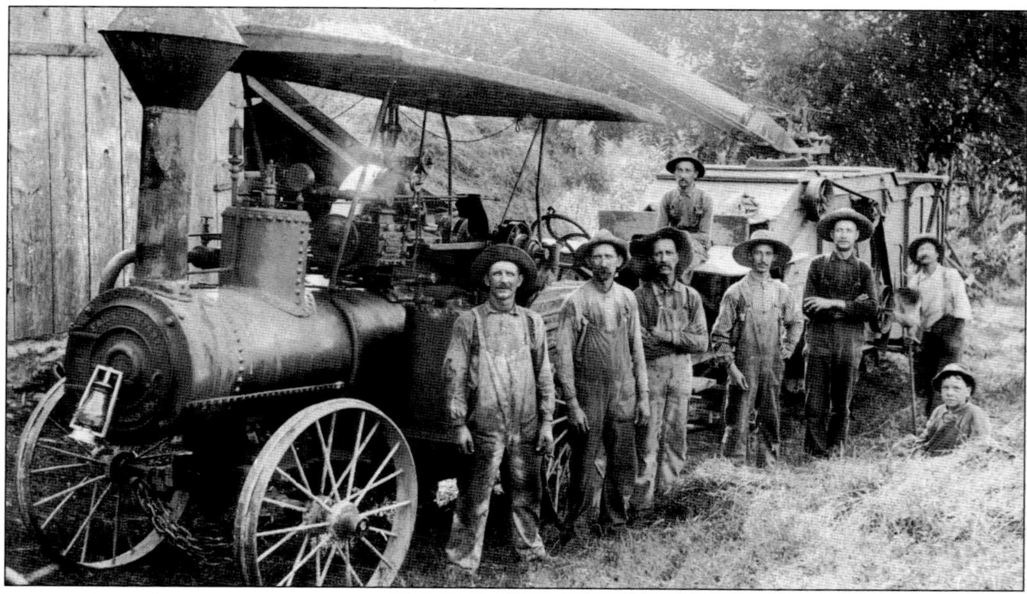

This early-19th-century photograph shows David Helwig's Frick steam engine and his thresher being used on a farm in the Murkle Road area. Helwig used his equipment to thresh other farmers' crops, a common practice during the late 1800s and early 1900s. Local farmers always helped each other. From left to right are David Helwig, Nathaniel Zepp, and other farmers from the area. (Photograph by Theodore J. Myers; courtesy of Catherine Zepp Miller.)

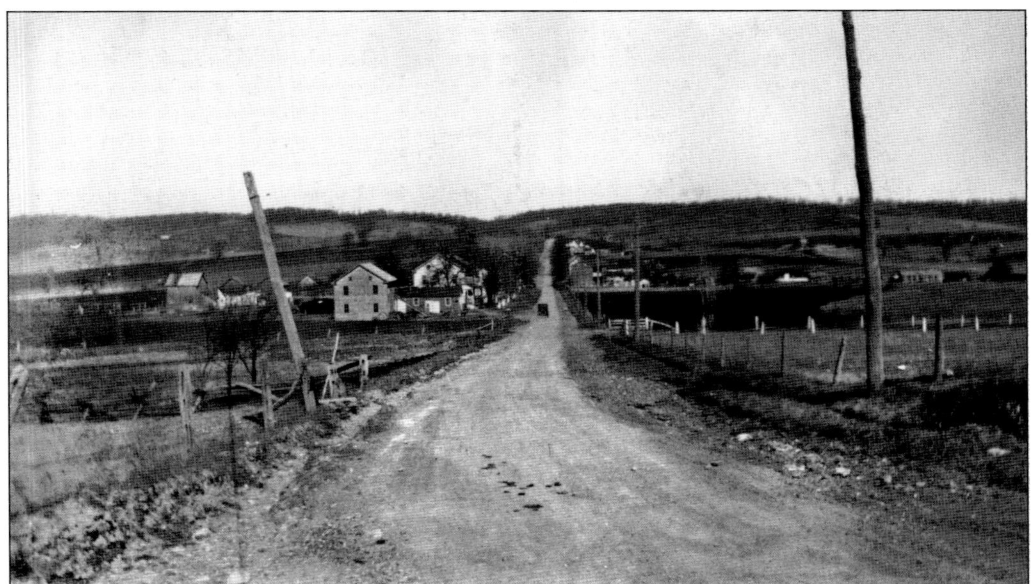

In the 19th and early 20th centuries, many farms in Carroll County were isolated by poor dirt roads. This photograph shows the back view from the Tracy Farm. The road leads to Melrose. (Courtesy of Helen Shaeffer Totura.)

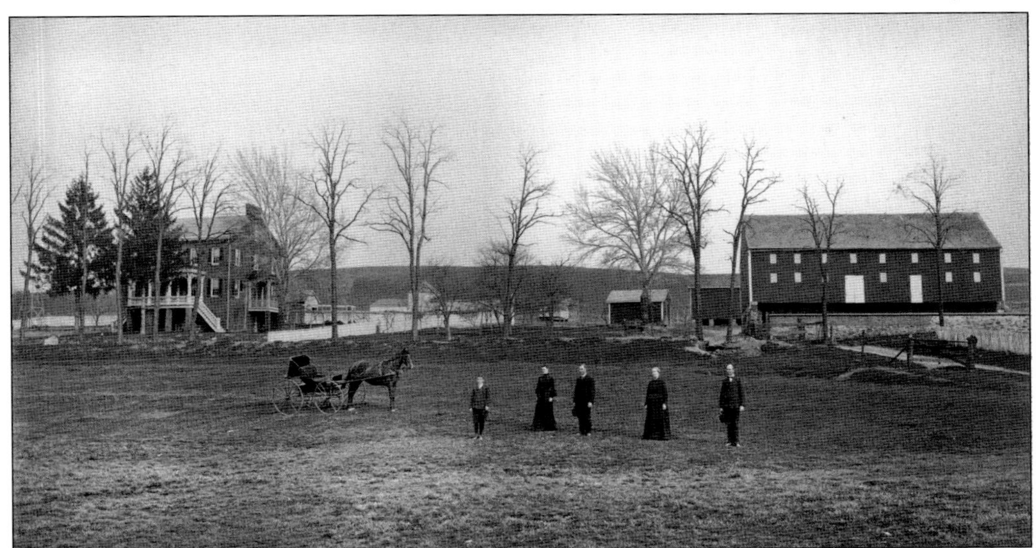

The J. Elhannon Englar family is pictured on their New Windsor farm in the late 1800s. The Englars built the barn in 1863 and the house in 1873. It was common for farmers to build the barn before the house because their livelihood depended on their crops and animals. Englar was also a miller and built a mill on the property. Richard Snader (Englar's grandson and the fourth generation) and Trudy Jo Hahn Snader own the farm today. (Courtesy of the Snader family.)

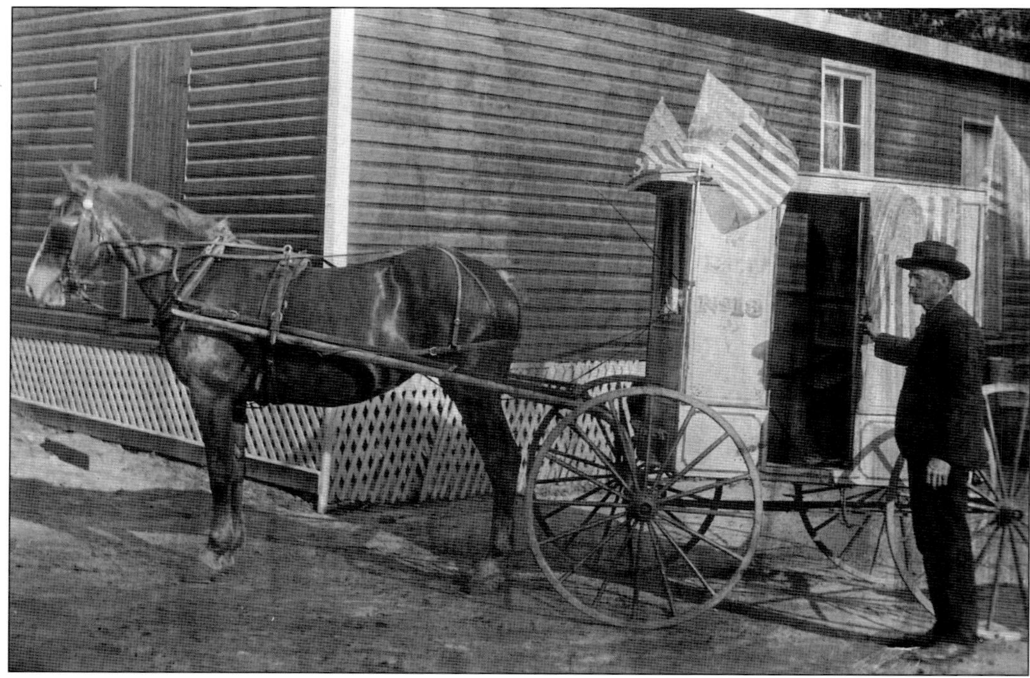

On December 20, 1899, Carroll County became the first county to have complete Rural Free Delivery. Philetus Haight stands beside a Rural Free Delivery (RFD) wagon in December 1899. Beginning in Oakland at 6:00 a.m., he carried the mail to Haight, Eldersburg, and Sykesville, covering 19 miles. (Courtesy of the Historical Society of Carroll County.)

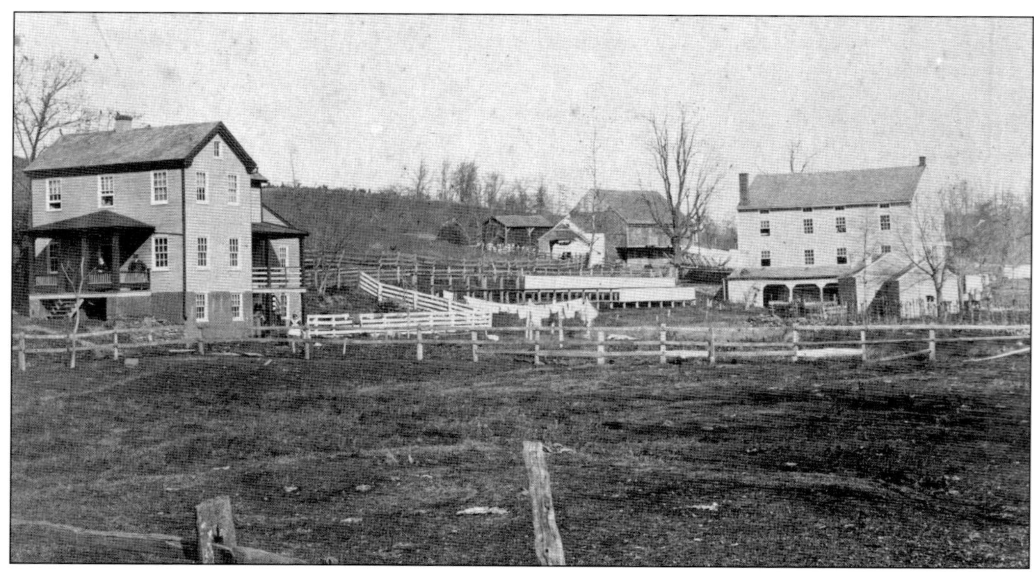

This is a late-1800s photograph of the Hibberd Mill. The Hibberds were a Quaker family of millers who arrived in New Windsor (then a part of Frederick County) in 1796. In addition to grinding grain, the family wove merino wool and sawed lumber. The mill building, in the background on the right, was torn down in 1919. (Courtesy of G. Hibberd.)

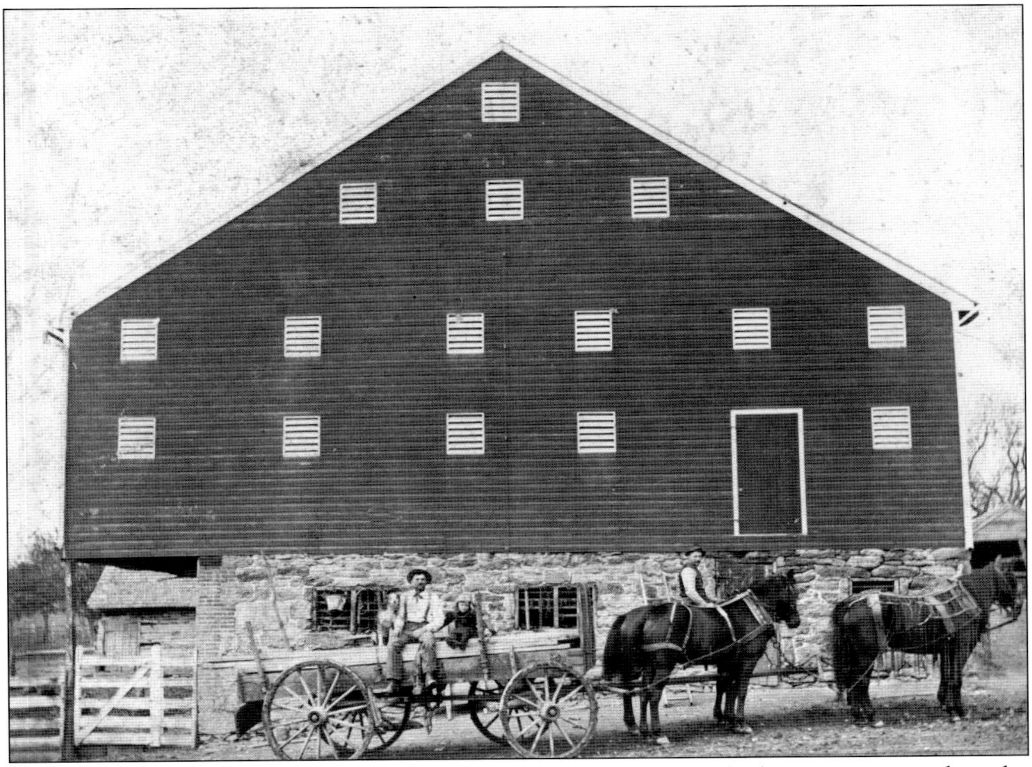

Denton S. Warehime (on the wagon) and a hired hand sitting on the horse are pictured on the Walter and Norma Warehime farm in 1910 on Old Bachmans Valley Road. (Courtesy of the Shipley family.)

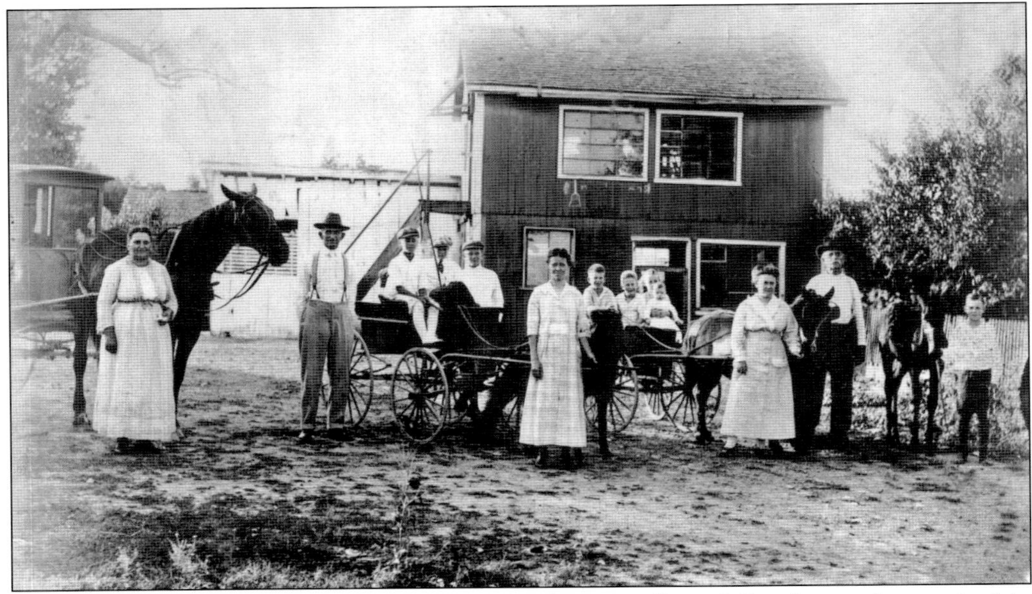

This is an early photograph of the Ed Burns family in Smallwood. Family members arrived in buggies and farm wagons. (Courtesy of Donald Dell.)

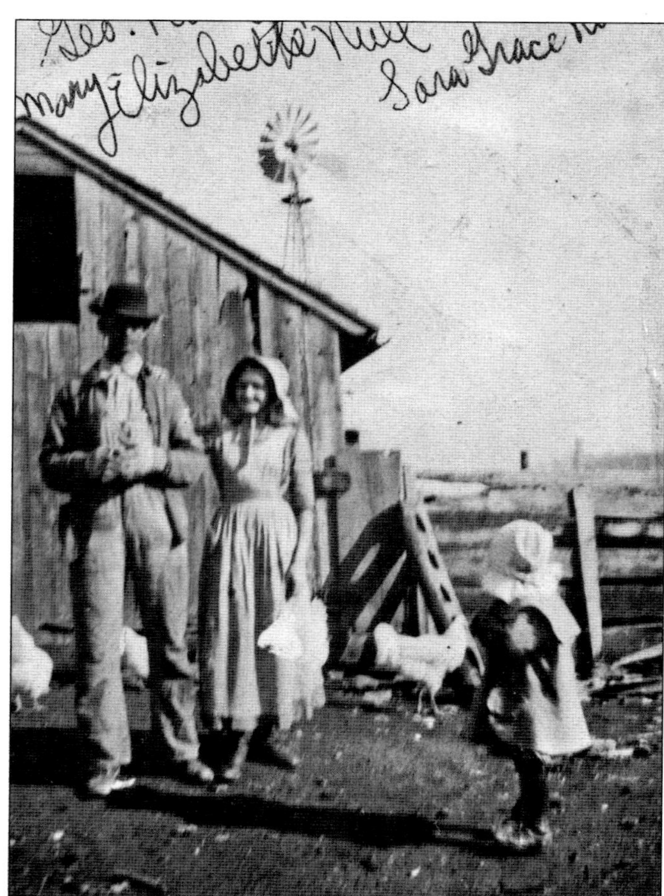

From left to right, George Null, Mary Elizabeth Null, and Sara Grace Null are pictured on the Jacob Null farm around 1915. In 1976, the Null farm was recognized by the Department of Agriculture as a "Bicentennial" farm, meaning that is has been in the family for at least 200 years and since the signing of the U.S. Constitution. Windmills, like the one in the background, provided power to pump water from deep underground to the house or barn. Early windmills had blades made out of wood. In the late 1800s, Thomas Perry designed sheet metal sails that doubled the efficiency of the windmill and are still used today. (Courtesy of the Null family.)

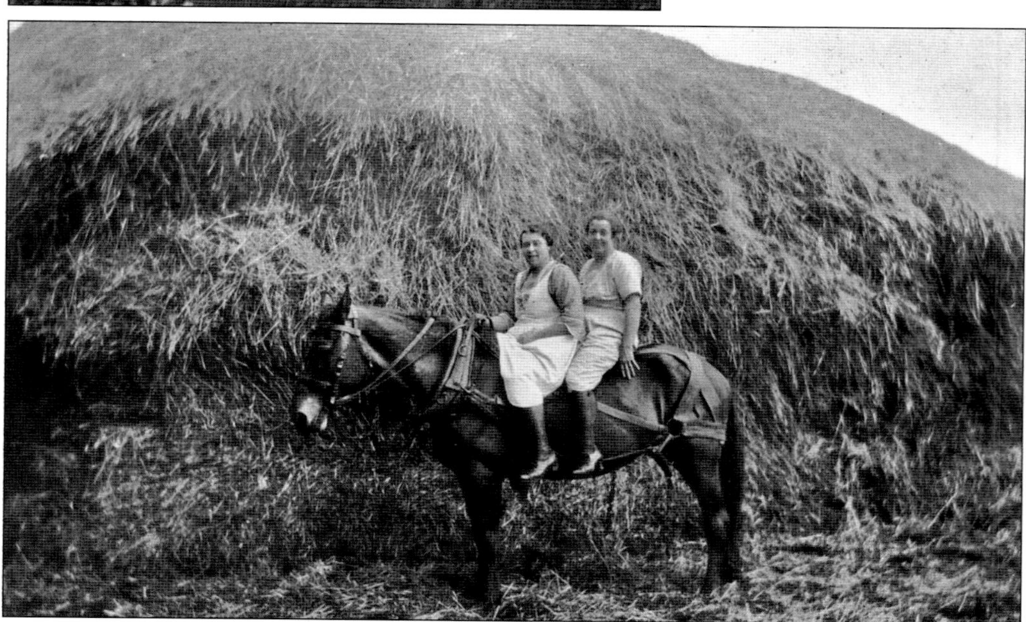

Rosella Hess Stull (left) and her sister Henrietta Hess Koontz posed for a photograph on a work horse beside a mammoth straw stack on the Stull farm in Keysville. (Courtesy of Mildred Stine.)

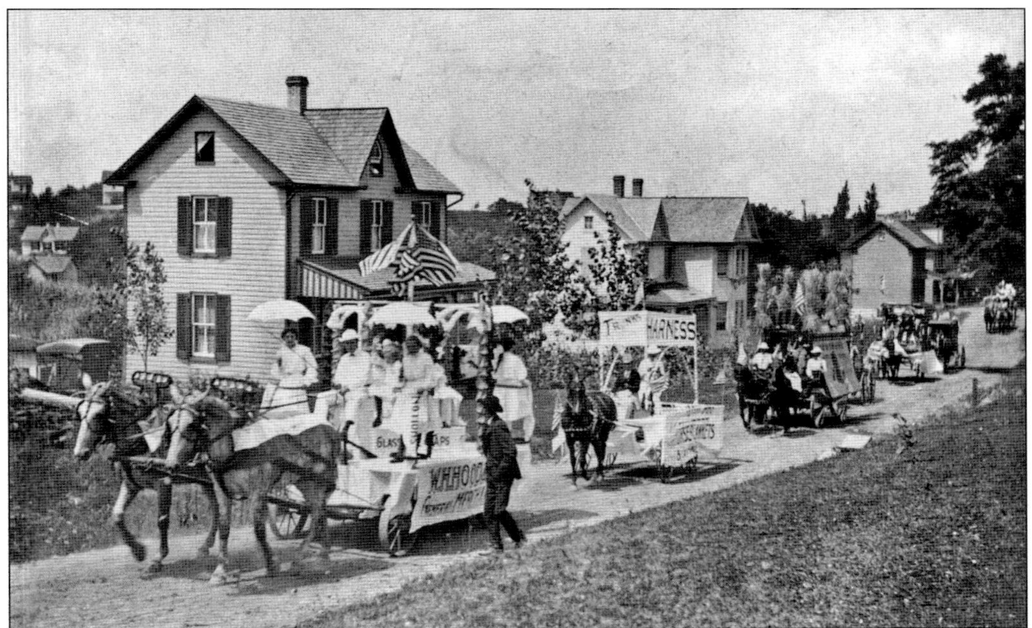

On August 18, 1905, the Farmers Parade in Mount Airy came down Park Avenue at Dorsey Avenue. The parade included a homemakers float, a harness makers float, and a hay float. (Courtesy of the Historical Society of Mount Airy, Maryland.)

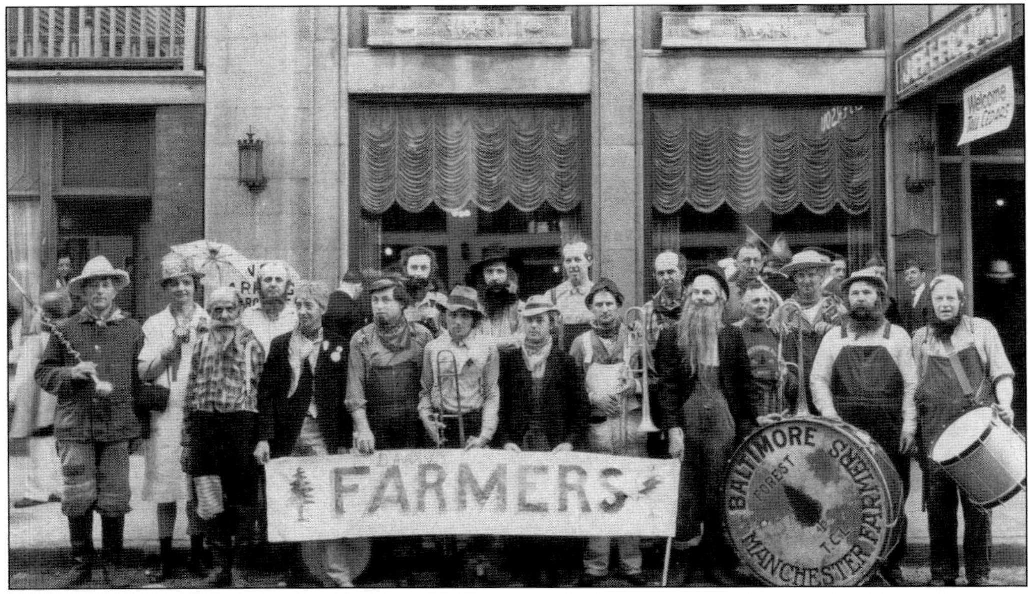

The Farmers Band in Manchester was associated with the Baltimore Forest Tall Cedars League. Civic and fraternal organizations, as well as businesses, often sponsored musical groups. In Westminster, the William F. Myers Marching Band was sponsored by the butchering business. (Courtesy of the Manchester Historical Center and the Joe Getty family.)

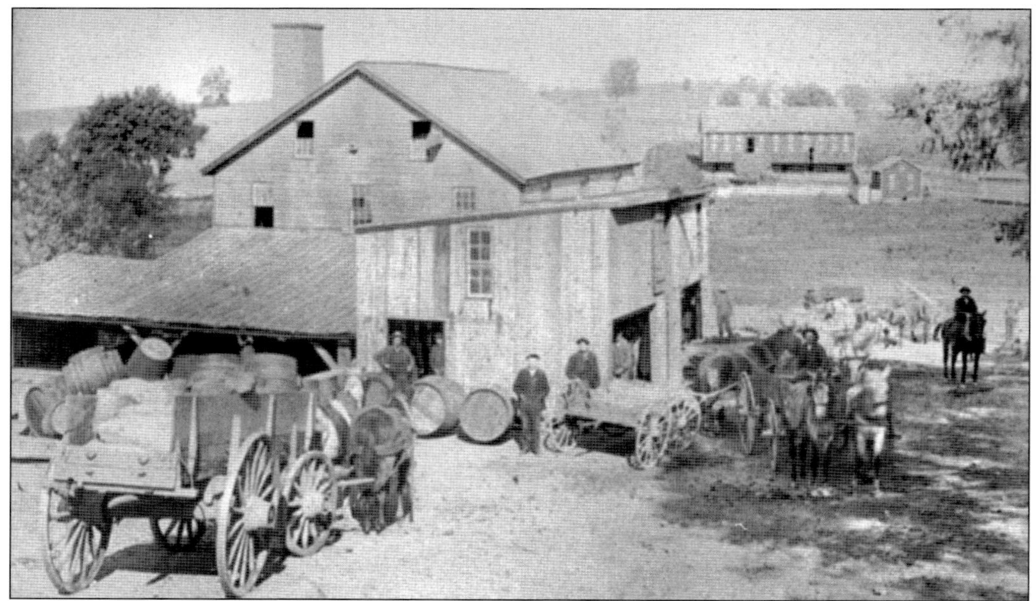

This is a view of Joseph P. Yingling's cider and vinegar mills in the village of Pleasant Valley. He had a 200-acre farm with an extensive apple orchard outside of the village. In addition, many farm families lined up around the mills on special days and had their own apples processed. The Yingling mill also made apple butter for each family according to their own family recipe. (Courtesy of Dennis N. Yingling.)

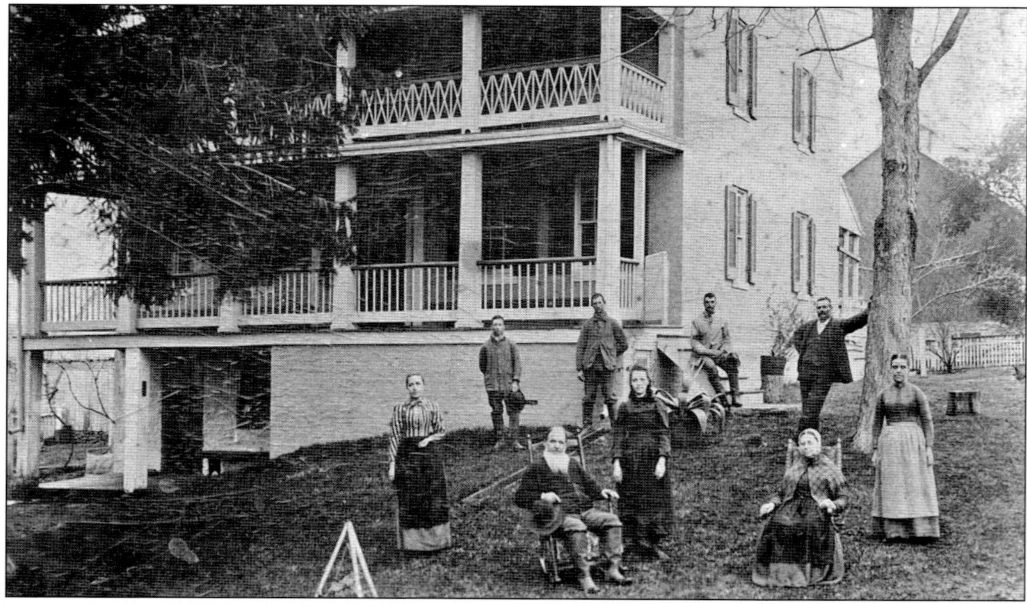

The Roop family poses for a photograph in 1895 at their Uniontown Road farm. Pictured are (first row) David and Henrietta Ocker Roop; (second row) their daughters Anna and Fanny and unidentified; (third row) three unidentified farmhands and H. Scott Roop. In 1886, H. Scott Roop (standing by the tree) planted a mahogany bean tree (Kentucky coffee bean) tree that is seen in the photograph. The farm was purchased from Dr. Thomas Boyer by David Roop in 1832. At that time, the farm was part of Frederick County; in 1883, the farm was passed to David J. Roop and then to Scott and Kate Roop in 1922. (Courtesy of the Historical Society of Carroll County.)

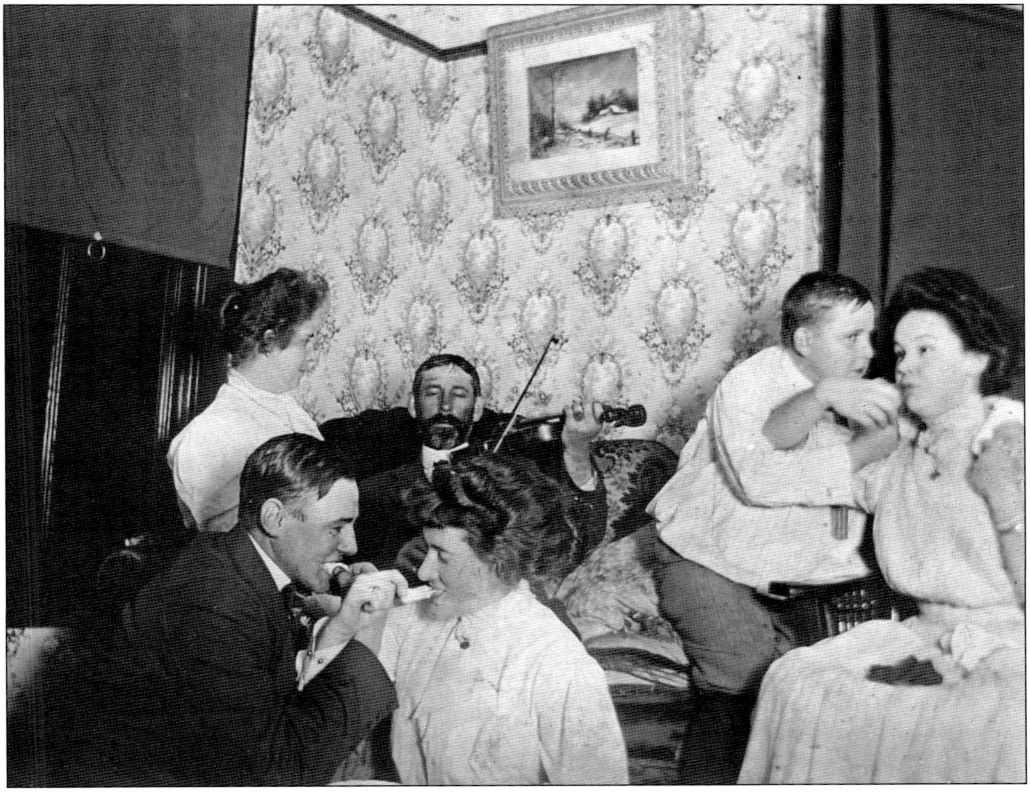

An early-1900s farm family gathers in Carroll County. The man with the violin was farmer Abdiel Bollinger. (Courtesy of Edna Bollinger.)

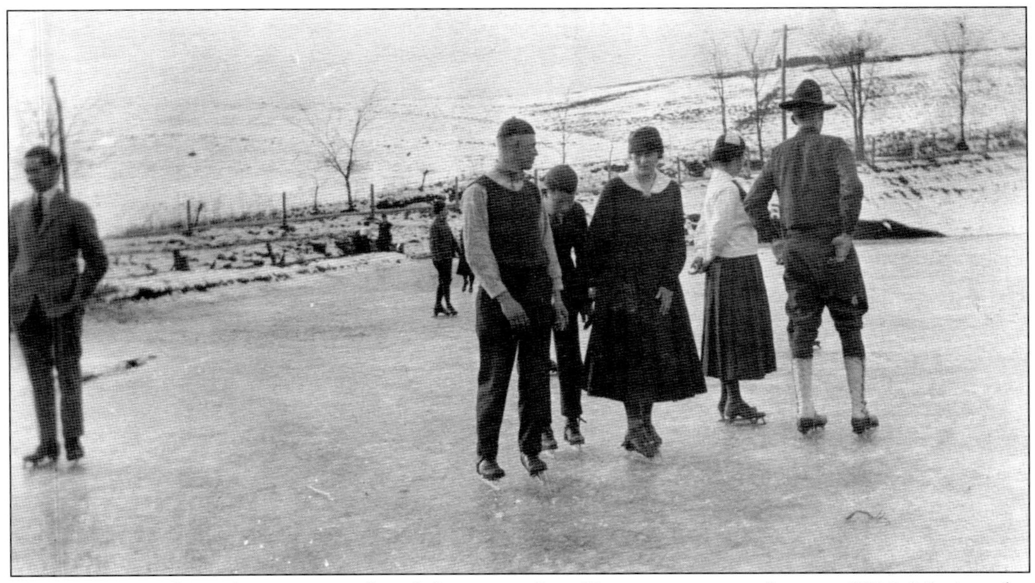

This picture of ice-skating on a local farm pond in Dennings was taken in 1916. Notice the man wearing the World War I army uniform and one man wearing a suit and tie while skating. (Courtesy of Judy Naill.)

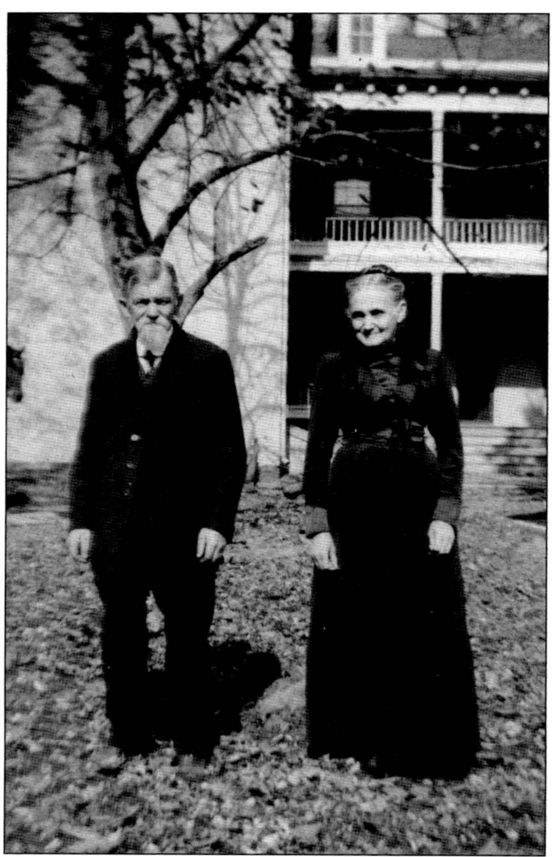

Successful farmers Alfred Stevenson and his wife, Helen Alice Schweigart Stevenson, are pictured in 1915 on one of their seven farms in the Westminster area. The Stevensons had 10 children. Big families were common on family farms. (Courtesy of Lyndi McNulty.)

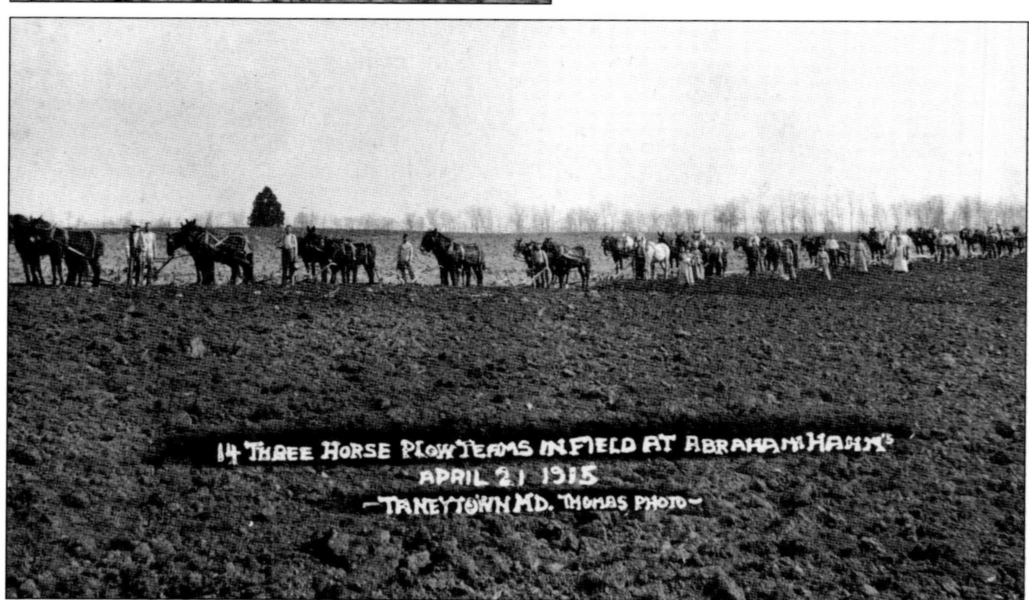

Taken on April 21, 1915, this is a photograph of 14 three-horse plow teams on the Taneytown farm worked by Abraham Hahn (a tenant farmer) and owned by the Crapsters. They were plowing a cornfield in Taneytown. Abraham Hahn was ill, so his neighbors and family came to plow the fields. (Courtesy of the Carroll Hahn family.)

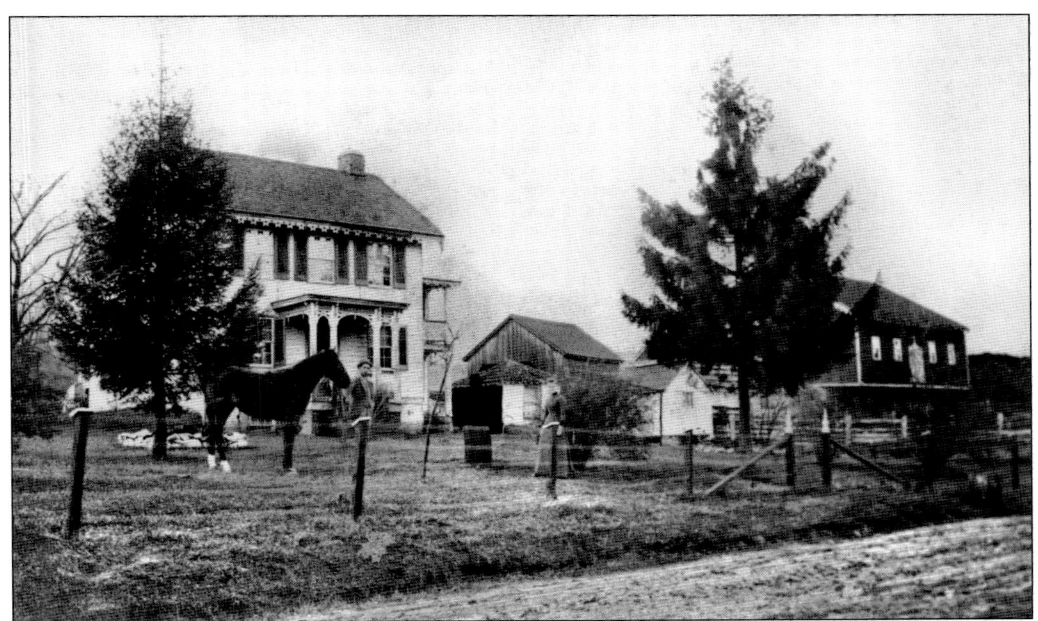

In 1890, Jackson and Florence Myerly stand in front of their farm, now at the intersection of Bond Street and Route 27. George Harris and Katie Myerly, their daughter, ran a dairy farm there from World War II until 1963. George and Katie's son George and Mildred Harris raised chickens and sold eggs until the 1980s. Today Kenneth Harris and his family raise and sell vegetables from a roadside stand at their family farm. The original spring still waters the vegetables. (Courtesy of Kenneth and Barbara Harris.)

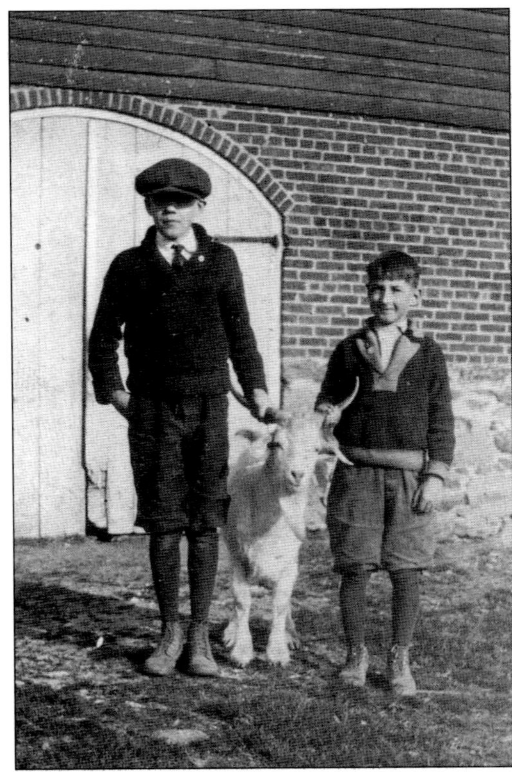

Theodore W. Owings (left) and Chris Owings are pictured on a visit to the John Owings farm near Warfieldsburg in 1920. They are standing with a pet goat. (Courtesy of Virginia Lambert.)

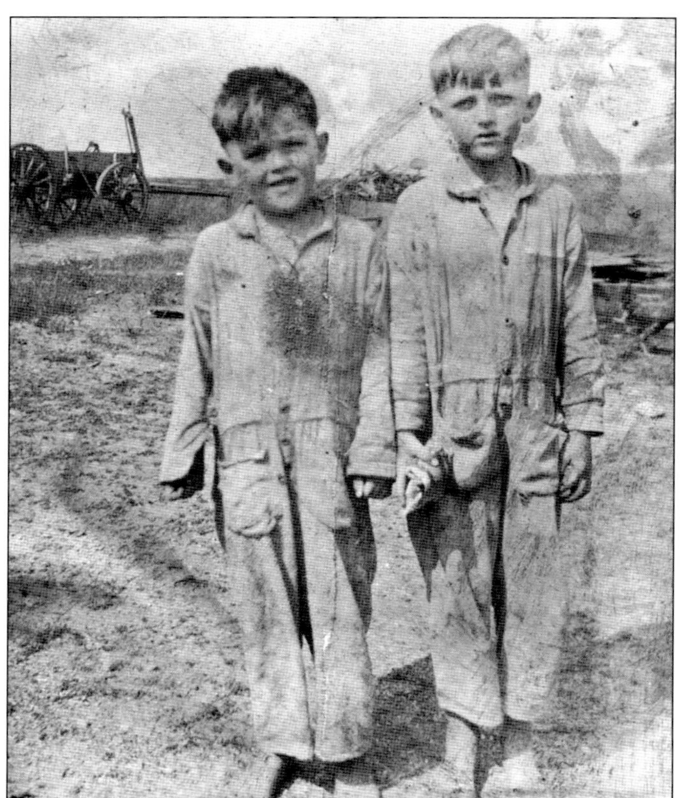

Stanley Bollinger (left) and Edward Bollinger Jr., farm boys, have their picture taken on one of the three Edward and Jeanette Bollinger farms around 1927. Jeanette gave Edward the rag in his hand and told him to wipe off his little brother Stanley's face for the photograph. (Courtesy of Edna Bollinger.)

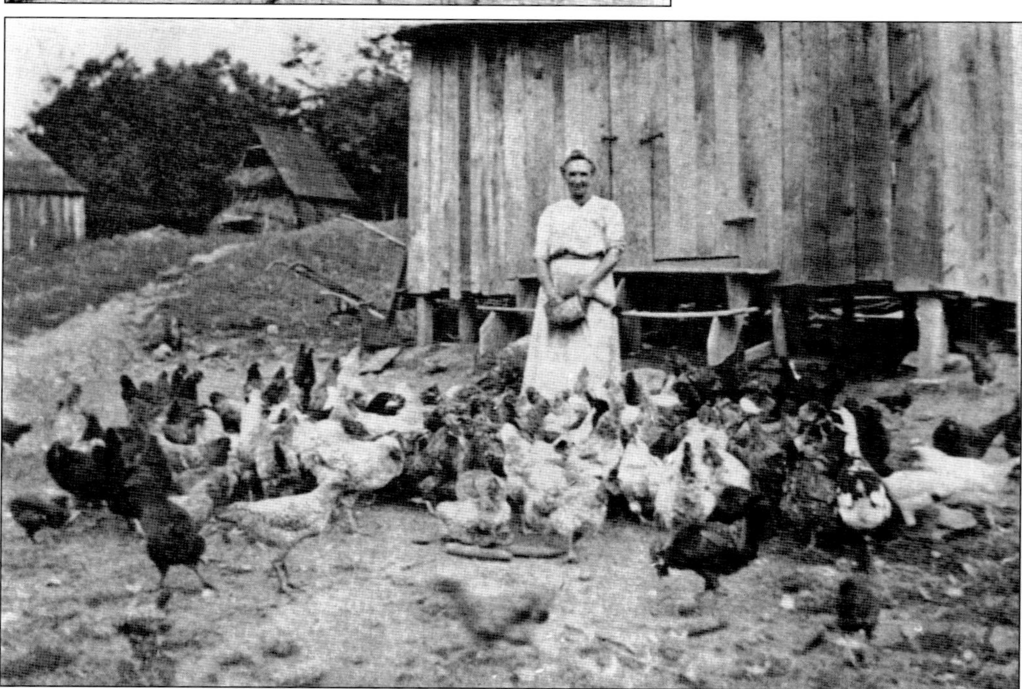

Eva Baginsky, born in Poland around 1920, is pictured in a barnyard in Sykesville, Maryland. Chickens roamed free in the barnyards in the 19th and early 20th centuries. (Courtesy of the Sykesville Gate House Museum.)

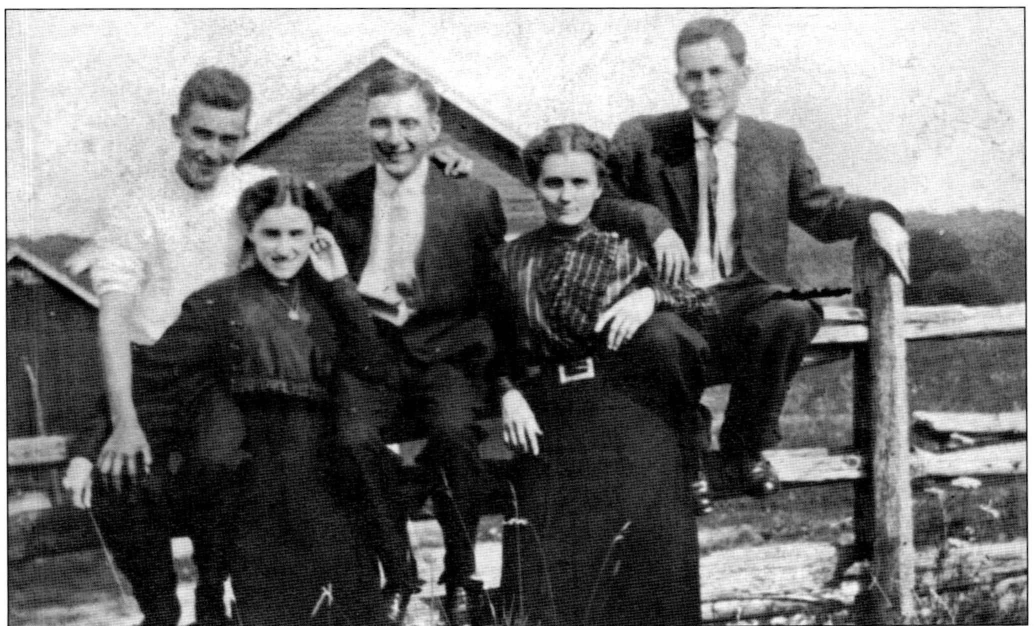

In 1928, Cora Anders and cabinetmaker Tim Anders of Westminster (left), Emory and Myrtle Berwager (center), and Fred Mathias of Westminster (right), enjoy themselves at the Leister/Mathias reunion on the Grover/Morelock Farm near Frizzellburg and Taneytown. Still popular today, reunions were a rare chance for leisure for farm families and allowed them to exchange news and stay close. (Courtesy of Gary R. Brauning.)

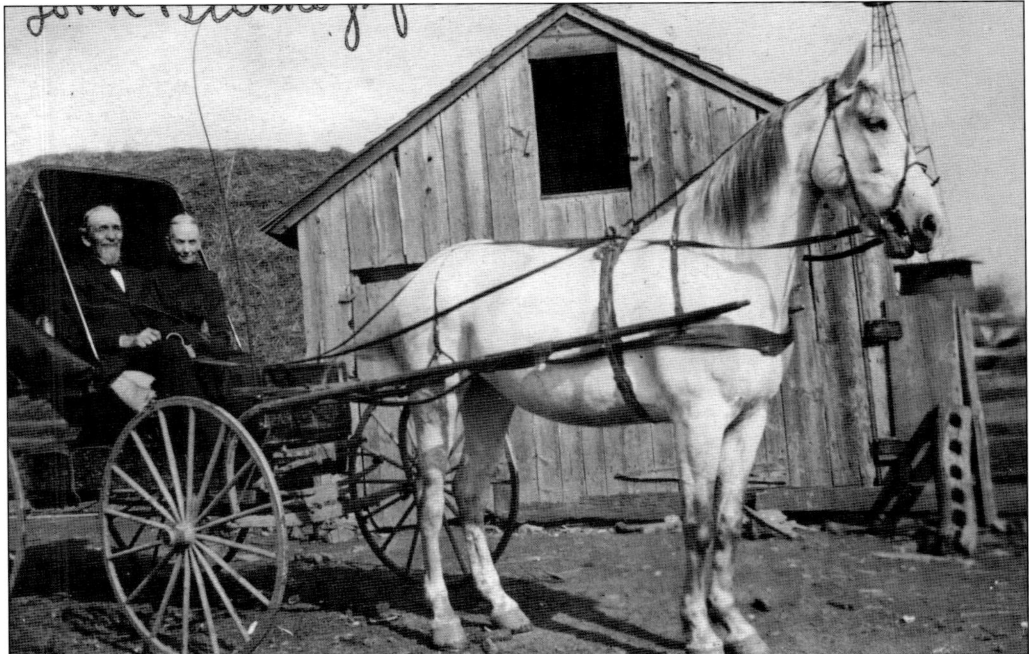

Luther (left) and Alice Bushey are pictured visiting their friends on the Jacob Null farm in Taneytown around 1912. Before 1812, the Bushey family took over the Forest Farm on Bushey Road in Winfield. The farm was originally deeded to the Hudson family from the king of England. (Courtesy of the Null family.)

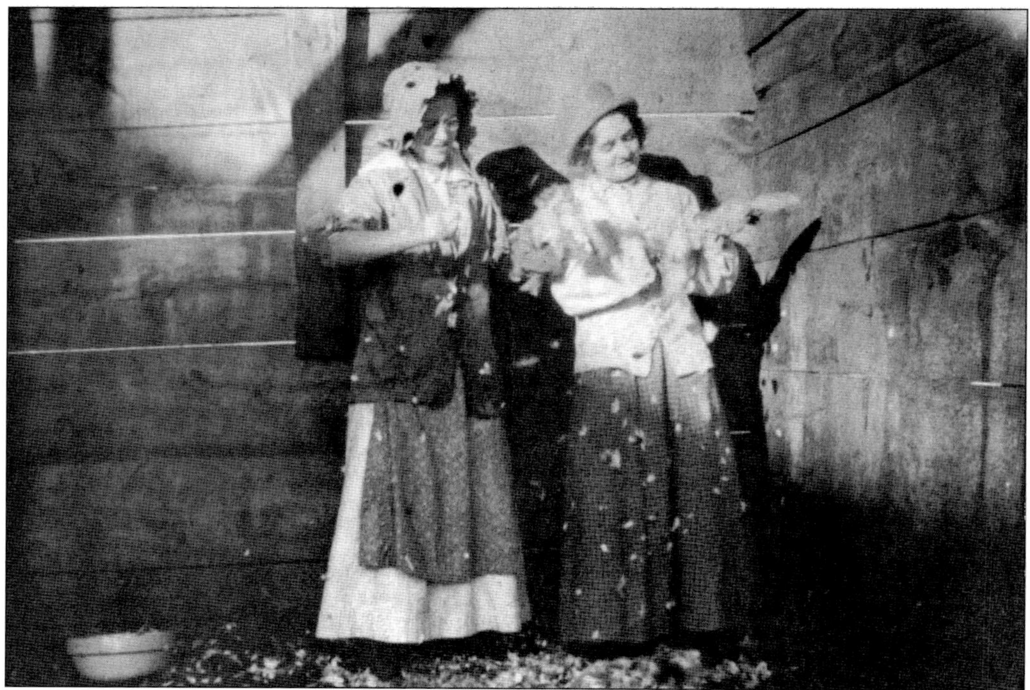

Women pluck chickens in the barn on the Jacob Null farm in Taneytown around 1916. Almost every farm had a few chickens for eggs, for a Sunday chicken dinner, and to sell both for extra cash. (Courtesy of the Null family.)

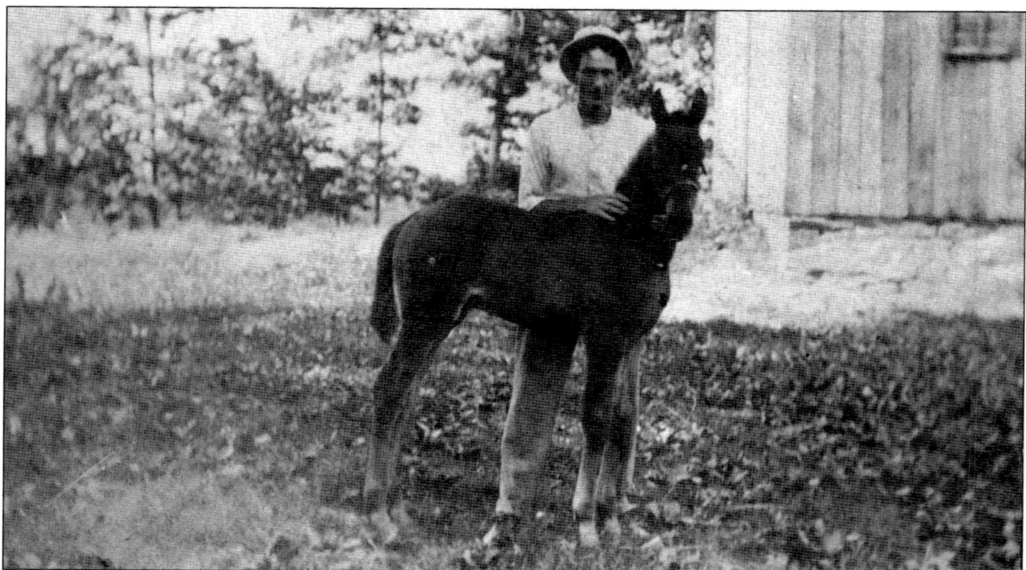

William Mordecai Gist Jr. stands with a colt on the Gist family farm in Cedarhurst (formerly Asbestos) around 1920. The family hauled their milk as far as Emory Church, using a horse-drawn sleigh in the winter. Woodrow Hubbard Gist, his son, paid $5 a month to ride the school bus from Finksburg to Westminster. When he took over the farm, he had a small orchard with fruit trees, including apples, peaches, pears, and plums. He sold the fruit by word of mouth and a sign on the road. Every fall, he made apple cider to sell. Seven generations have lived on this farm since the mid-1800s. (Courtesy of the Gist family.)

Oliver Brown and his 1½-year-old daughter June have their photograph taken during corn-husking time in 1928 on the 60-acre family farm between Mayberry and Pleasant Valley. It was 2 miles to Tyrone, Mayberry, or Pleasant Valley on dirt roads and a long walk to the school bus for June when she got older. The family did not have electricity until June was 12 years old. They did not have a tractor, only three horses, and they had six cows for milk. It was during the Depression, and June raised ducks in the summer for spending money, but she didn't need much because she only went to church. (Courtesy of June Brown Bollinger.)

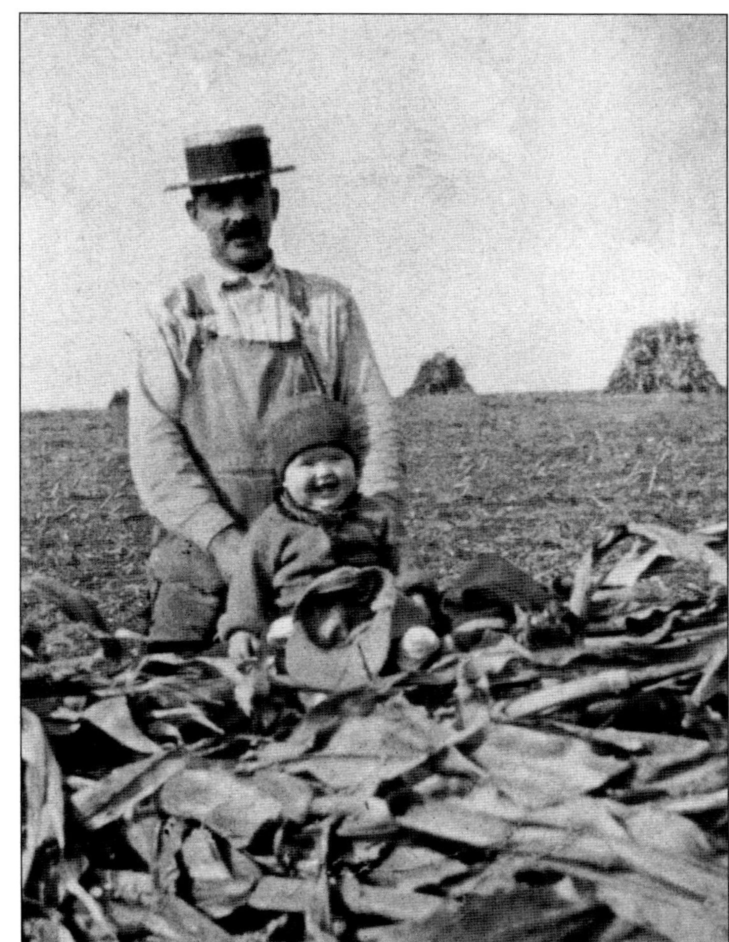

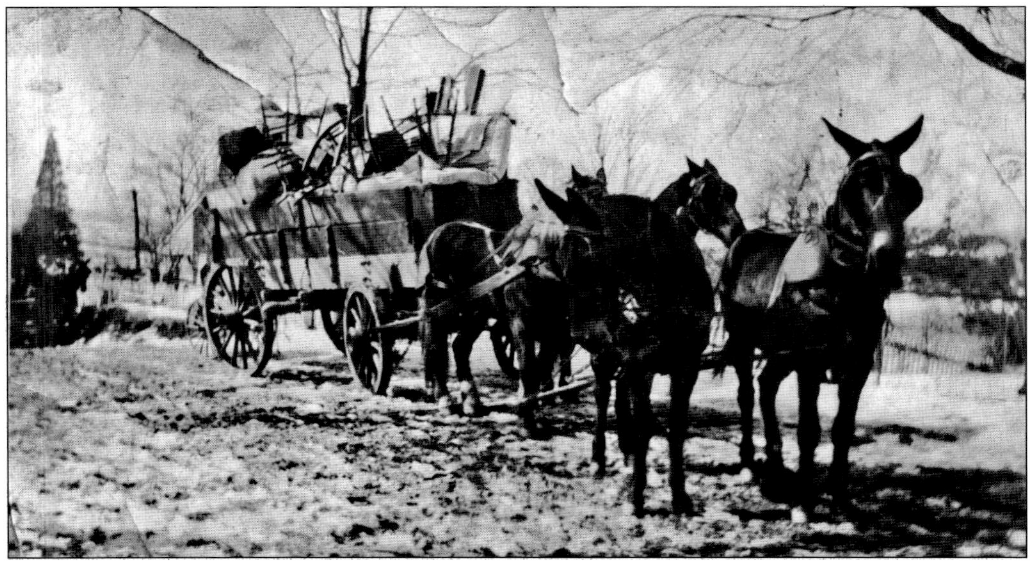

When a farm family moved in the 19th and early 20th centuries, they loaded all their possessions on their farm wagon. (Courtesy of Helen Tracy Totura.)

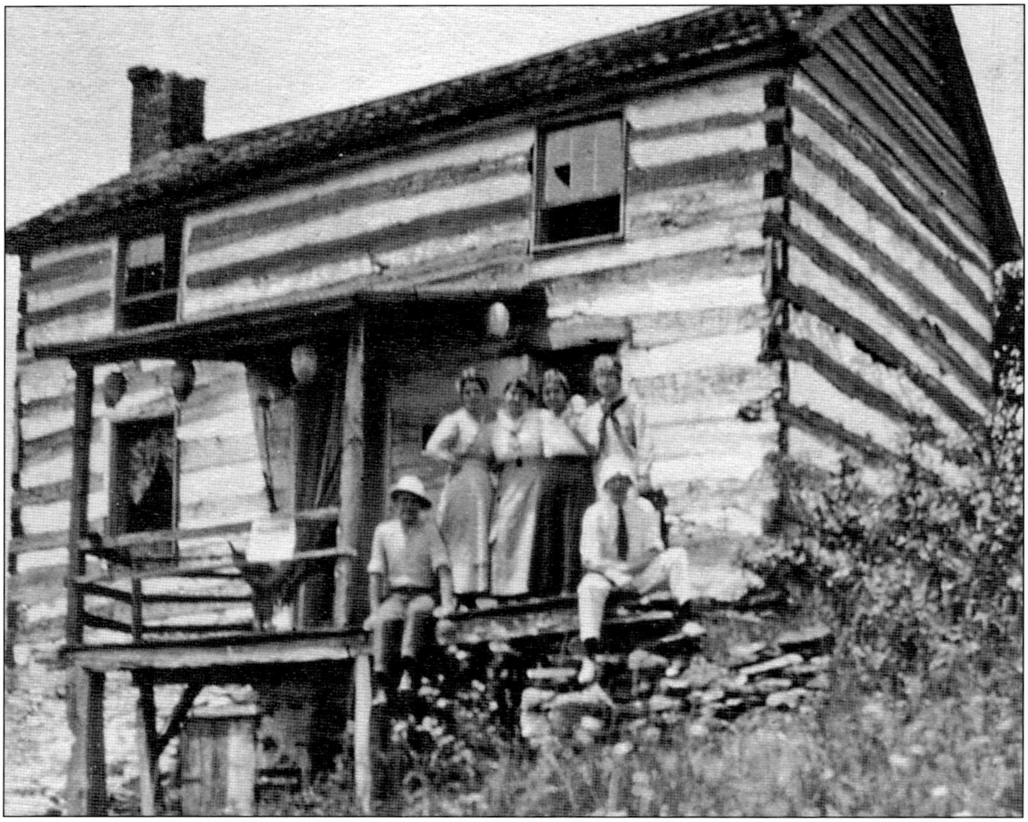

This log farmhouse on the Lauterback Farm near Oakland Mills was destroyed by construction of the Liberty Reservoir. (Courtesy of the Historical Society of Carroll County.)

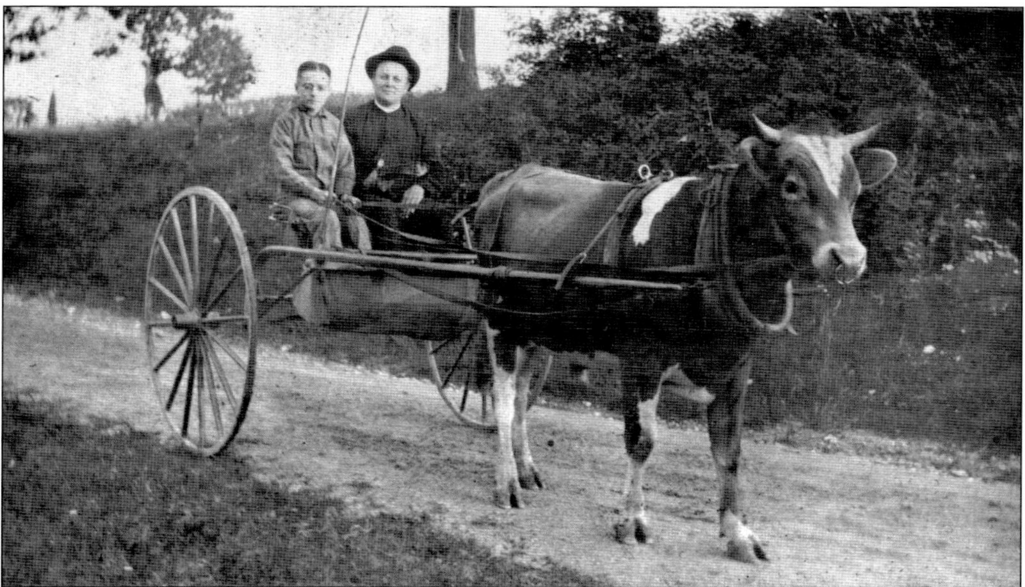

Wilber Naill (born 1901) and preacher ? Martin are taking a ride in early-1900s Dennings. A visit from the country preacher was a welcome sight in rural Carroll County during the last century. It was a reason to make a big Sunday dinner and get out the best china. (Courtesy of Judy Naill.)

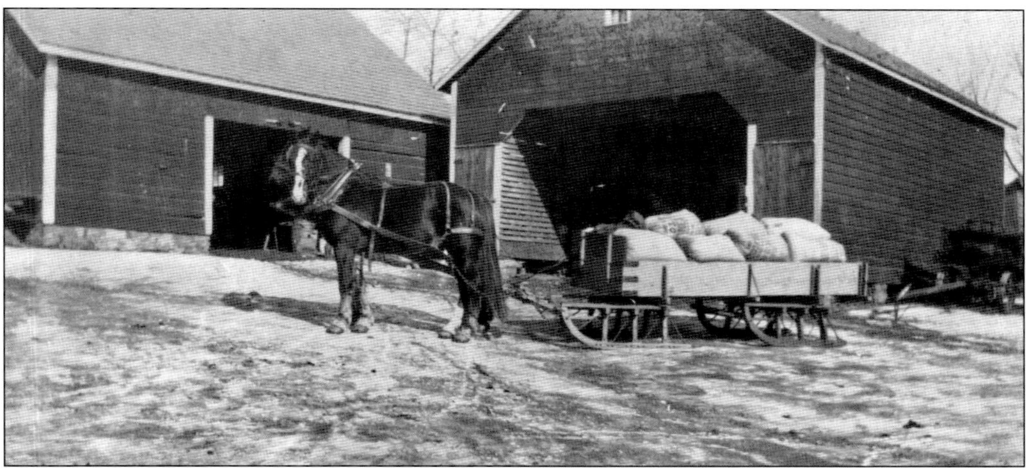

In the 1920s, this team of horses on the Charles Tracy farm near Melrose is pulling a sled with bobs attached to it. Often farm wagons had attachments with runners for winter called bobs. The icehouse is the building on the left. (Courtesy of Helen Tracy Totura.)

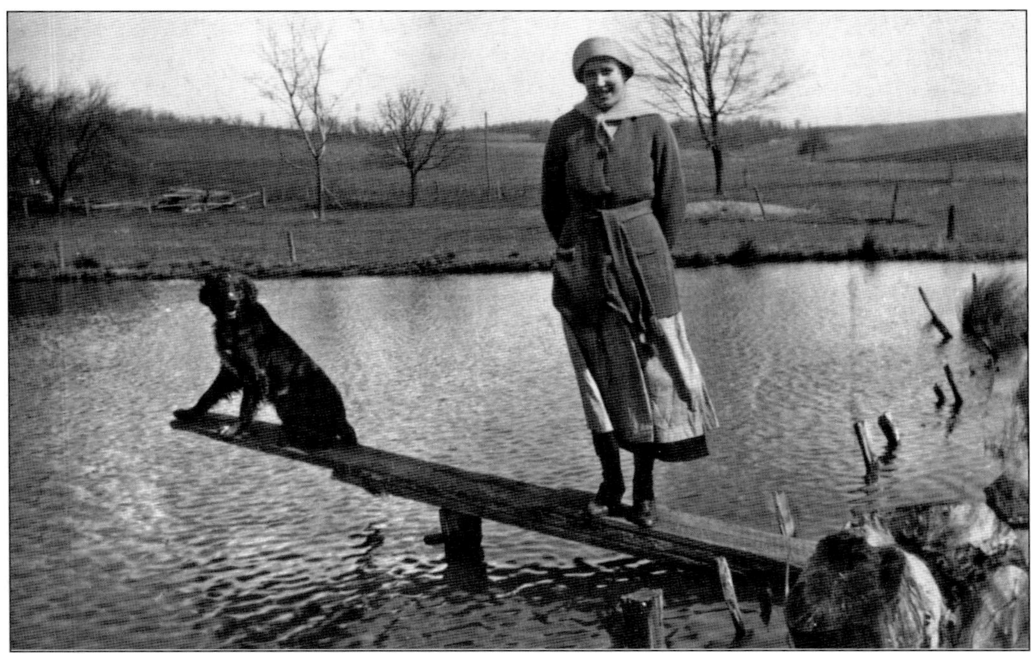

This is a 1930s photograph of Mary Noble Tracy standing by the pond on the Charles Tracy farm near Melrose. The family harvested ice by cutting blocks of it from the pond. The pond froze at least a foot deep. They stacked ice blocks in sawdust in the icehouse on the farm. The ice lasted all summer back then. (Courtesy of Helen Tracy Totura.)

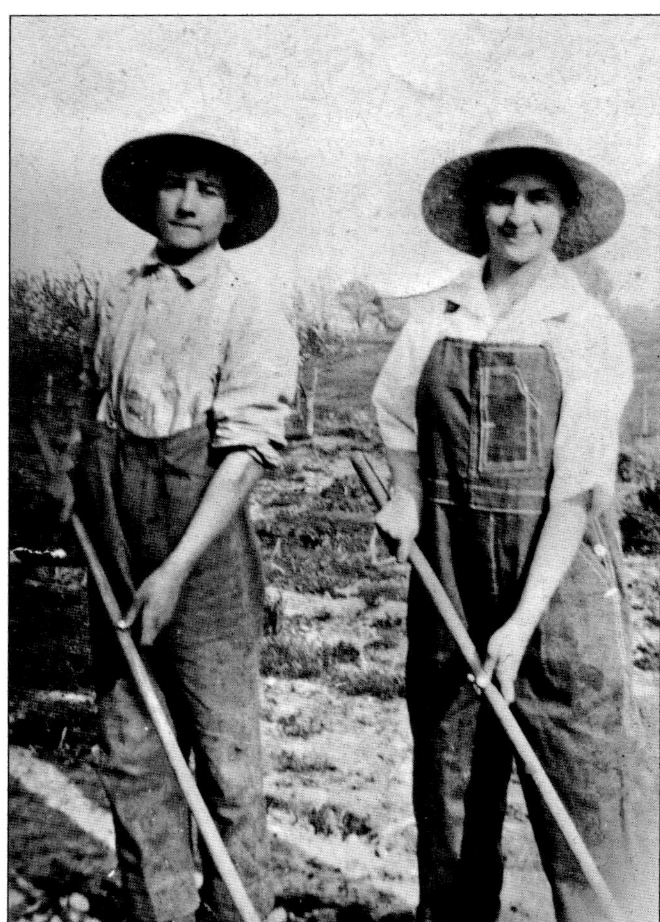

Hubert and Anna Null work on the Jacob Null farm in Taneytown in 1916. Work days were long and hard on local farms with hand tools. (Courtesy of the Null family.)

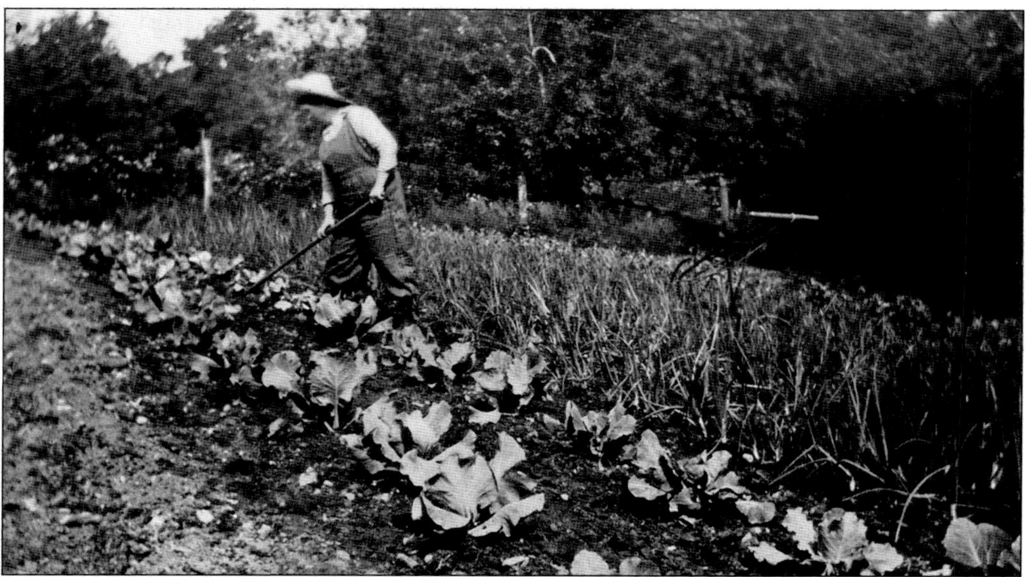

In the early 1900s, Rosella Hess Stull of Keysville hoes the family truck patch garden used to produce vegetables for canning, herbs, cabbage, and lettuce. (Courtesy of Mildred Stine.)

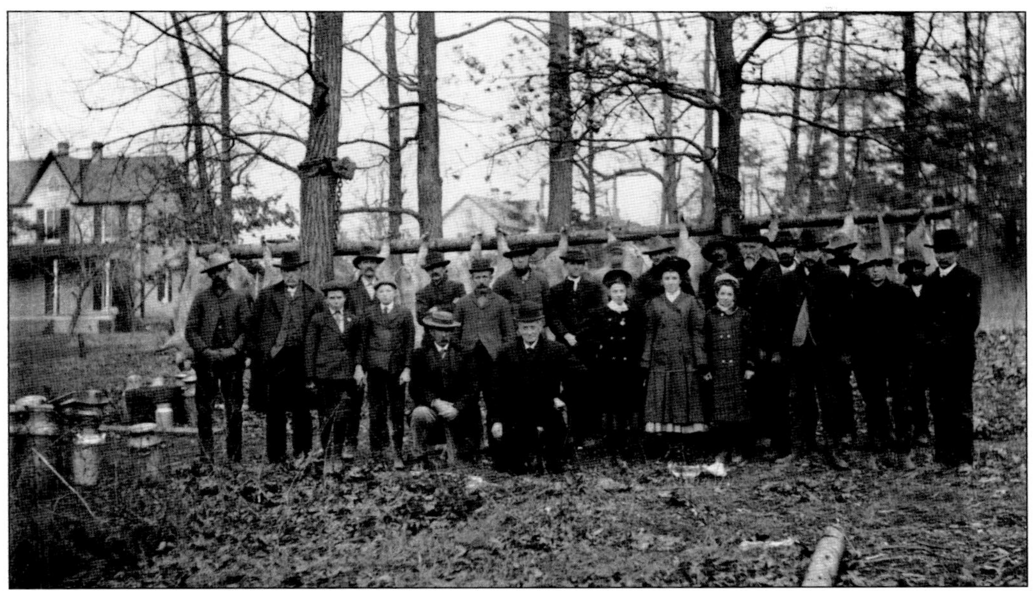

These 1904 photographs show the Clay and Clary families, who butchered their hogs together. It was common for families and neighbors to butcher together in the fall when there was less work and the cool weather helped preserve the meat. These photographs were taken at the end of East and Church Streets in Mount Airy. (Courtesy of the Historical Society of Mount Airy, Maryland.)

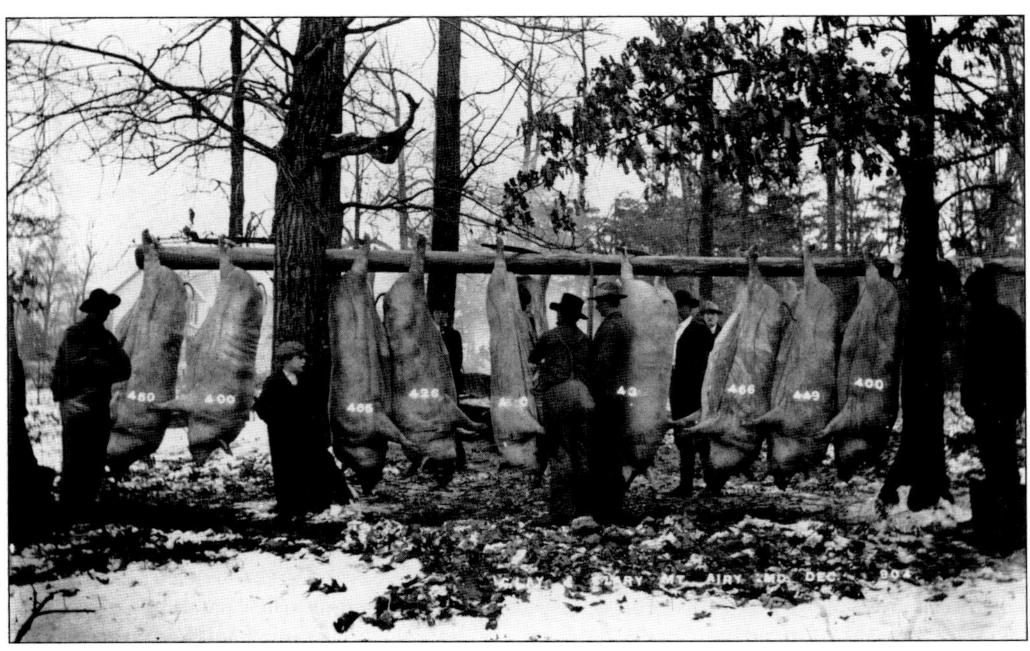

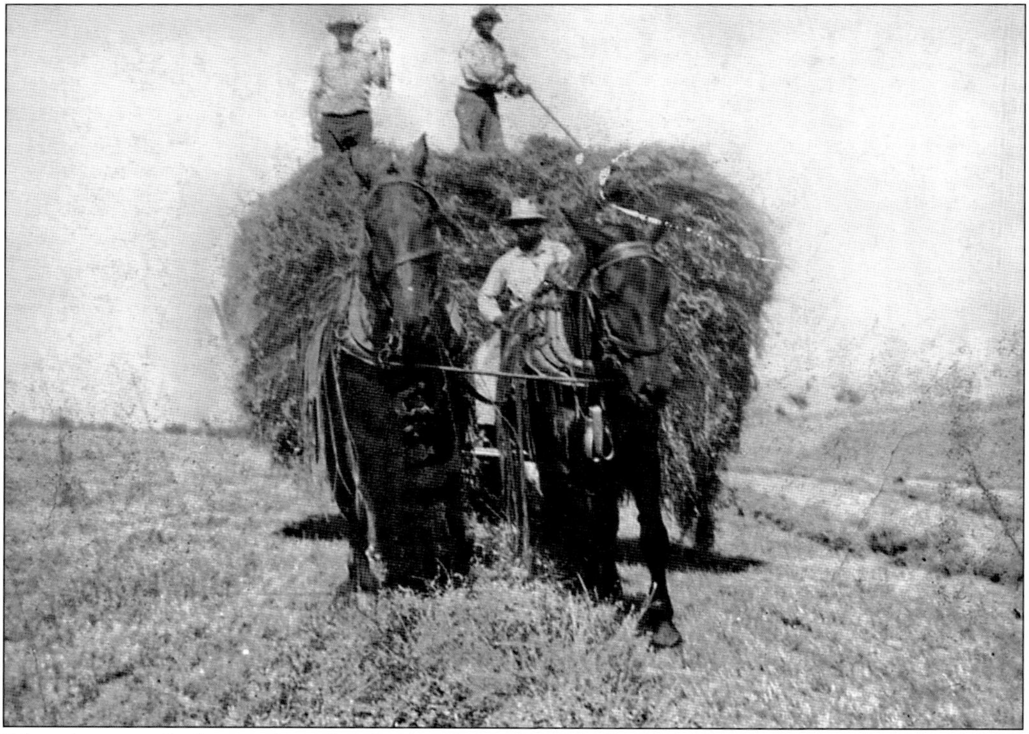

This photograph shows a huge load of hay being brought back to the barn, where it will be stored in the hay mow. (Courtesy of the Sykesville Gate House Museum.)

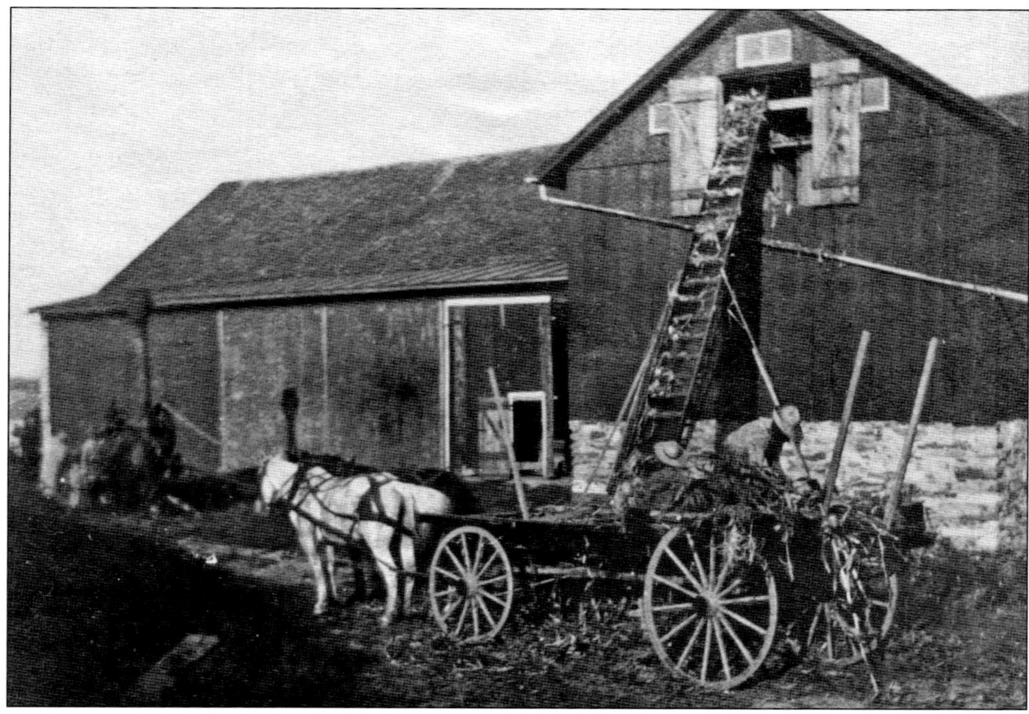

These men are loading a barn with an elevator on the John Ecker farm near New Windsor in the early 1900s. (Courtesy of the New Windsor Heritage Committee.)

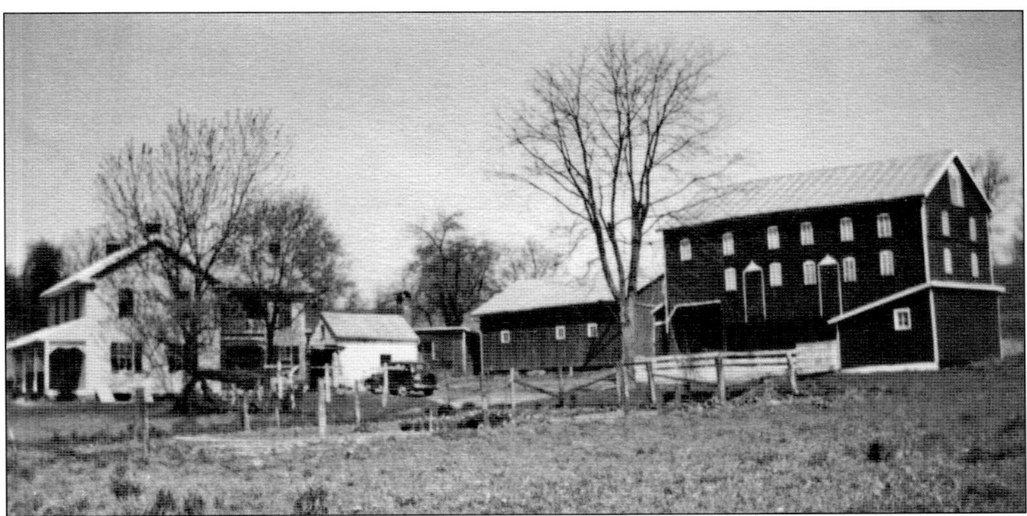

This is the Upton Harvey and Alice Motter Myers farm on Stone Road, which was farmed by the family from 1906 to 1940. Myers was a huckster. He gathered eggs, poultry, and vegetables from local farms and loaded them onto the train. Then he hired a team of horses in Baltimore, met the train, and sold his wares door-to-door. When they got home, he and his son Ernest ate mush, cornmeal and water cooked all day. (Courtesy of Ray Brown.)

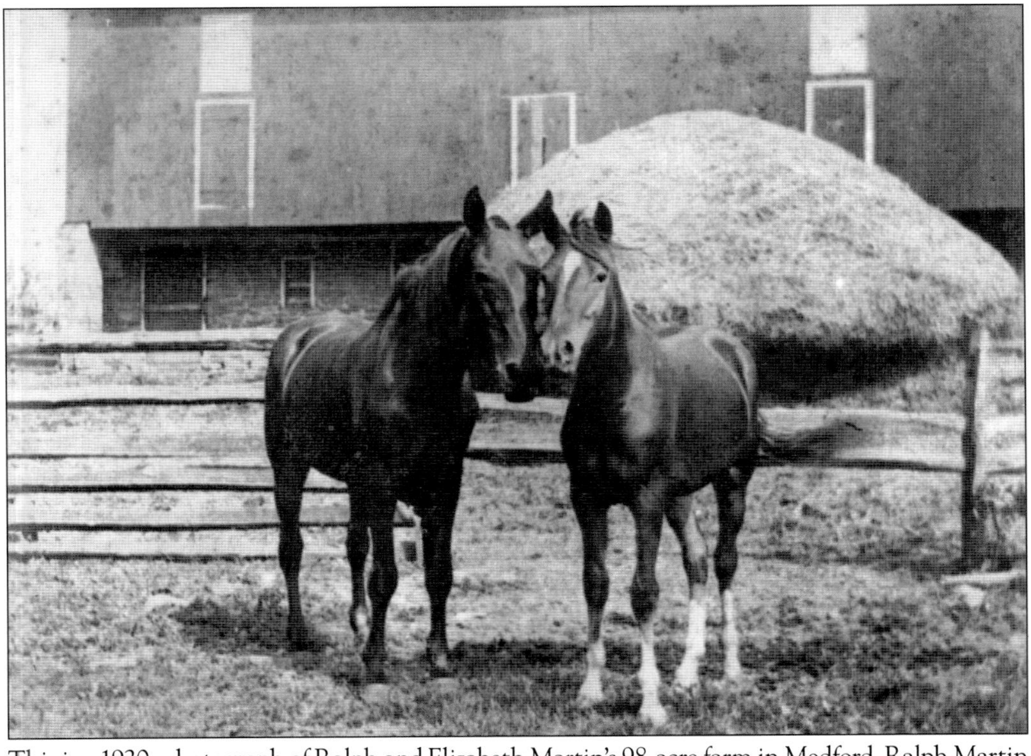

This is a 1920s photograph of Ralph and Elizabeth Martin's 98-acre farm in Medford. Ralph Martin passed away, leaving his wife a widow with three children. A family friend arranged to auction the farm and place her two sons in a boys' home, without asking her. She was furious and, with the help of two hired hands, ran the farm herself. (Courtesy of Dottie Martin Haschert.)

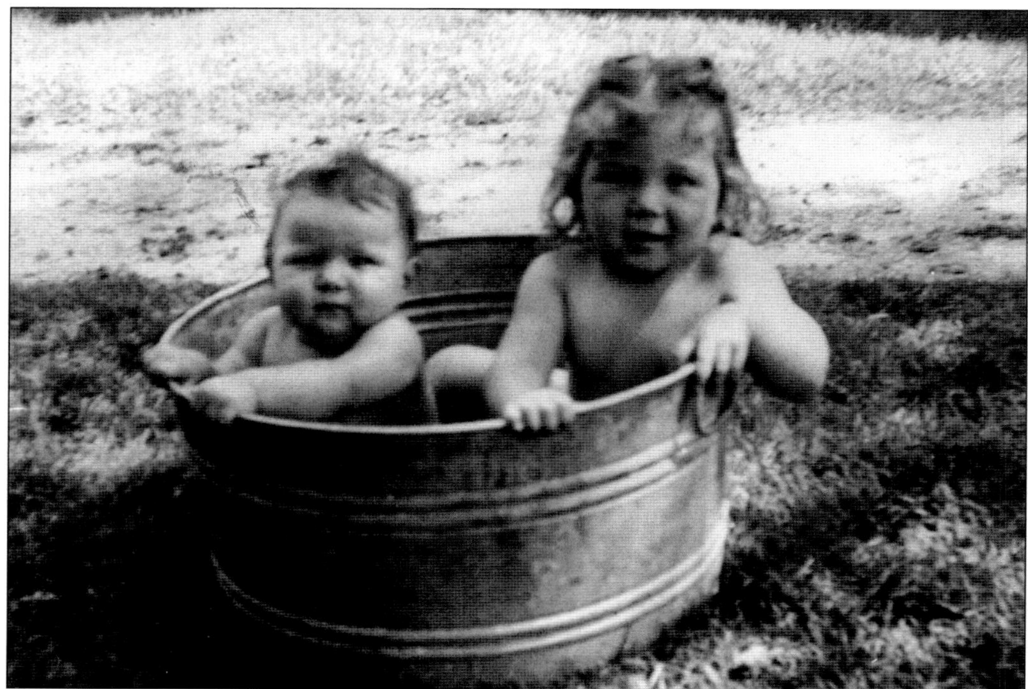

From left to right, Linda Hampshire (Bowdler) and Jeanne Hampshire (Link) are getting a bath in 1949 on the Maurice B. and Marguerite Wells Hampshire farm in Hampstead. Clarence and Edna Hampshire, Maurice's parents, purchased the farm in 1918. The Hampshires had a Home Comfort wood stove on which they cooked. They did not have indoor plumbing except in the kitchen. They put the children in a galvanized tub in the summer house to give them baths. There was never a bathroom or running water in the house. (Courtesy of the Hampshire family.)

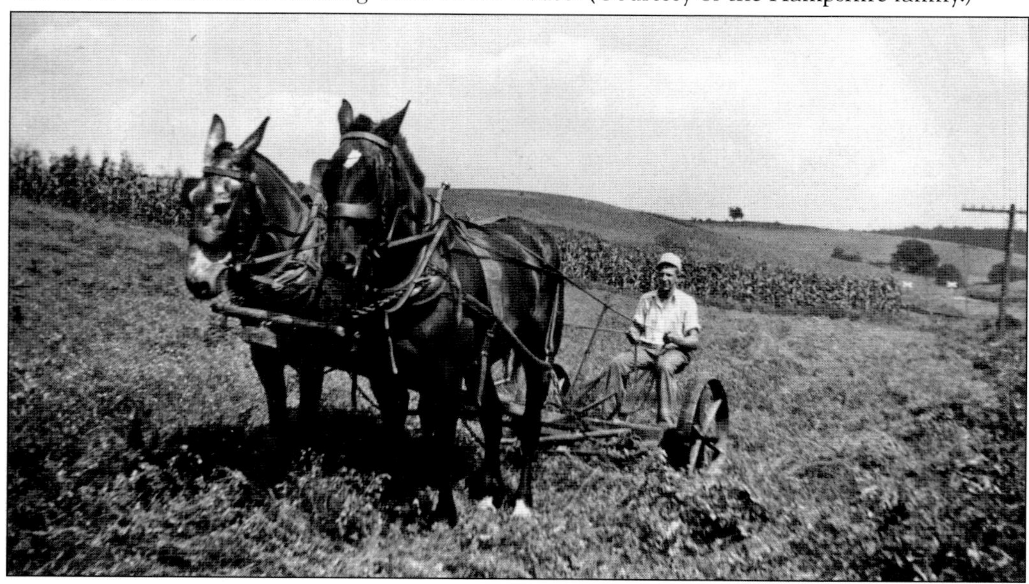

In 1942, Russell Warner was mowing a field on a small tract of land his uncle Raymond Warner owned in Lineboro. Raymond Warner's primary farm was near Manchester on Roop and Watertank Roads. It was the remaining part of a 2,000-acre land grant the family acquired in the 1700s. A section of this farm is still in the family. (Courtesy of Mary Kathryn Warner Babylon.)

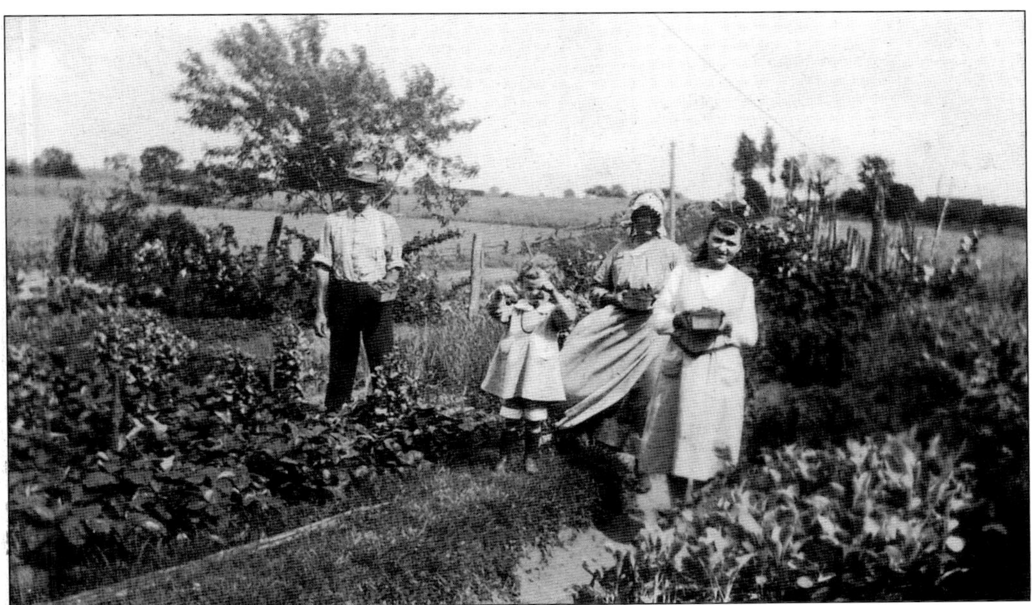

This farm family is picking strawberries around 1922 on the Brown Farm on Harney Road. Berries were used to make jams and jellies that were canned for use throughout the year. Tasty pies were made from many of the berries. Pictured from left to right are ? Brown, Mildred Stine, ? Brown, and unidentified. (Courtesy of Mildred Stine.)

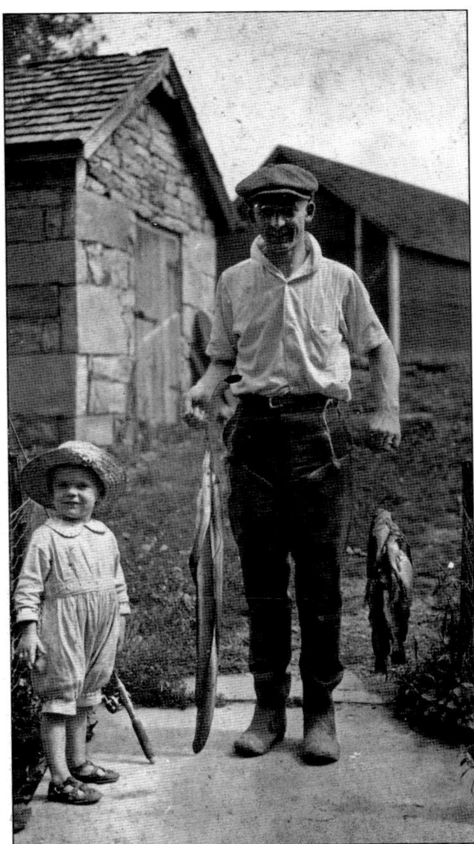

Bill Sell shows off the catch with his cousin Mildred Stull on the Byron Stull farm in Keysville around 1921 after a fishing trip to the Monocacy River, which runs behind the family home. Behind them stand the smokehouse and the wagon shed. (Courtesy of Mildred Stine.)

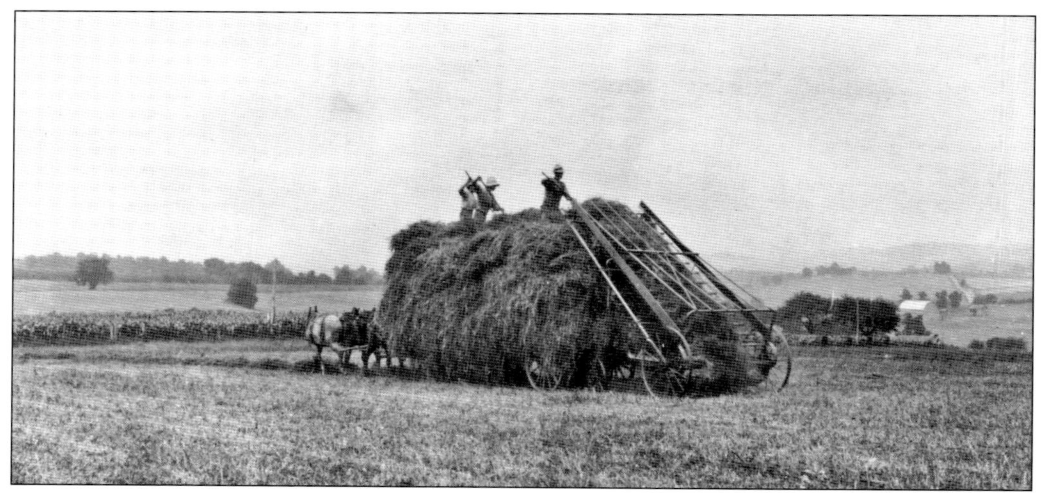

Men stack a mountain of hay in 1921 onto a horse-drawn hay wagon. A hay loader is pulled behind it, loading the cut hay as they move across the field. (Courtesy of the University of Maryland Cooperative Extension Office, Carroll County.)

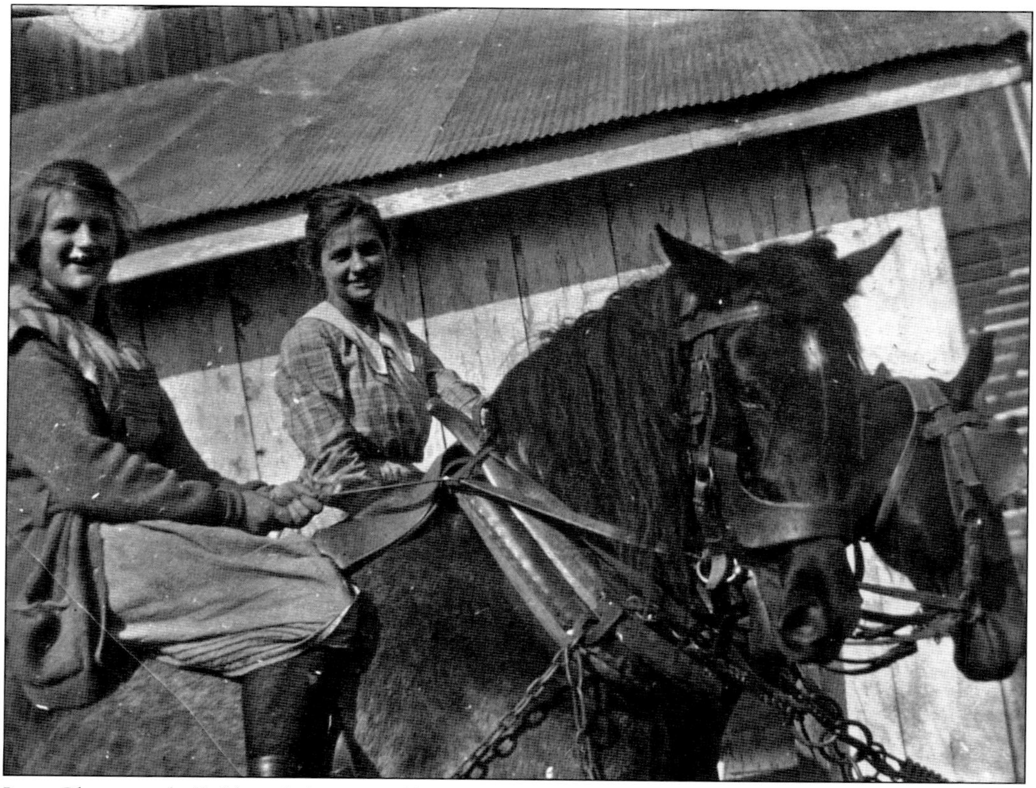

Jane Chenoweth (left) and Anna Null are riding draft horses in Taneytown around 1918. Most farms did not have horses suitable for riding, so the work horses occasionally did double duty. (Courtesy of the Null family.)

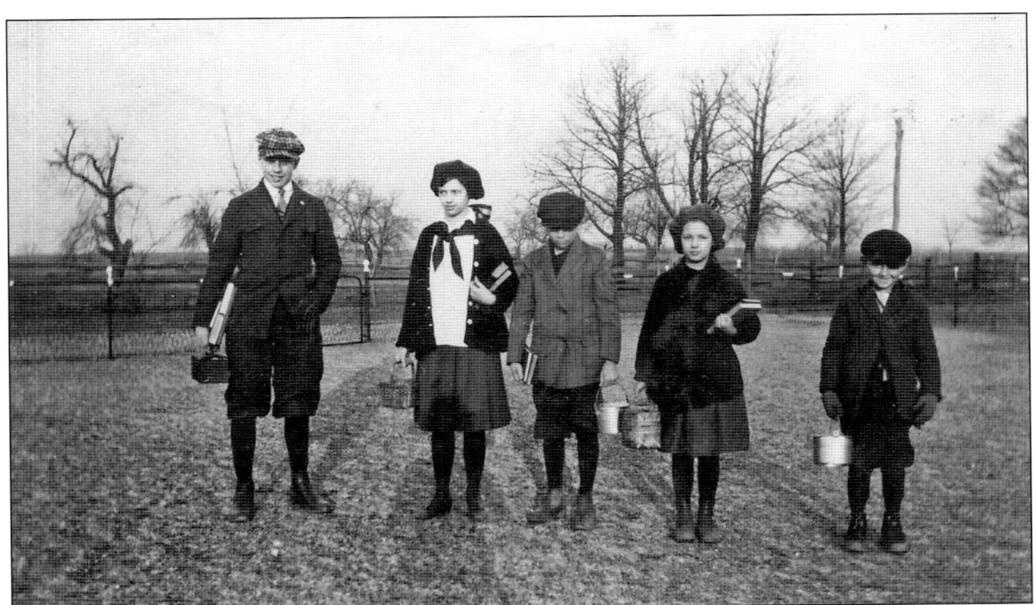

The Maurice Wilhide children are going to the Detour School around 1917. From left to right, Lloyd, Louise, Merhrle, Dot, and Carroll are pictured. They carry tin pails holding their lunches. (Courtesy of the Wilhide family.)

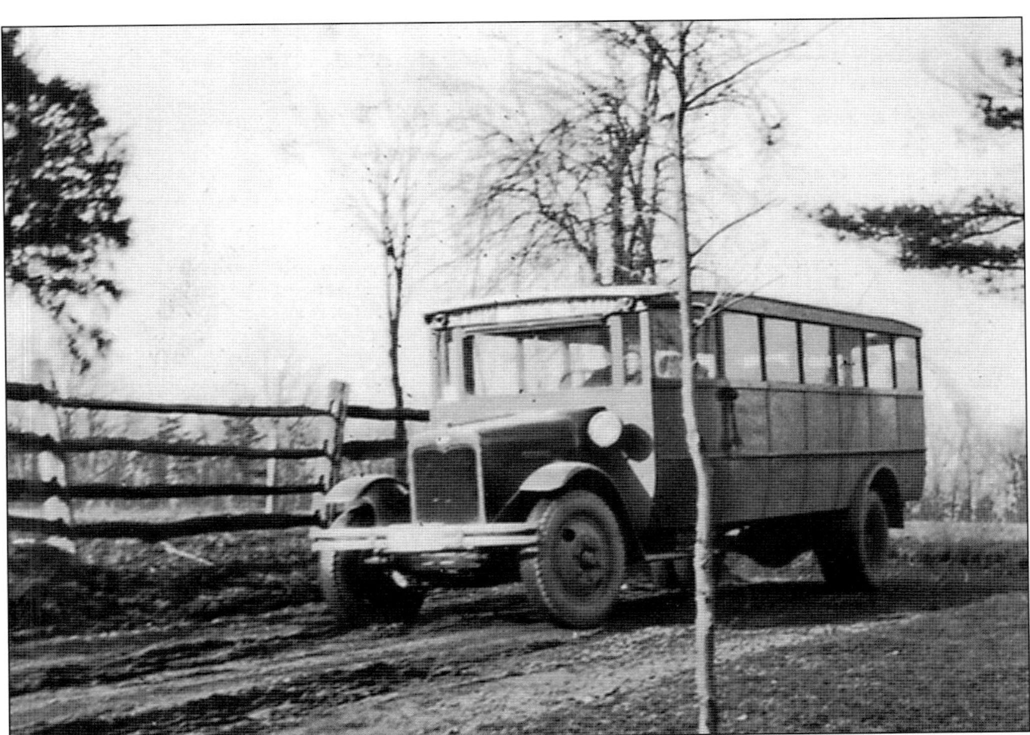

Farm children in Keysville went to a one-room school until sixth grade. When the school was closed, they still had to walk to Keysville to catch the bus to school in Taneytown. Children walked to school or to the nearest bus route until a hard road came by their farm. This school bus came to get farm children in Keysville. (Courtesy of Mildred Stine.)

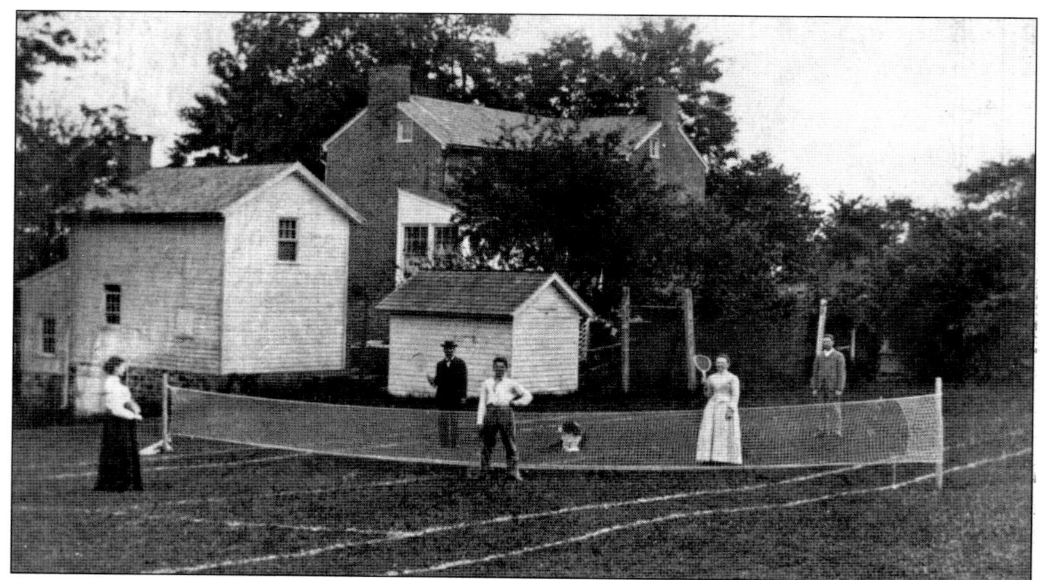

The tennis courts behind the house at the Overbrook dairy farm in New Windsor, owned by J. Frank Getty, were a rare sight in Carroll County. Pictured from left to right are two unidentified, Herbert Getty, Virginia Getty, and J. Walter Getty. (Courtesy of Sole Hoke.)

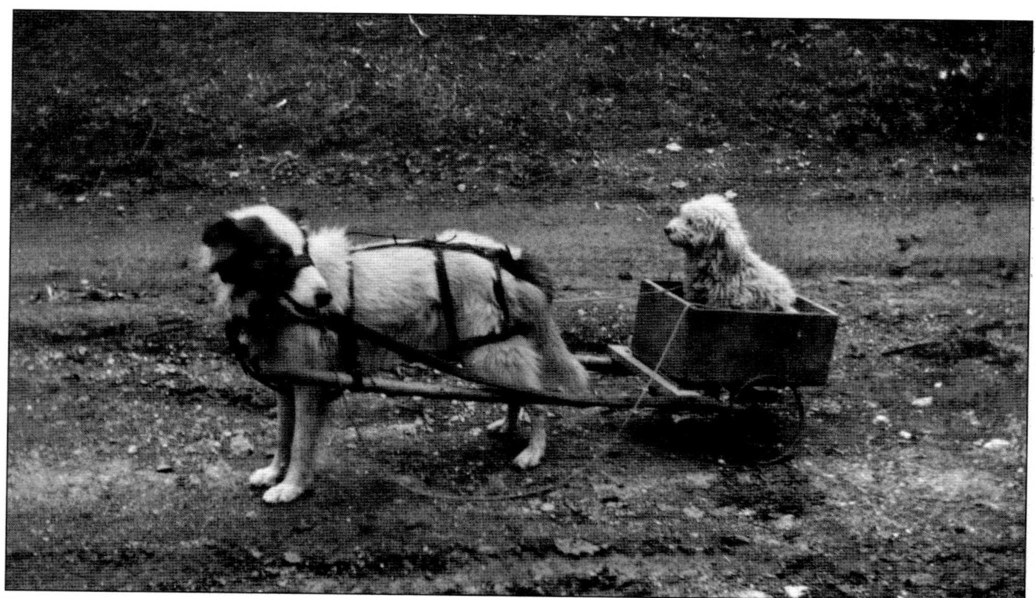

Raymond Louie's dog pulls Fuzzie the poodle in the early 1930s. Louie built the cart himself. (Courtesy of Elinor Hull.)

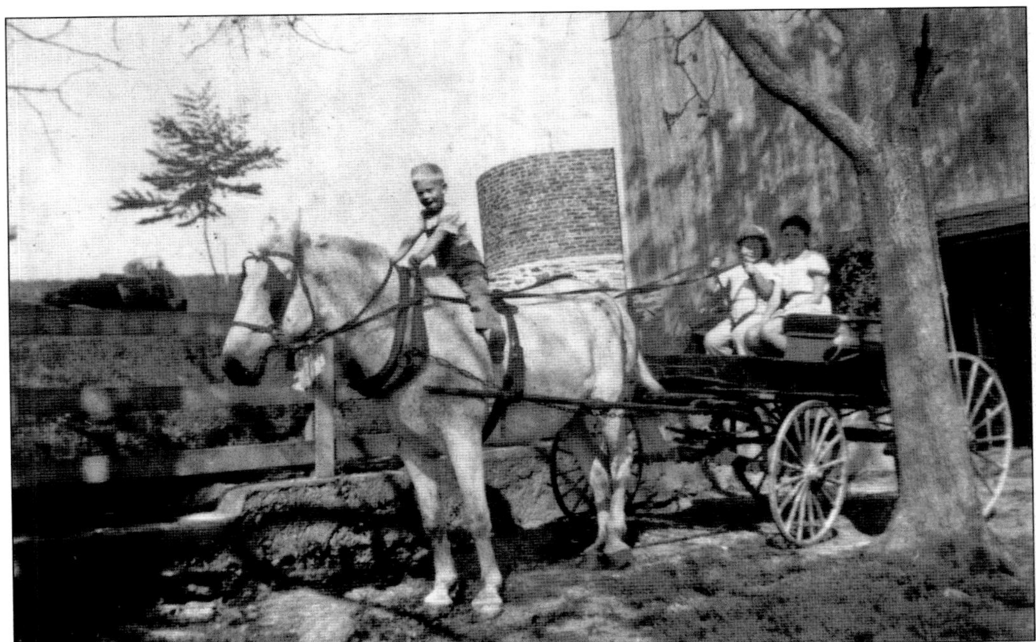

Bill and Joan Conaway hold the lines (left) and Peggy Beall drives the milk wagon on the Gordon Conaway Sr. farm around 1946. Milk cans are in the back of the wagon. (Courtesy of the James C. Conaway Sr. family.)

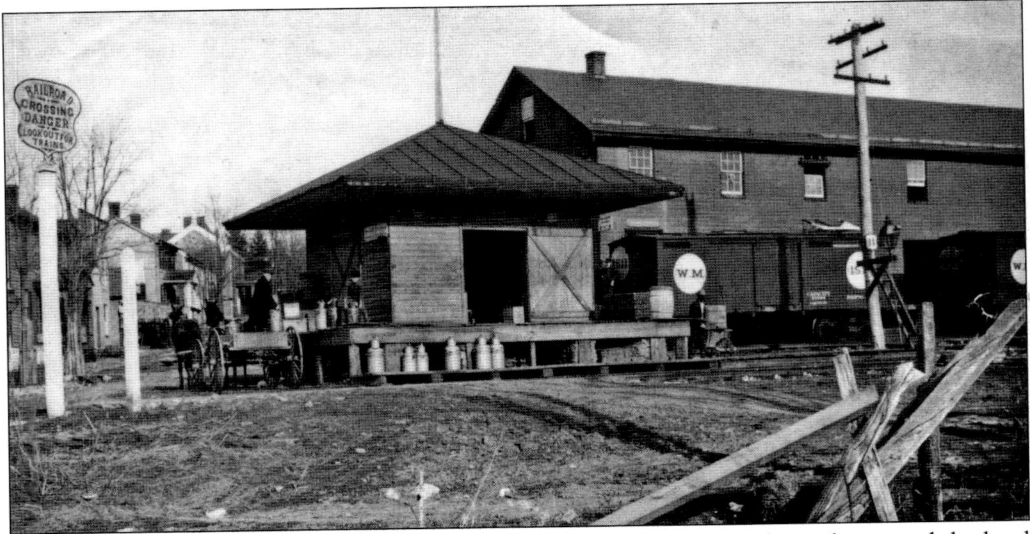

The *c.* 1900 freight house in New Windsor was built by David Paul Smelser, who owned the land beside the railroad. A local farmer is delivering milk cans that will be picked up by the train and delivered to Baltimore. Notice the building is halfway into the street. (Courtesy of the New Windsor Heritage Committee.)

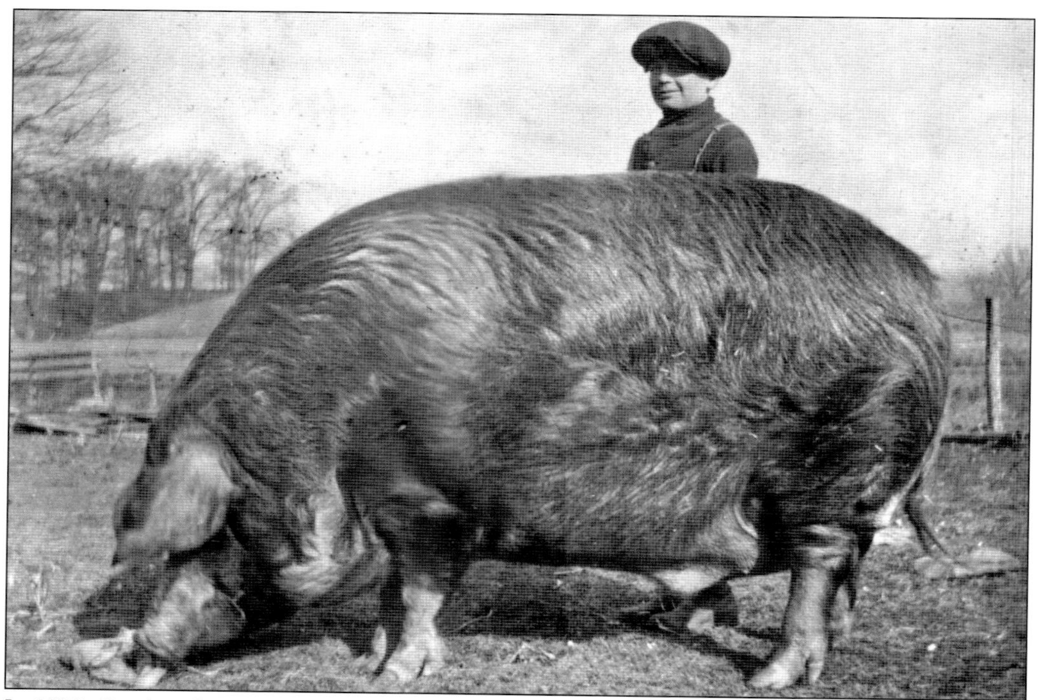

In 1922, Gordon Conaway Sr. is photographed with his enormous hog. According to the county agent's report in 1924, Carroll County produced more hogs than any other county in the state. At that time, with the encouragement of the county agent, pig clubs were formed to introduce more purebred hogs into the county. Ninety-nine purebred sows and 40 boars were sold in the county that year. (Courtesy of the James C. Conaway Sr. family.)

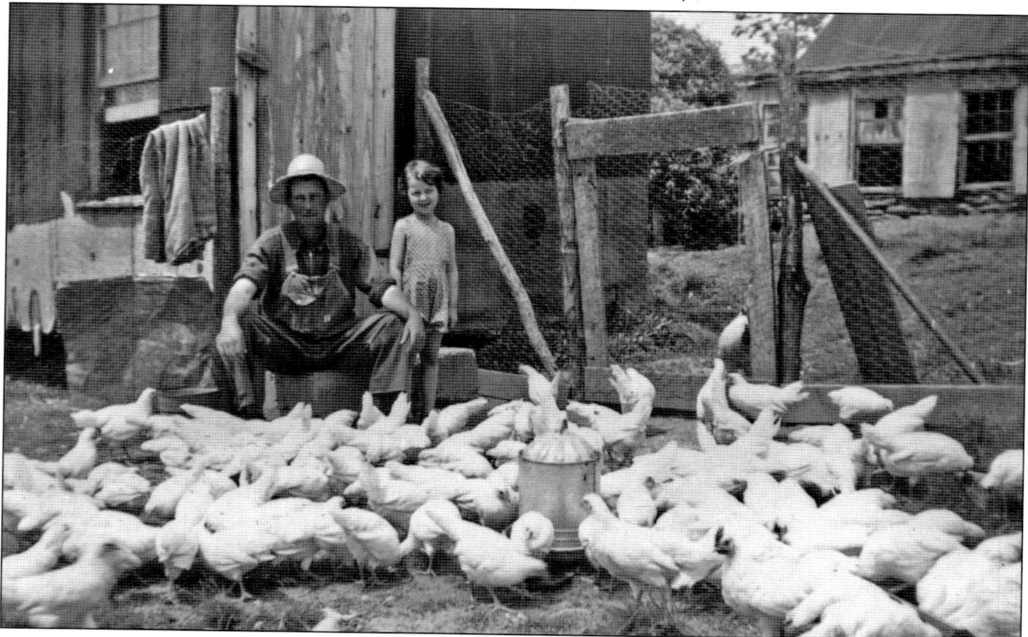

Herman and Bonnie Hoff (Fold), seen here in 1951, are in the chicken yard on the Francis and Ada Hoff farm in Gamber, which was purchased in the 1920s. They raised 100 chickens, and local people stopped by to buy eggs. (Courtesy of Bonnie Fold.)

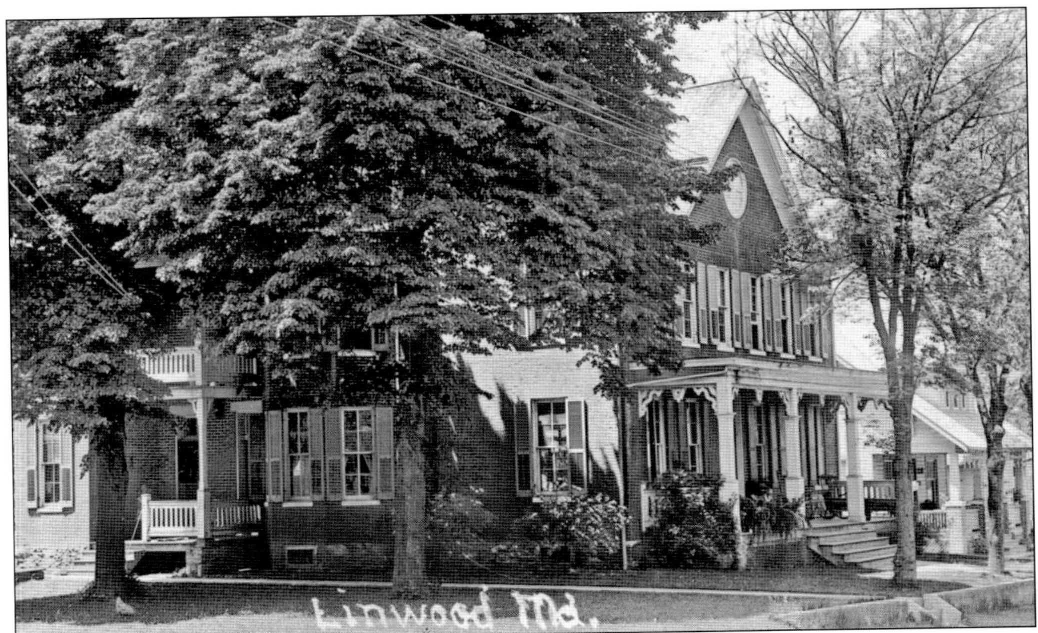

James Robert Etzler was a farmer in New Windsor. He made so much money in World War I in one year as a tenant farmer selling wheat that he bought this big brick home in Linwood. After his passing, his son, Robert, ran the farm, and his widow, Laura Carter Etzler, lived off the income from the farm. His daughter, Helen Etzler (Stevenson), took the train from Linwood to Westminster to attend Western Maryland College and graduated in 1917. (Courtesy of Lyndi McNulty.)

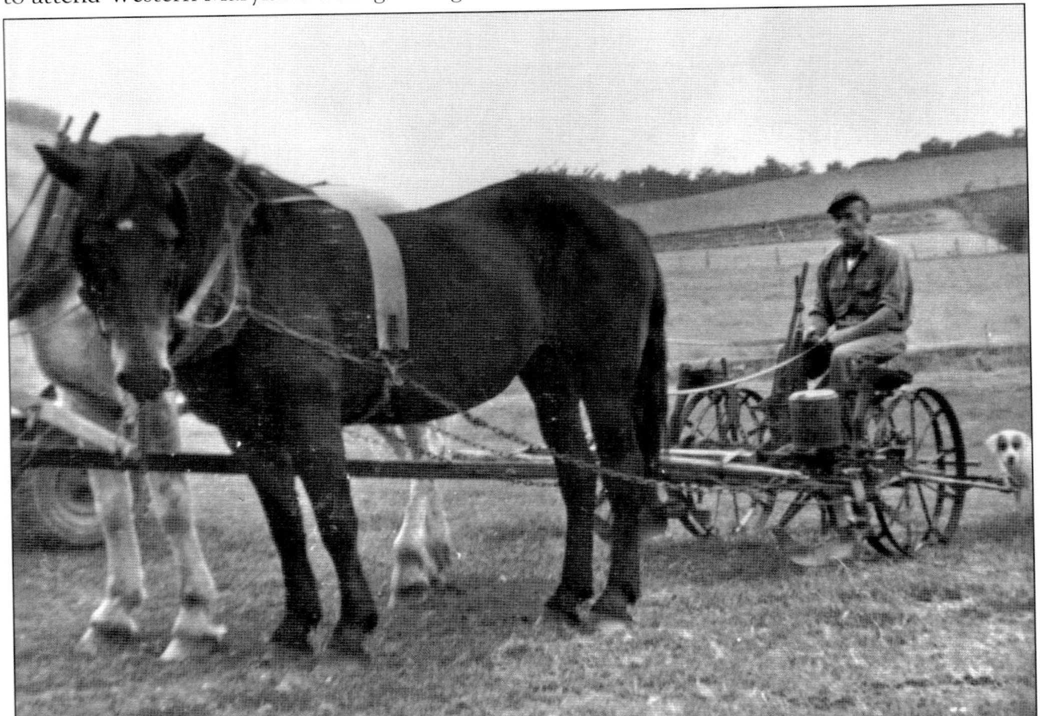

Gordon Conaway Sr. is planting corn with a horse-drawn corn planter on his farm in Berrett around 1950. (Courtesy of the James C. Conaway Sr. family.)

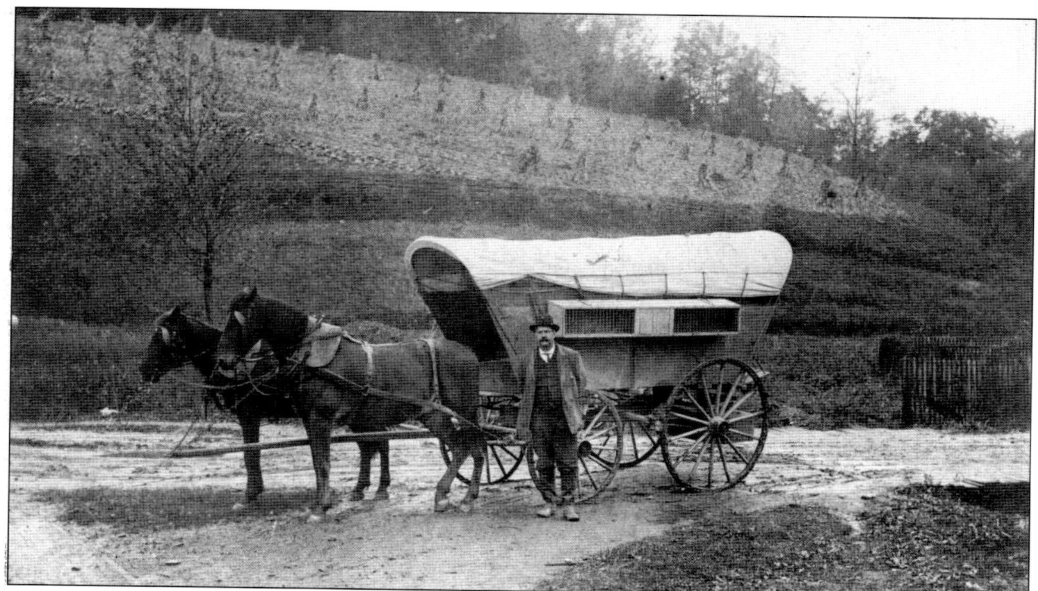

In the late 1800s, the Lantz brothers purchased local produce, milk, eggs, and other farm products from farmers, and John Lantz drove this huckster's wagon to Baltimore. Hucksters were a common sight throughout the county, providing both fresh food for the city and much-needed cash for small farmers. (Courtesy of New Windsor Heritage Committee.)

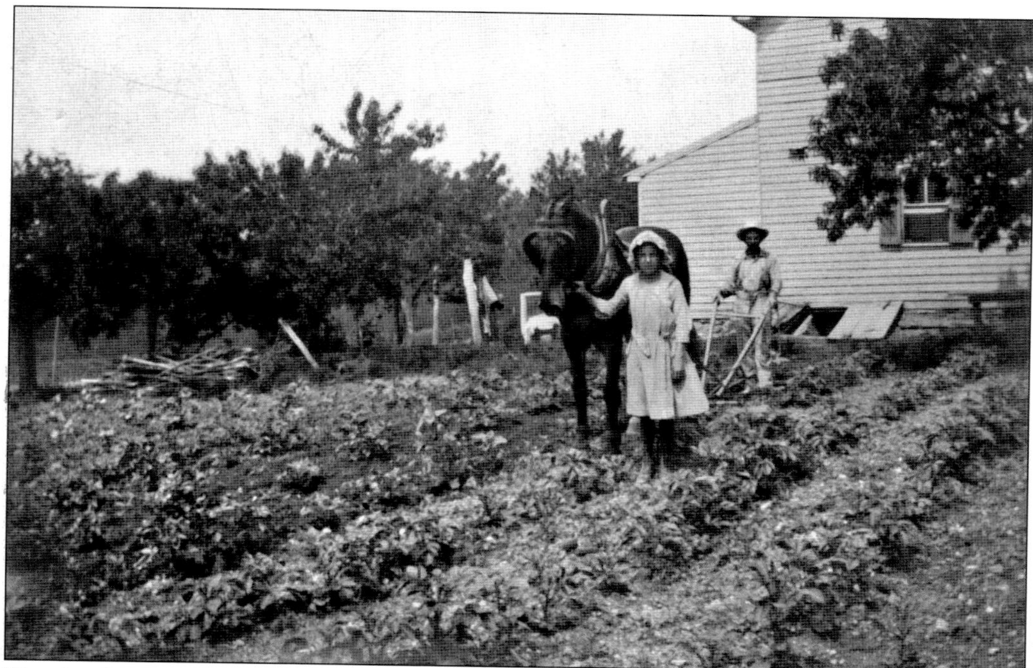

This kitchen garden was on the David H. and Annie Zile farm near Gypsy Hill. As with other farms, tomatoes, cucumbers, onions, and more were grown for the family. The girl was leading the plow, making sure the horse did not step on the vegetables. Extra produce was sold from the farm or by a huckster who picked up the produce and sold it, often in Baltimore. (Courtesy of Judy Naill.)

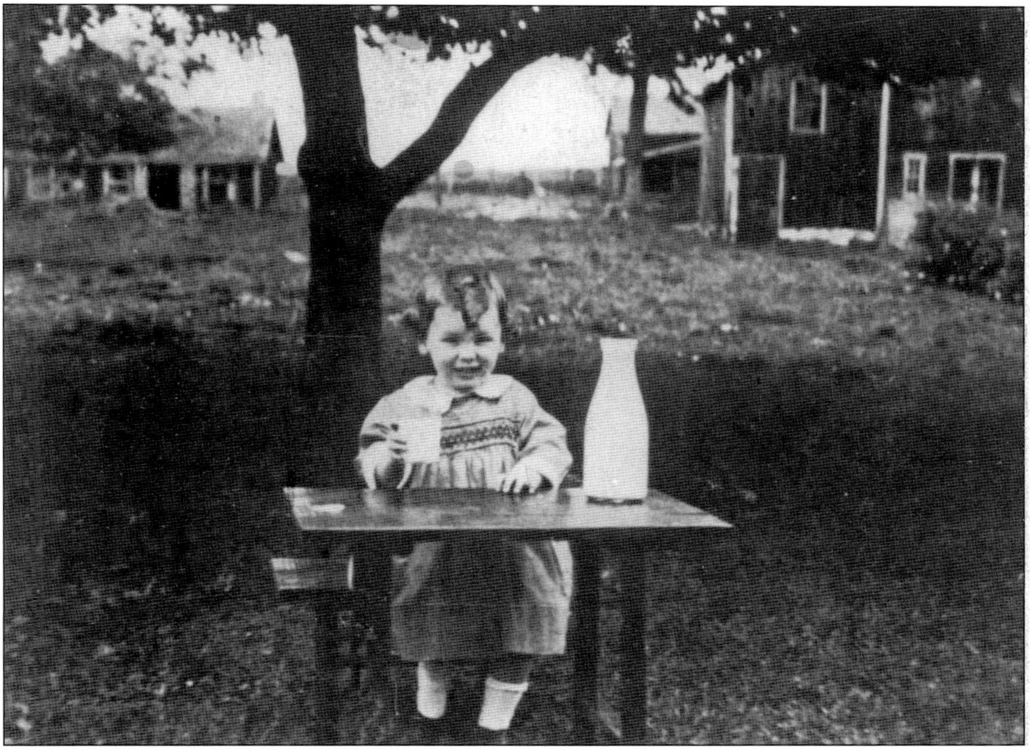

Nancy Getty (Haifley) shows off the grade-A milk from the Herbert Getty dairy farm in New Windsor in 1922. The family delivered milk and quarter-pint jills or gills (5 ounces) of cream and butter to the houses in New Windsor. (Courtesy of the Hoke family.)

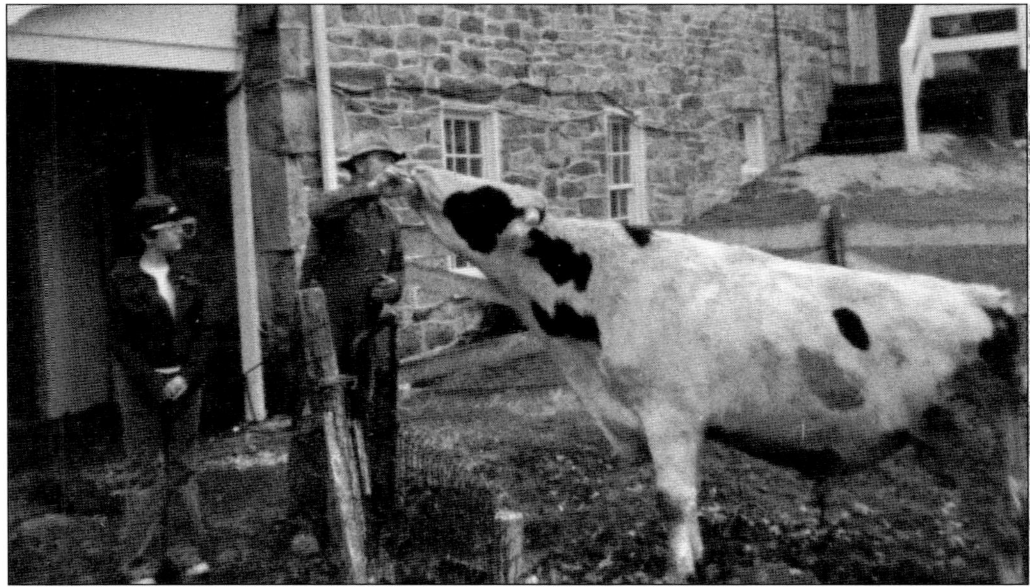

Gilbert Stein, seen here around 1980, always drank Pepsi at the farm and shared it with the bull, Junior, who loved Pepsi but would not drink Coca-Cola. (Courtesy of Mildred Stine.)

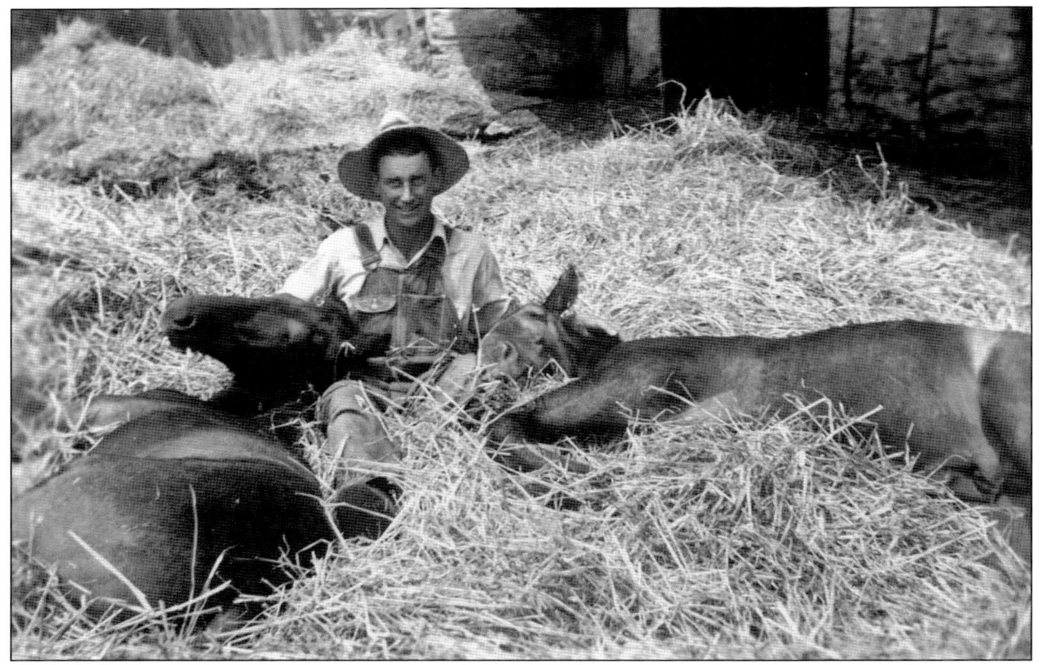

Herman Hoff is pictured with a rare pair of twin colts on his farm in Gamber in 1939. (Courtesy of Bonnie Fold.)

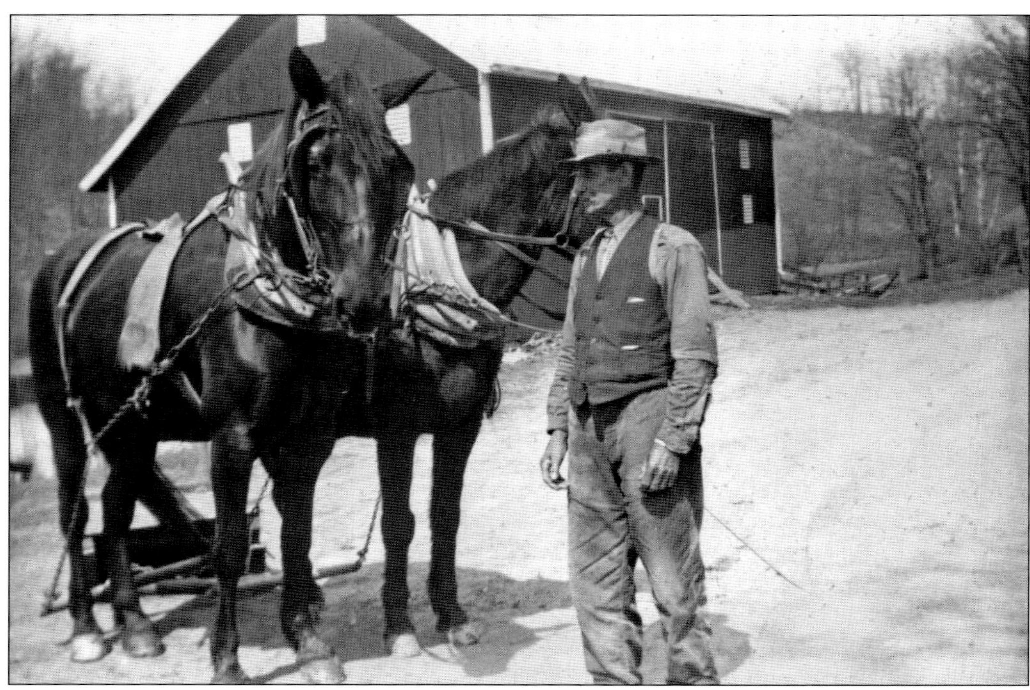

This picture was taken on Easter morning in April 1941 of William Nicolas Barber. He farmed on Jim Bowers Road in Bird Hill. Barber often did hauling with his horses. (Courtesy of Bonnie Fold.)

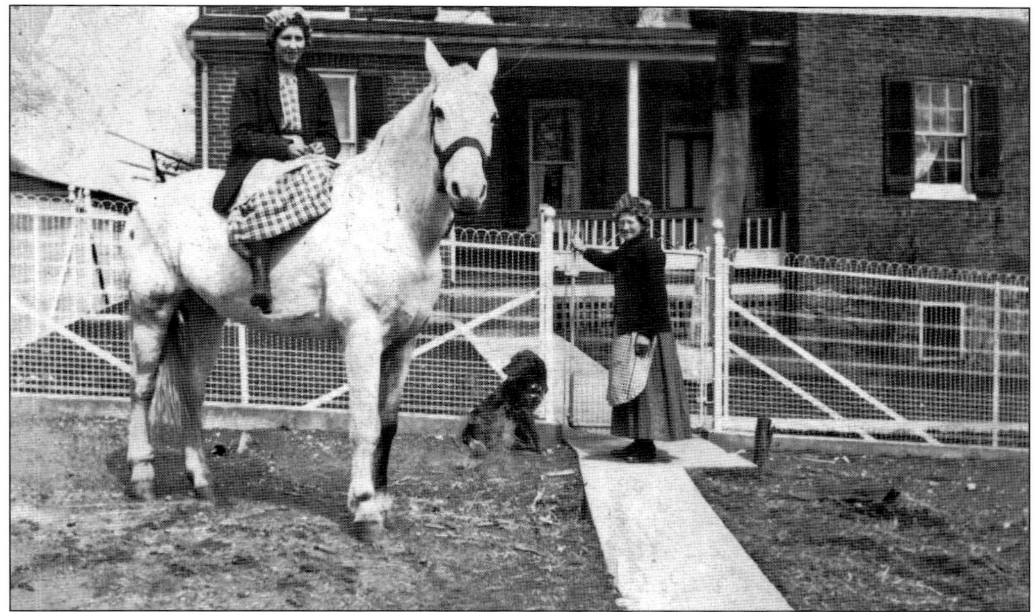

Mary Noble Tracy sits on a white horse, and Letilda Trone Tracy opens the gate on the Charles Tracy farm near Melrose in the 1920s. They are wearing their dust bonnets to keep their hair clean while they work. (Courtesy of Helen Tracy Totura.)

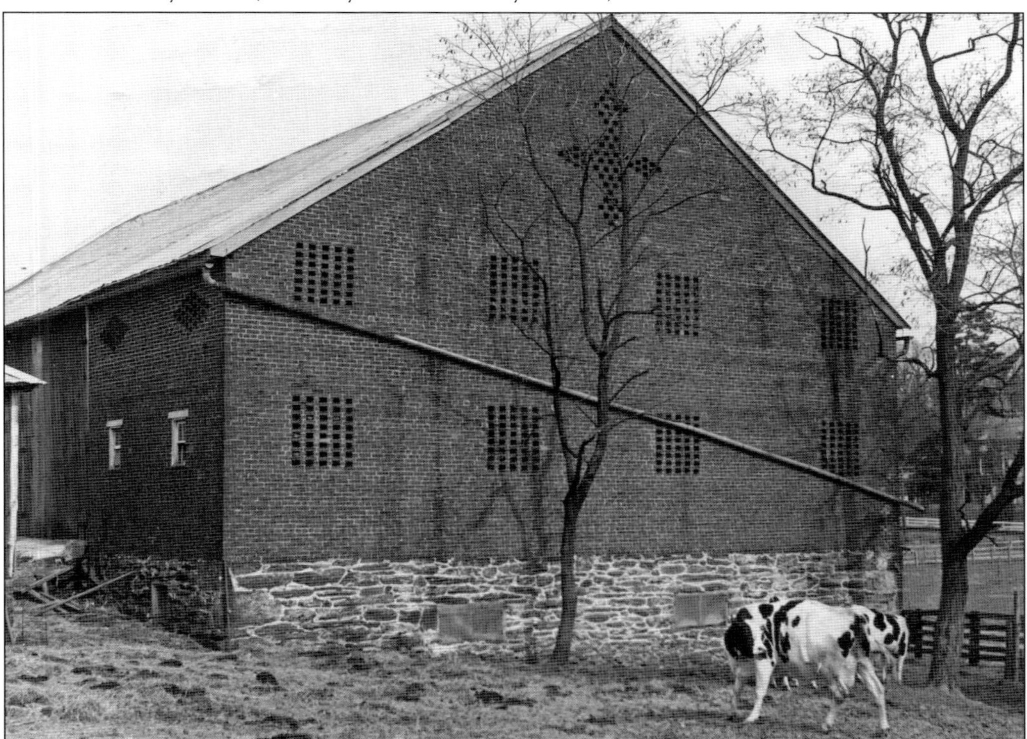

This brick-end barn in Union Bridge is one of several hundred that are unique to northern Maryland (Carroll County) and southern Pennsylvania. These barns have brick ends with symbolic designs that also provide ventilation. Master masons went to the farms and made the bricks there for both the barn and the farmhouse. (Courtesy of the Historical Society of Carroll County.)

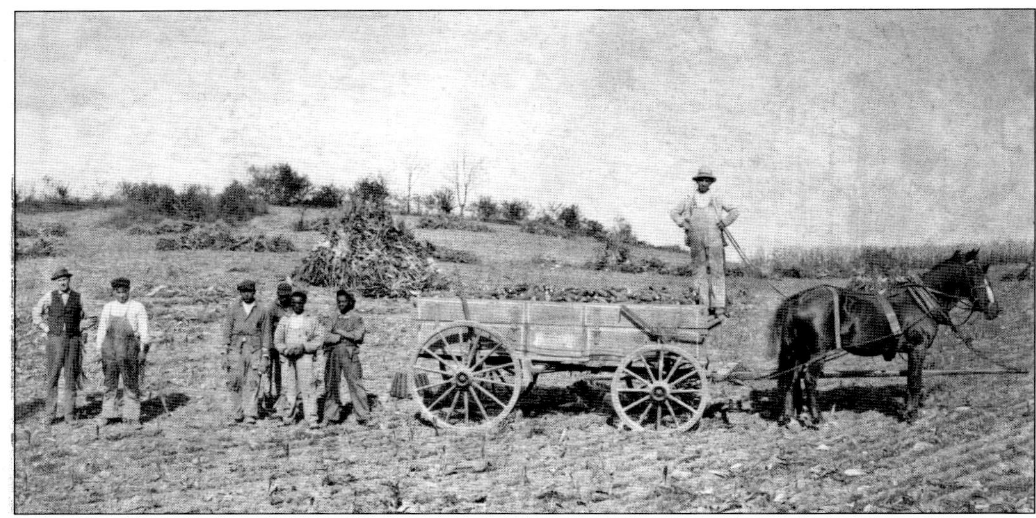

This is one-third of a panorama of a day on the Sunny Side Farm on Wakefield Valley Road in New Windsor when 34 neighbors gathered to help C. Scott Bollinger. On this day in 1910, they came to harvest the fall field corn by hand. The neighborhood women prepared a feast for dinner for all. C. Scott Bollinger is standing on the wagon. Guy Babylon is wearing the white shirt, and farmhands Oscar ? and Fletch ? are closest to the wagon. The others are unidentified. (Courtesy of Sandra Hughes.)

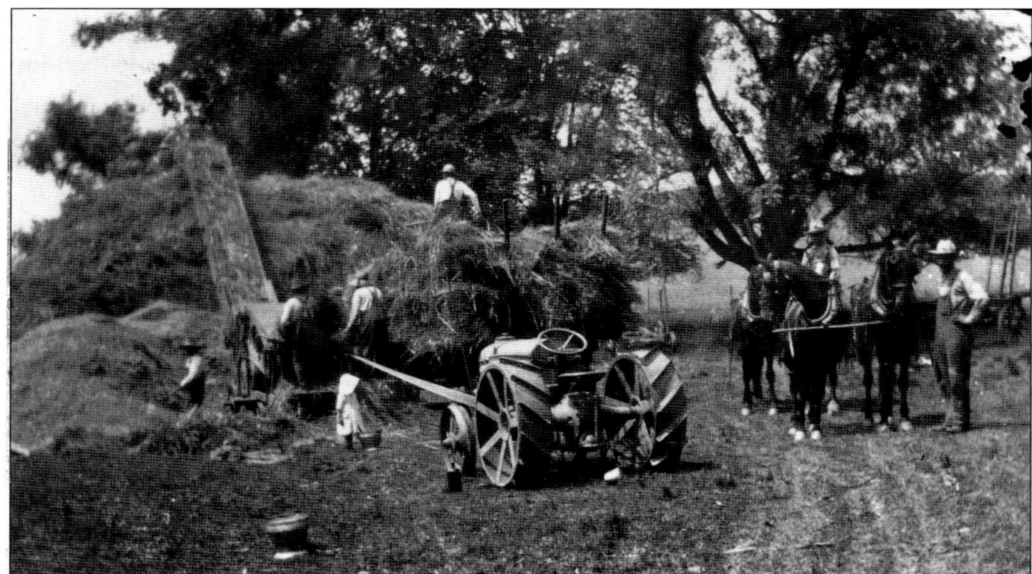

These men are threshing wheat on a Tracy farm in Bachmans Valley. George Tracy owned the thresher, and Jesse Tracy (his brother) owned the tractor. It was common for the farmers to share farm equipment. Neighbors and relatives came to help thresh. (Courtesy of Helen Tracy Totura.)

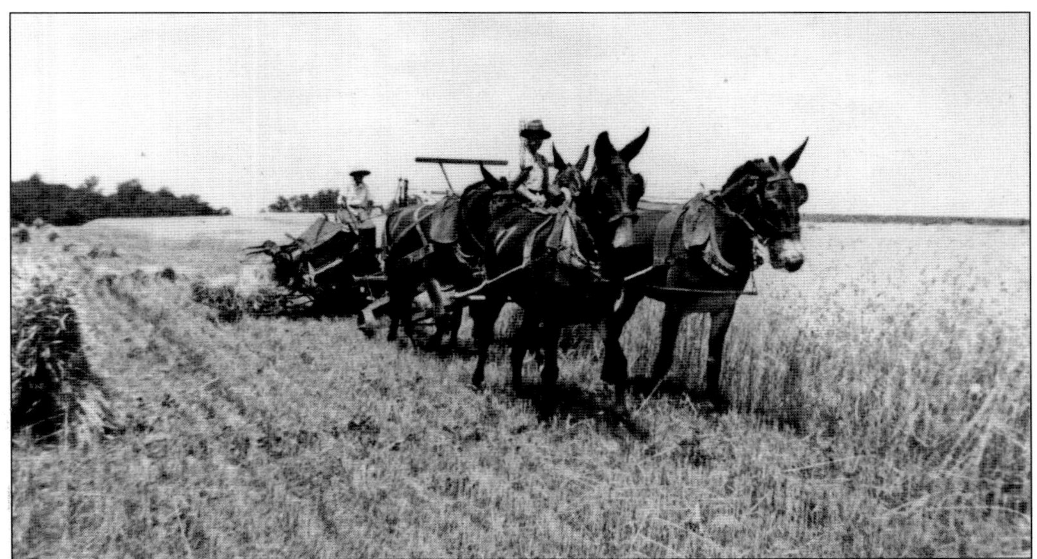

In 1933, Robert Myers is shown on a binder, and Charles R. Myers is guiding the team by riding the mule closest to the binder. They are on Charles Myers's dairy farm in Upperco on Emory Church Road. The farm was purchased in 1914 by Charles Myers and is now owned by Robert Myers. (Courtesy of Reatha Osborn.)

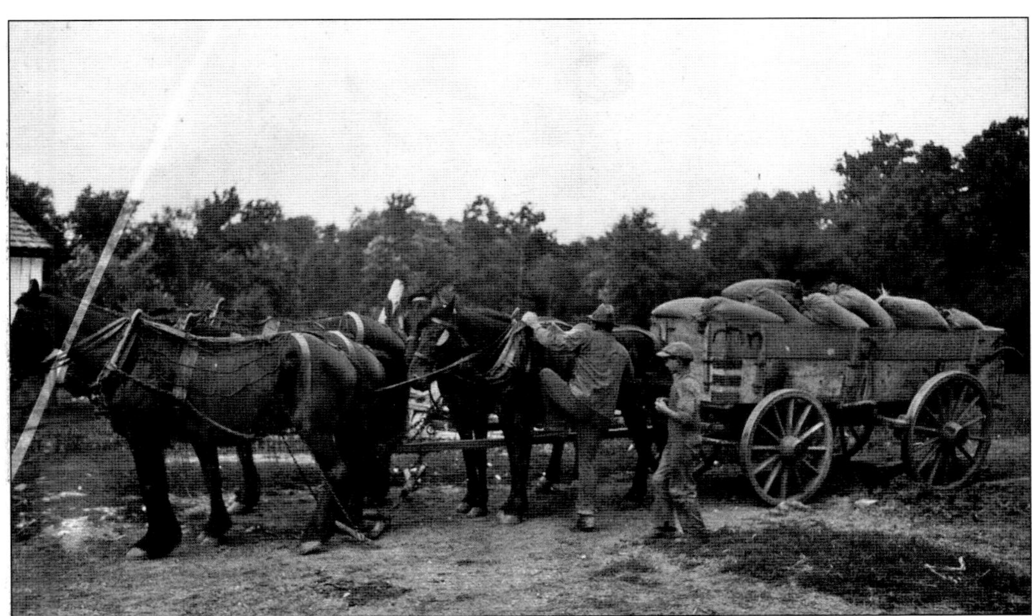

Byron Stull and his hired boy, Jackie Ridge, load wheat after it had gone through the threshing machine. It was put in bags and taken to the nearest mill. Mills dotted the Carroll County landscape because it was important for a farmer to be in close proximity to one. Millers often took their pay in flour instead of cash. (Courtesy of Mildred Stine.)

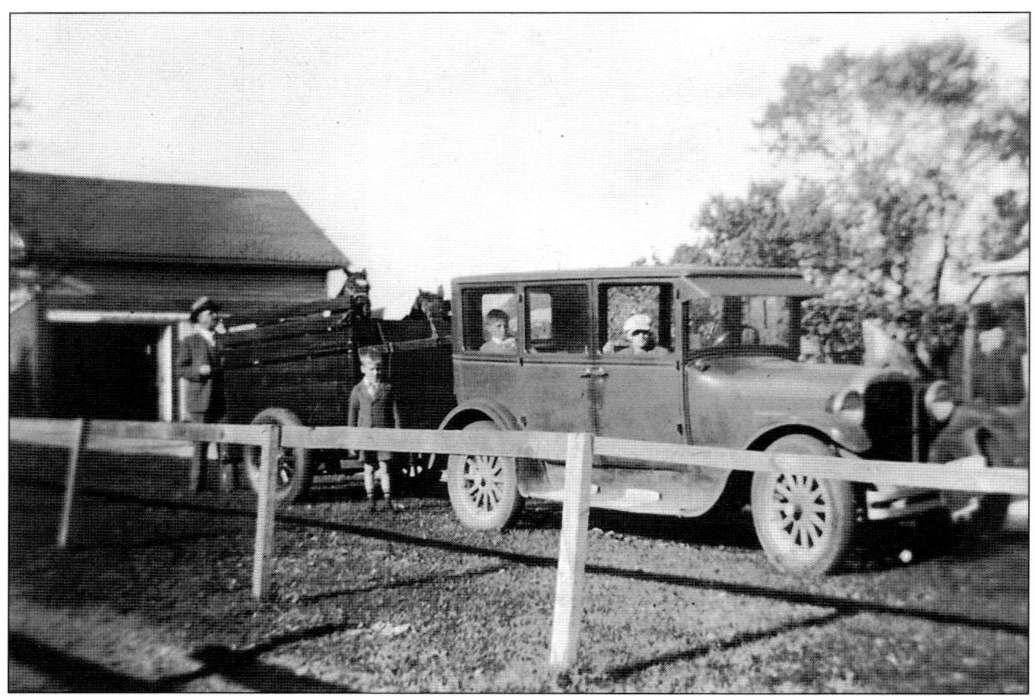

The Reifsnider family loads their horses for transport in a rare early horse trailer. (Courtesy of the Historical Society of Carroll County.)

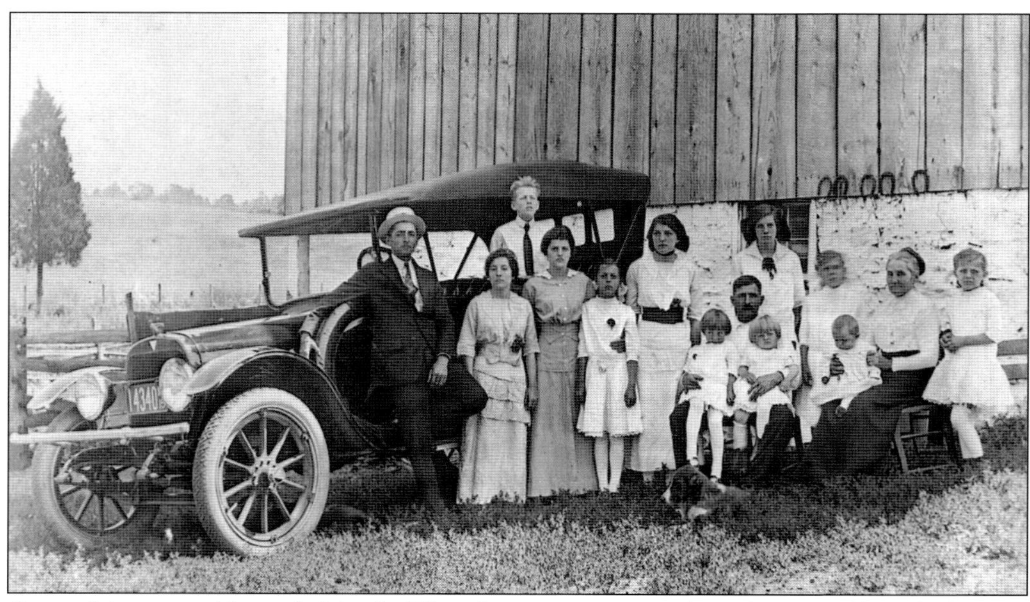

George Monroe and his wife, Martha Ellen Owings, are pictured standing proudly with their car and their family. They are on their first farm in Morgan Valley, Warfieldsburg. From left to right are George Monroe Jr., Mary Elizabeth, John, Jeanette, Susie, Myrtle, Gladys, George Monroe Sr., May, Helen, Evelyn, Martha, Ellen, and Bertie. (Courtesy of Edna Bollinger.)

Gordon Conaway Sr. and Ida "Louise" Conaway are pictured on the Gordon Conaway farm in Berrett around 1935. Roy and Georgie Conaway, Gordon's parents, bought Willow Wind Farm in Berrett near Sykesville. They raised dairy cattle, pigs, hay, chickens, and corn, and had a vegetable garden. They milked by hand. (Courtesy of the James C. Conaway Sr. family.)

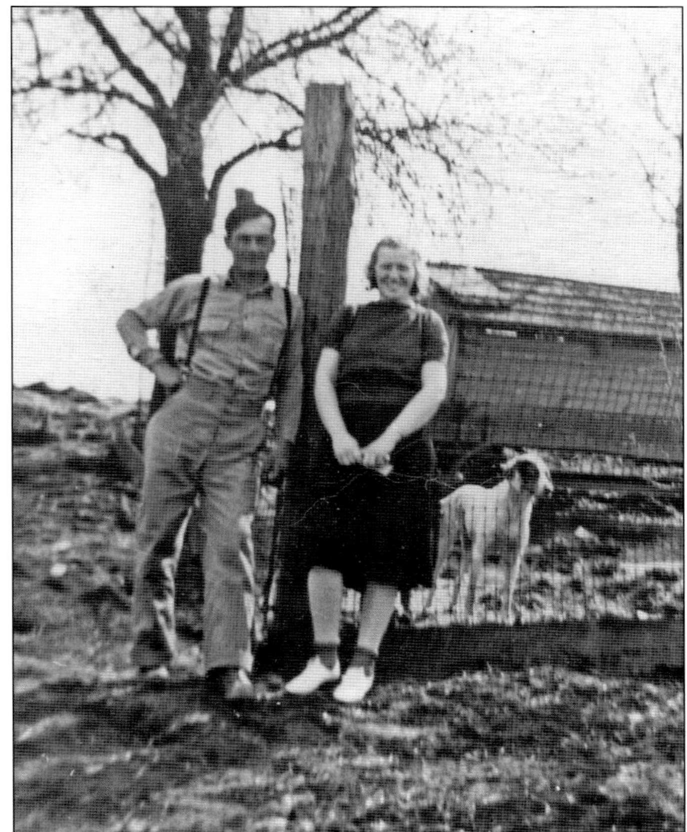

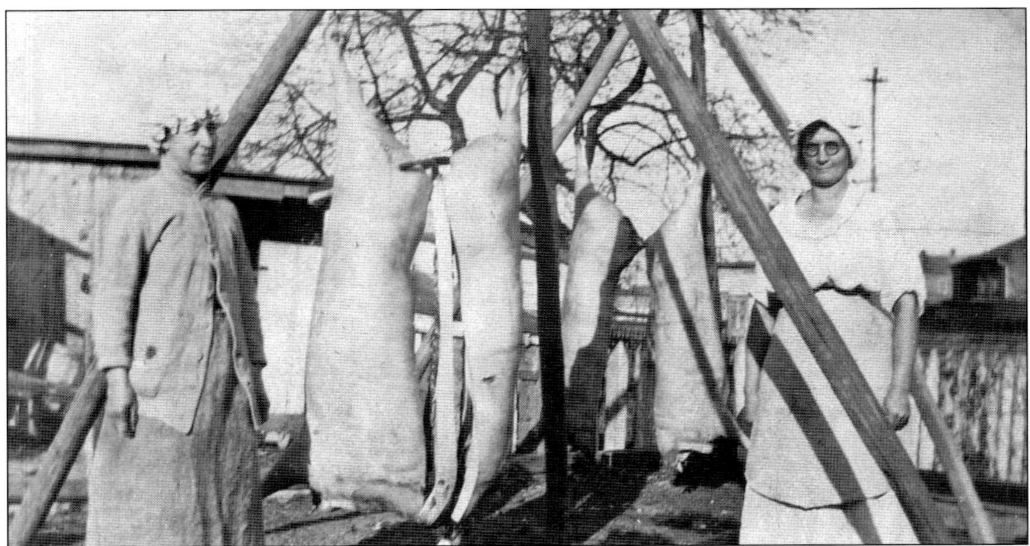

In the 1920s, the Stull family butchered hogs in the fall. After the hog was killed, it was put in a scalding trough full of hot water, and the hair was scraped off the hide. Then they cut the meat up and hung it to cool. Hams were sugar cured or salt brined in a big hogshead barrel. The salt brine was made so that it would float an egg. Then they smoked the meat with apple wood in the smokehouse to preserve it. The fresh meat was cured or canned in jars, while sausage or puddin' was put in a crock and covered with lard to keep it from spoiling. (Courtesy of Mildred Stine.)

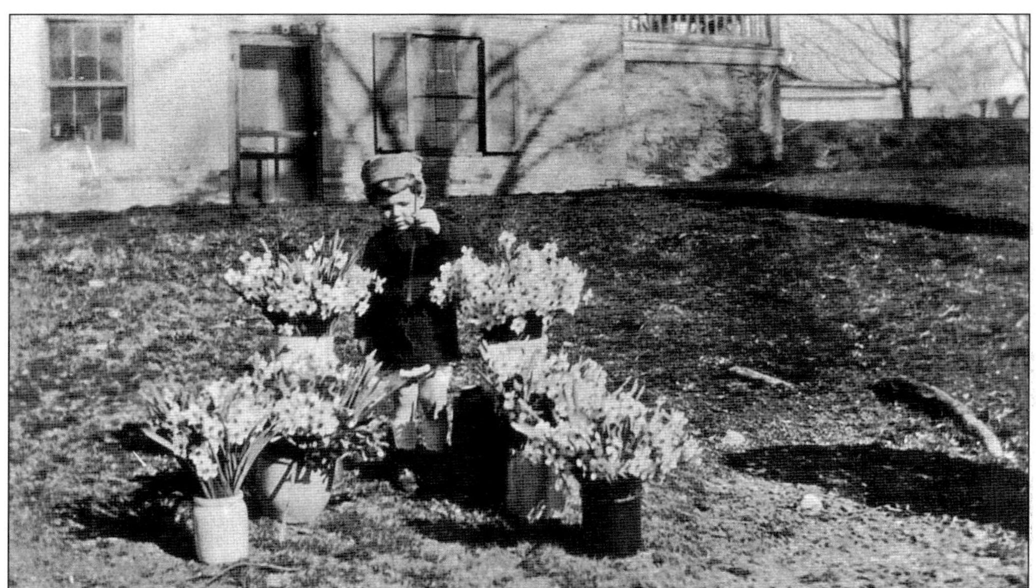

Stephen Morelock stands in the yard with crocks of daffodils for sale on the Harry Paul Morelock farm near Westminster in the early 1900s. They planted 3 acres of jonquils, tulips, narcissus, daisies, poppies, clematis, and magenta peonies. Orders were sold for 50¢ each to ladies in Westminster. When Stanley Tevis was a boy, he said flowers should cost more than that. (Courtesy of the Hull family.)

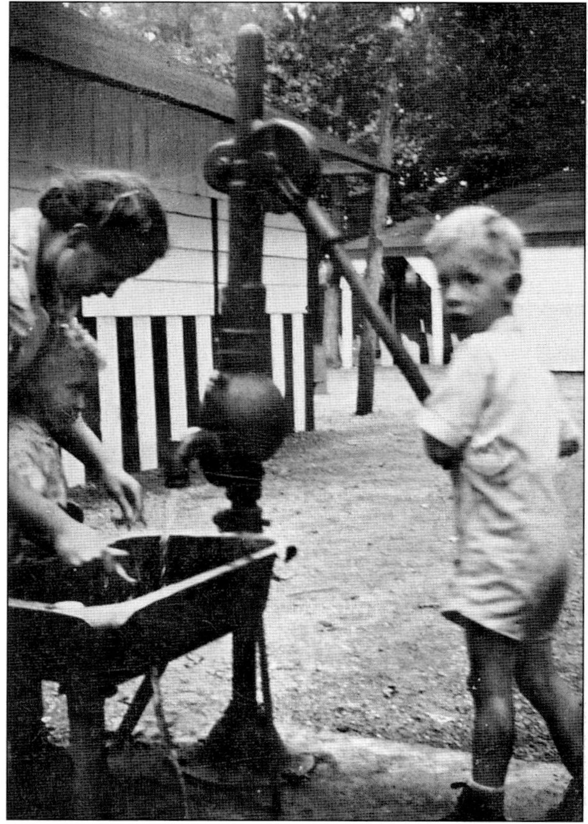

Richard Wilhide of Keysville is pumping water into a water trough on a family outing to Rocky Ridge Park. His mother, Edith, and brother Myron Wilhide are washing their hands in the trough. (Courtesy of the Wilhide family.)

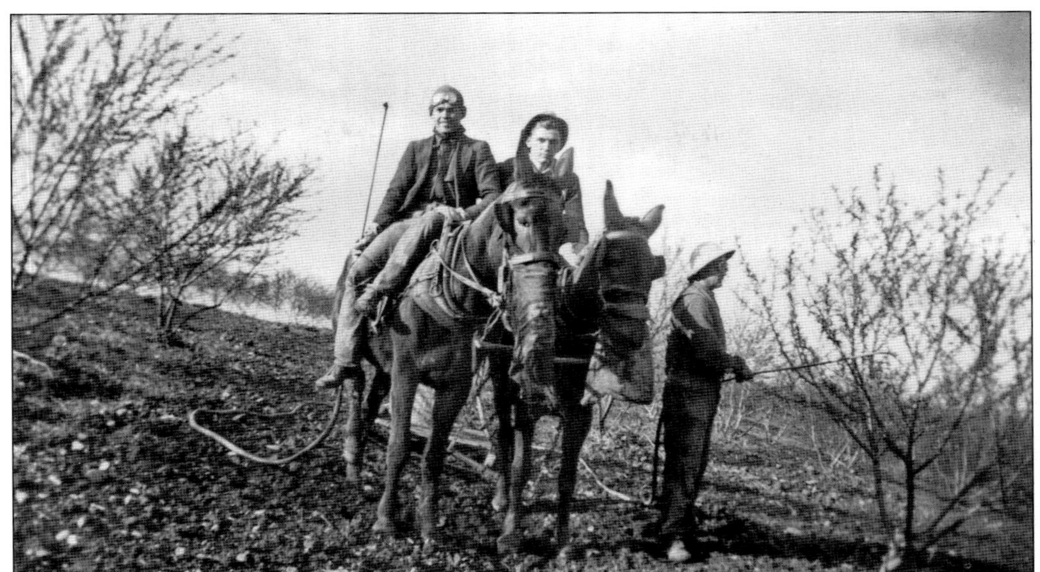

From left to right, Stanley, Edward Jr., and Edward Sr. Bollinger are spraying the peach orchard with a horse-drawn sprayer. The Bollingers owned three farms on Bollinger Road and its intersection with Deer Park Road. (Courtesy of Edna Bollinger.)

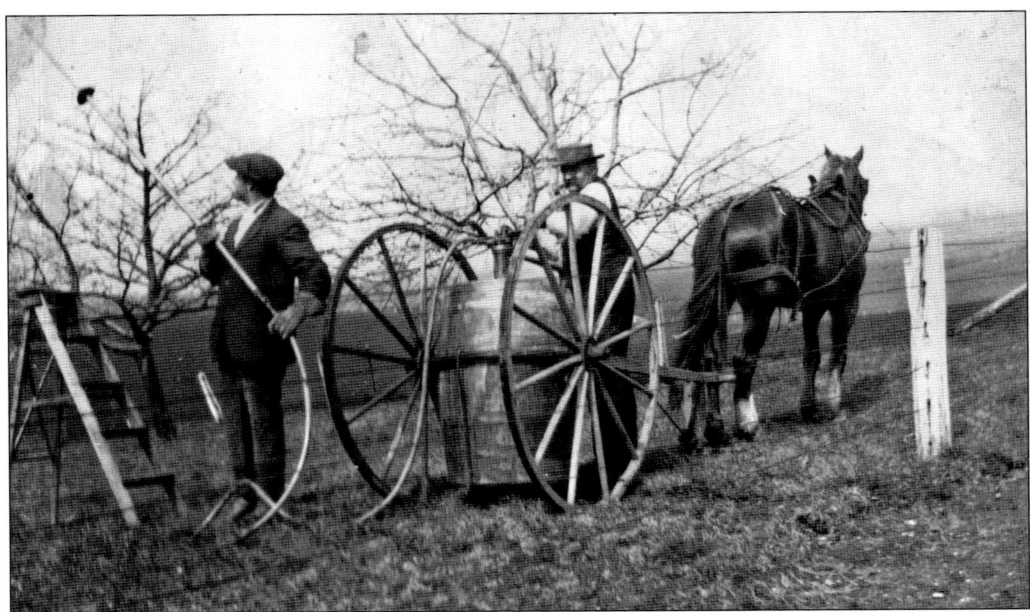

Jesse Tracy (left) and his father, Charles Tracy, are spraying fruit trees, including apricots, cherries, and apples, on the family farm in upper Bachman Valley. Only 3 miles away in lower Bachman Valley, it was too cold for orchards because cold air settles in the valley. (Courtesy of Helen Tracy Totura.)

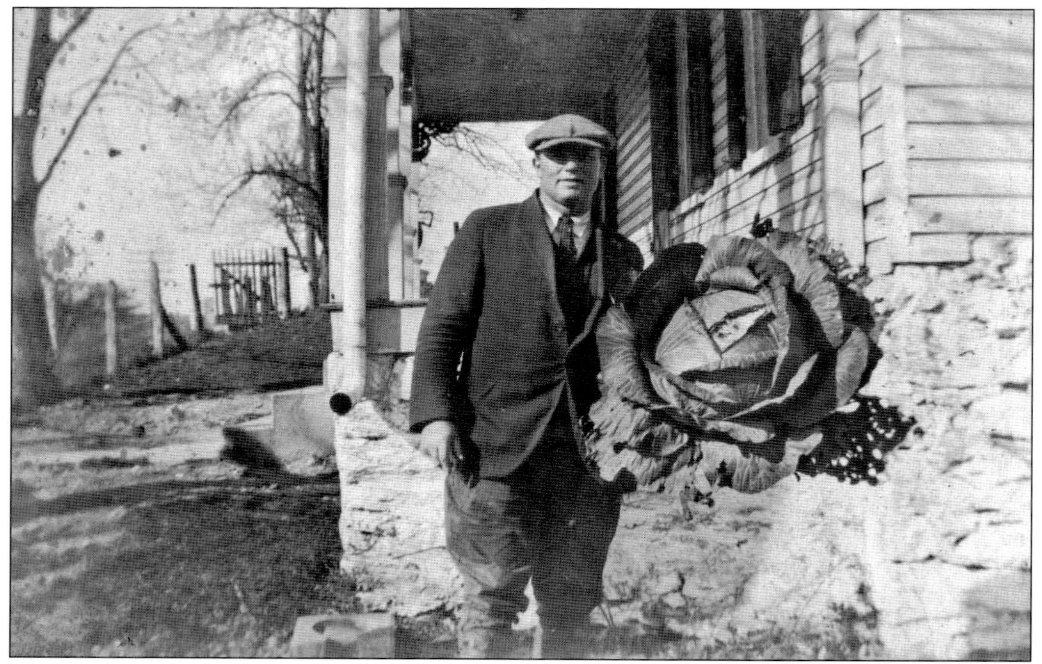

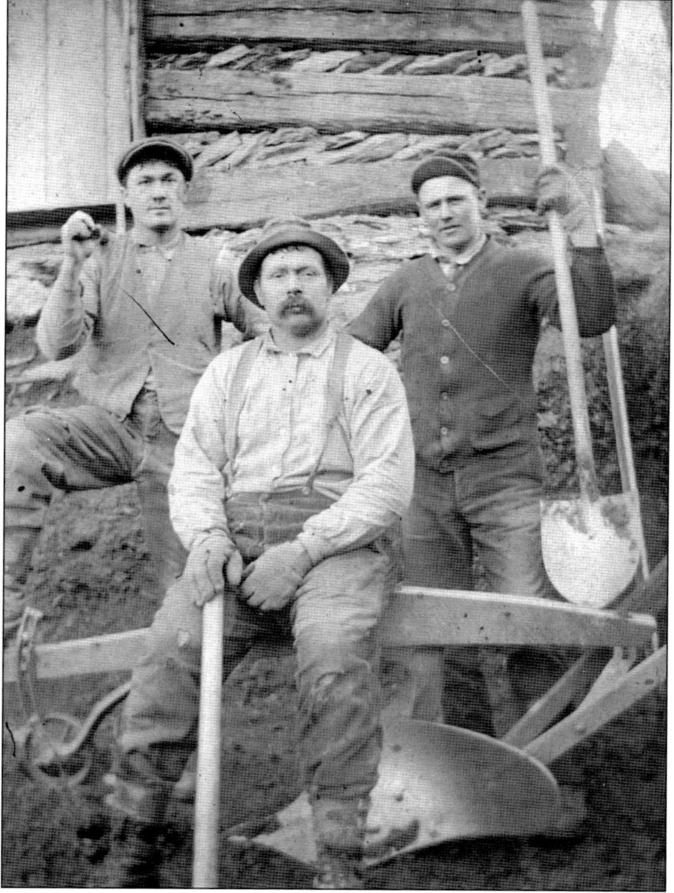

Clyde Ecker, pictured above in 1929, is displaying a giant head of cabbage he raised on his Old Westminster Pike farm. Improved farming techniques, new equipment, insecticides, fertilizers, and crop rotation helped farmers produce bigger and better crops as the century progressed. (Courtesy of Virginia Ecker Hierstetter.)

From left to right, Edward Bollinger Sr., Hayden Bollinger, and an unidentified man take a break for a photograph on a Bollinger farm in Carroll County. Hayden sits on a one-horse plow. Bollingers owned three farms in the Smallwood area on Deer Park and Bollinger Roads, and pursued a wide variety of farming and business enterprises, including owning a sawmill, a wormseed distillery, orchards, crops, and a pond and swimming pool recreation area. (Courtesy of Edna Bollinger.)

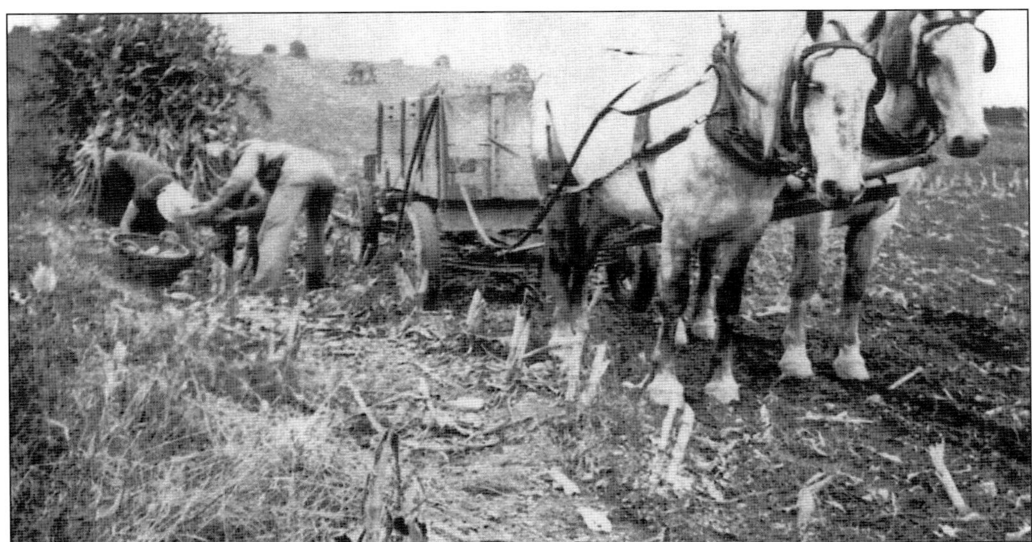

This photograph shows husked ears of corn being loaded into baskets. The baskets are then dumped into the wagon. From left to right, Lillian, Vernon, and Maurice Wolfe are pictured working on the Vernon Wolfe farm. (Courtesy of the Wolfe family.)

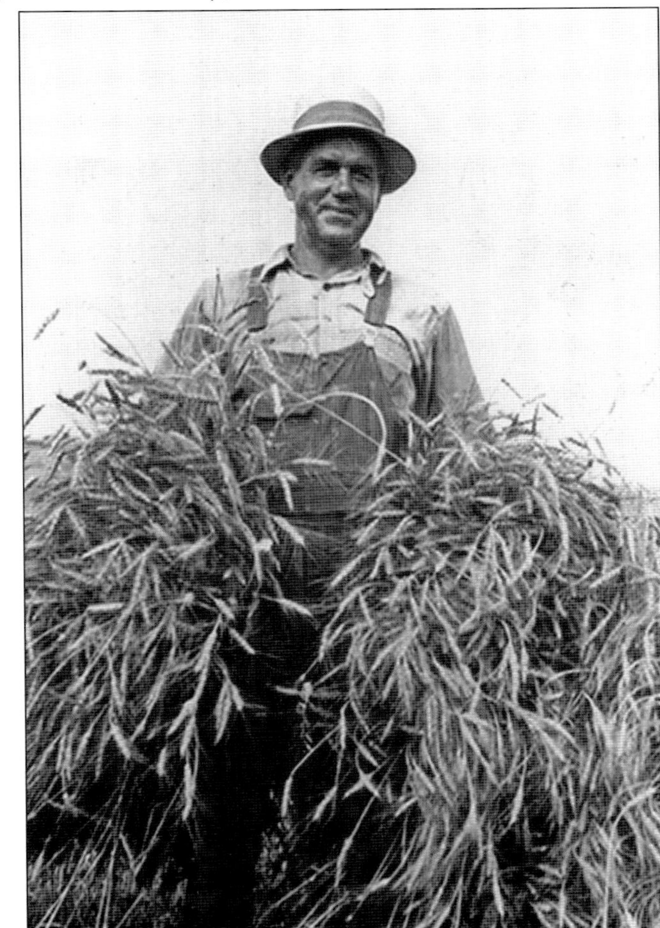

In the early 1940s, Johannes Lieb from Dettingen, Germany, shows off his wheat harvest on his farm named Good Intent, north of Keymar. He was a dairy farmer and also did general farming. This farm was originally part of Terra Rubra (meaning "red land"), the birthplace of Francis Scott Key. (Courtesy of the Lieb and Steffen families.)

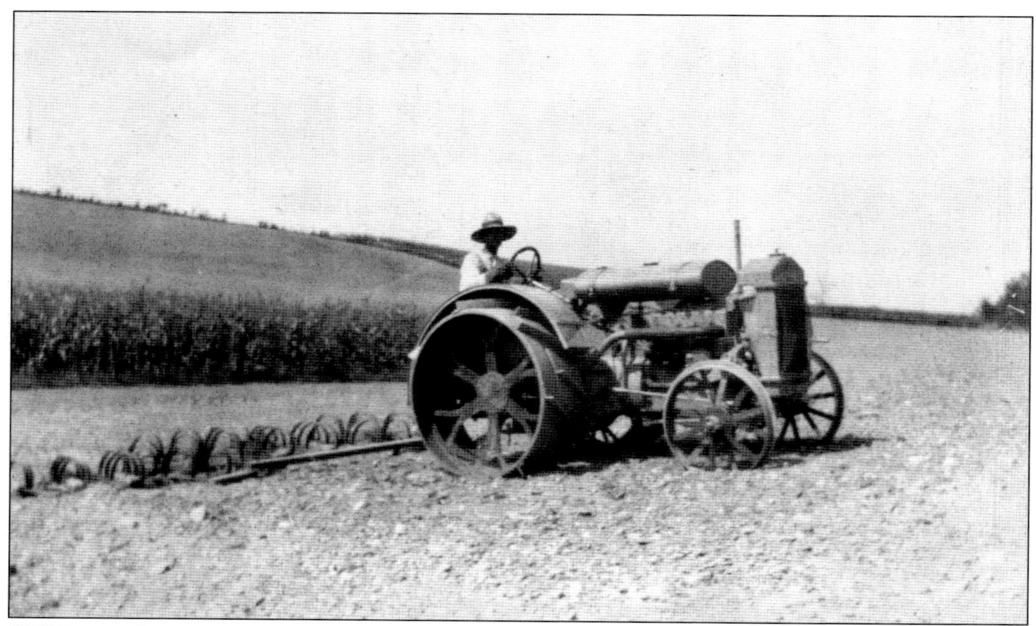

Will Farver harrows his land on his farm in Gypsy Hill on Route 27. Gypsy Hill was named for the Gypsies who camped there. Groups also camped in Bachmans Valley and were known to weave linen from locally grown flax. (Courtesy of Judy Naill.)

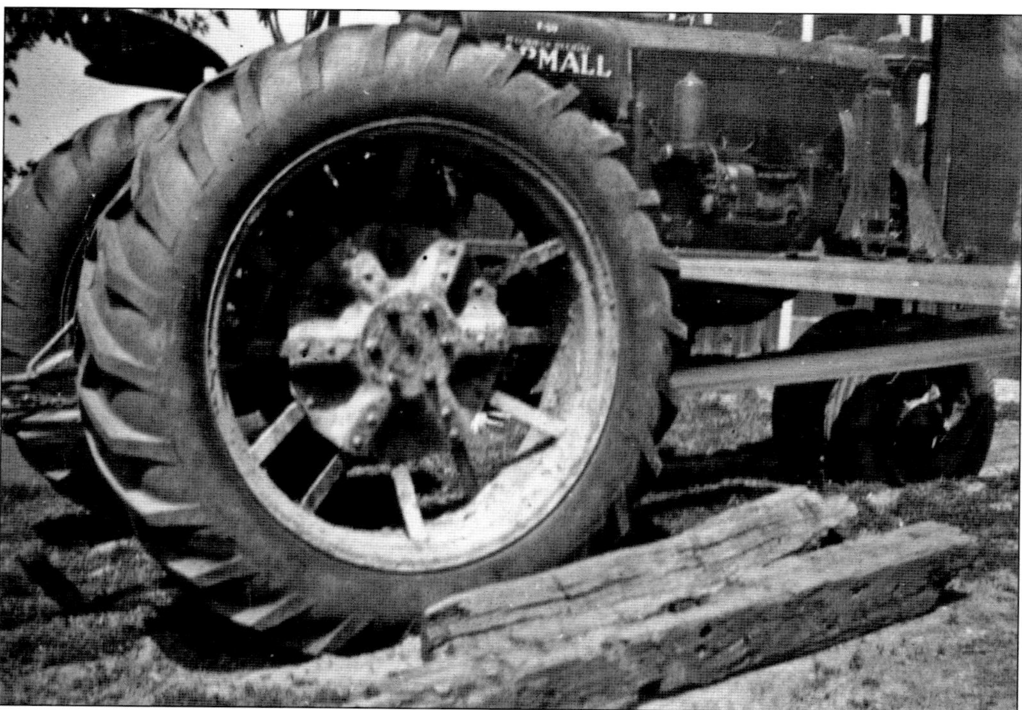

This is Carroll Wilhide's first F20 Farmall Tractor, which he purchased the year he started farming in 1937. It came with rubber tires on the front and steel wheels on the back. Since his steel wheels slipped, he had Crouse's Ford in Taneytown cut the rim for him, and he added rubber tires to the steel wheels. (Courtesy of the Wilhide family.)

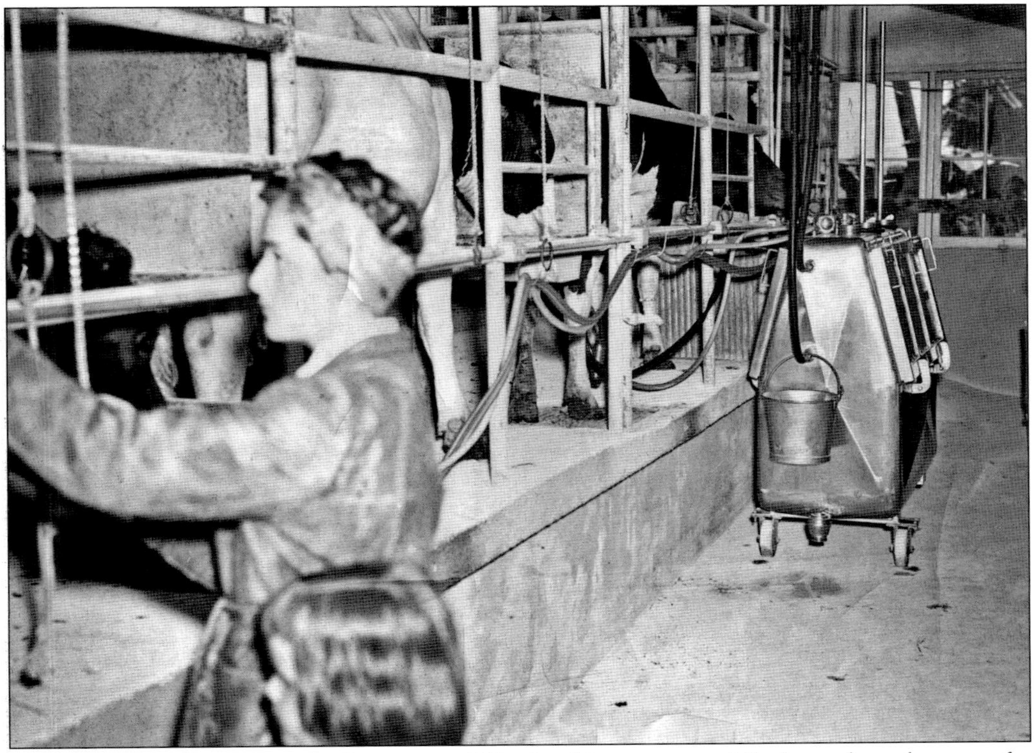

Before school, the Roop girls, Patricia and Shirley (the younger girl) cleaned up the cows for the W. Roger Roop dairy farm on Middleburg Road in Union Bridge around 1950. Shirley and Patricia were responsible for cleaning the cows and competed to see who dad said did the best job. (Courtesy of Patricia Roop Robinson.)

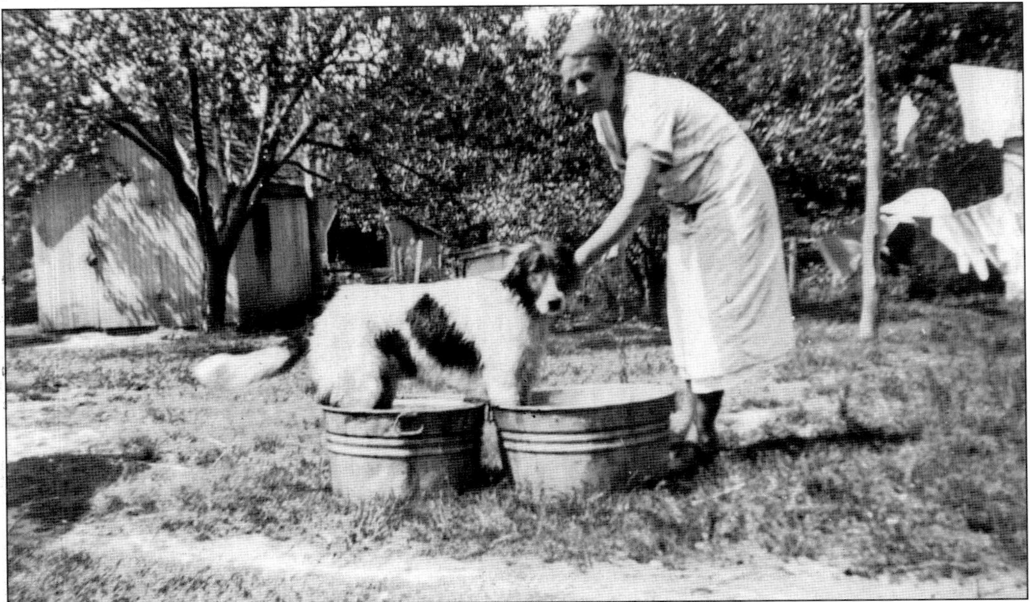

Katharine Hollingsworth is pictured washing the family dog at their farm in Finksburg. Jesse and Katharine Hollingsworth farmed 100 acres, raising dairy cattle, chickens, wheat, rye, oats, and corn. The farm was in the family from 1828 until 1946. (Courtesy of Ann Horvath.)

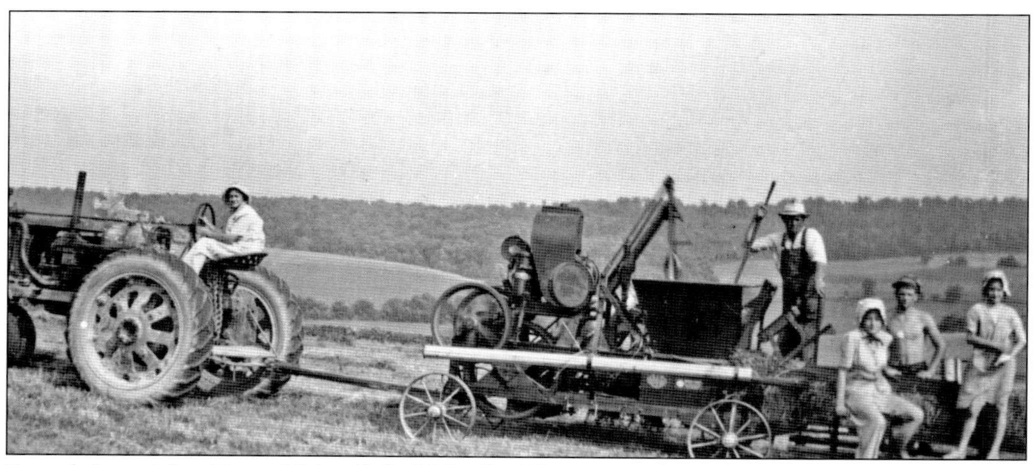

From left to right, Grace Hoke, S. L. Hoke Sr., Florence Hoke, Solomon Hoke Jr., and Fannie Mae Hoke bail hay in 1942 on the Wolf farm on Back Woods Road in Bachman Valley. Notice that some women wore dresses even in the field. (Courtesy of the Wolfe family.)

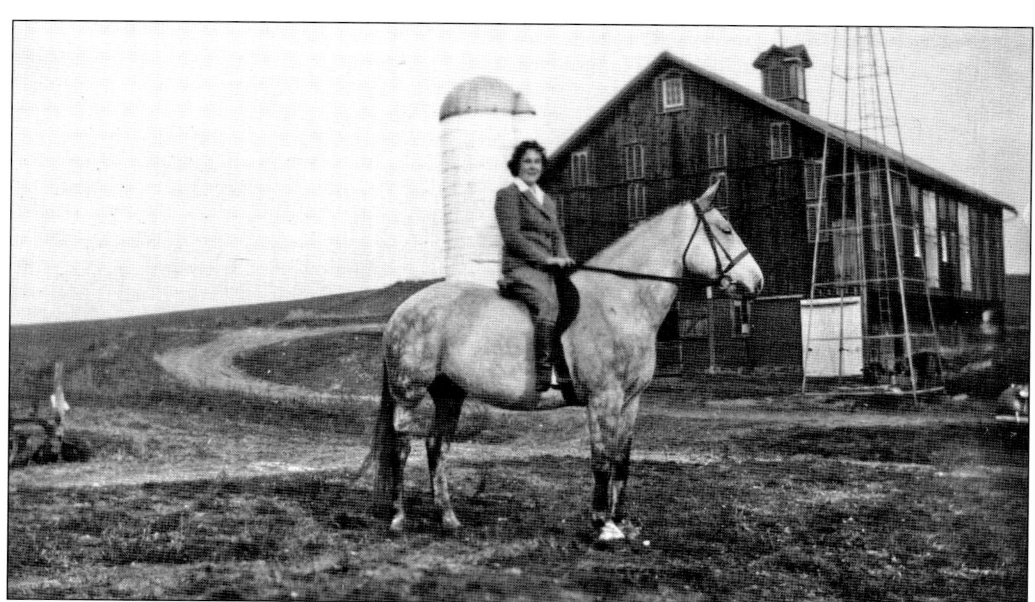

Grace Grabill Owings rides Queenie on the 150-acre Runnymede Farm in Uniontown in the 1940s. William H. Owings purchased it for $6,500 in 1942. When her husband, Theodore, passed away in 1988, Grace and her daughter, Virginia, took over the farm. They bought 700-pound cattle, fed them on grass until they were 900 to 1,000 pounds, and sold them as feeder cattle. (Courtesy of Virginia Lambert.)

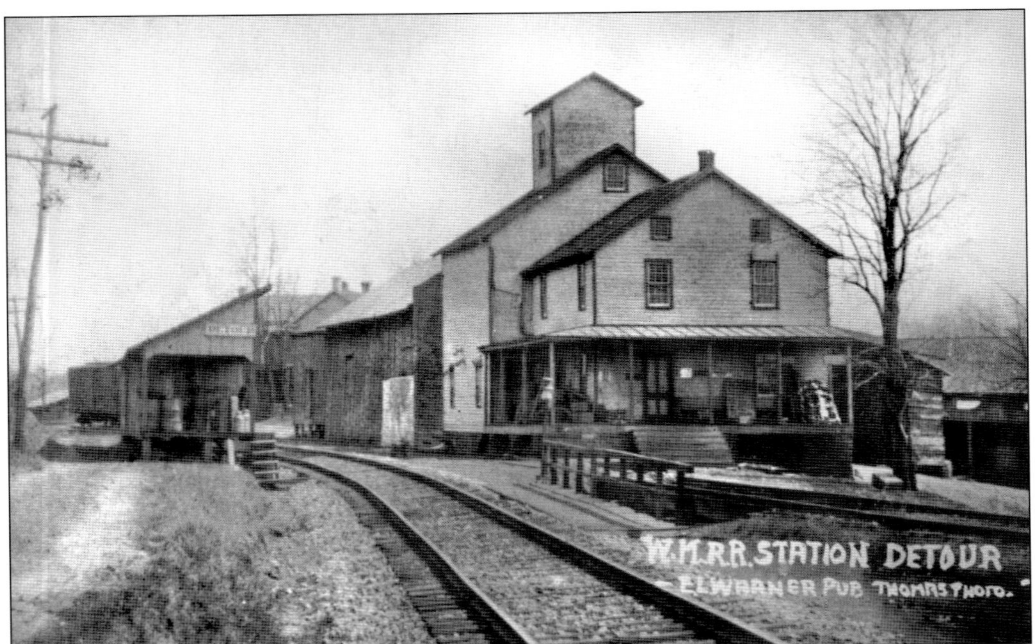

This is the Western Maryland Railroad Station in Detour with milk cans ready to be taken to Baltimore at 8:00 a.m. Maurice Wilhide sent four cans of milk a day. Sometimes they would spill and get dents in them. They stirred the milk and tried to cool it in the summer. If it turned sour before it got to Baltimore, they would send it back. (Courtesy of the Wilhide family.)

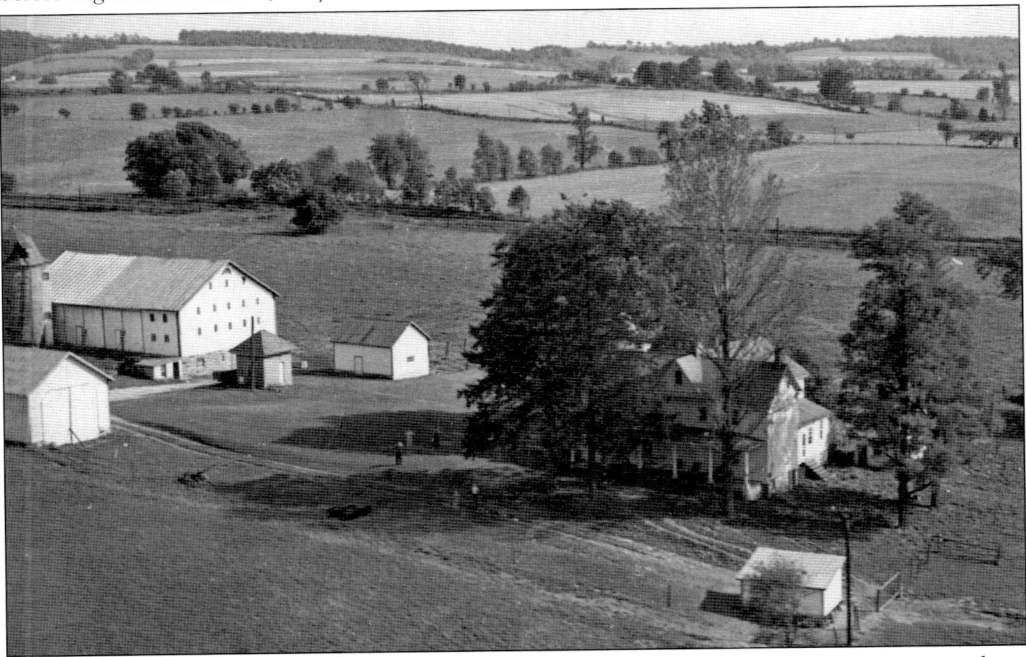

This farm in New Windsor was purchased by Herman and Olive Baile in 1930. It was a dairy farm until 1952. The Bailes took their milk to New Windsor in milk cans and put it on a truck to Baltimore. In 1969, they sold the farm to their son, Melvin, and his wife, Pat. The Bailes fed out 1,000 hogs and 160 beef cattle annually. Melvin and Joan Baile Jr. and their family moved to the farm in 1998 and began running a grain operation. (Courtesy of the Baile family.)

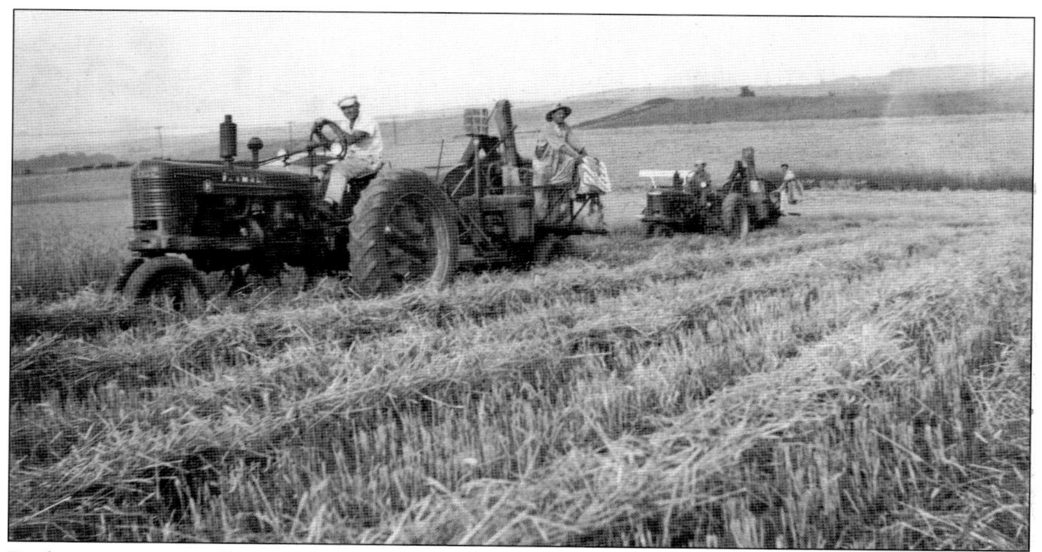

Both tractors are pulling combines, which are cutting off and threshing the grain out and leaving behind straw in a windrow on top of the straw stubble. They are cutting high enough to avoid running a stone through the combine, which would do some damage. During the war, tractors were in such short supply that people could get almost any price for a tractor. When the government made rules to stop this, they got around the law by selling a bale of hay at an auction and giving them the tractor free with it. (Courtesy of the Mathias family.)

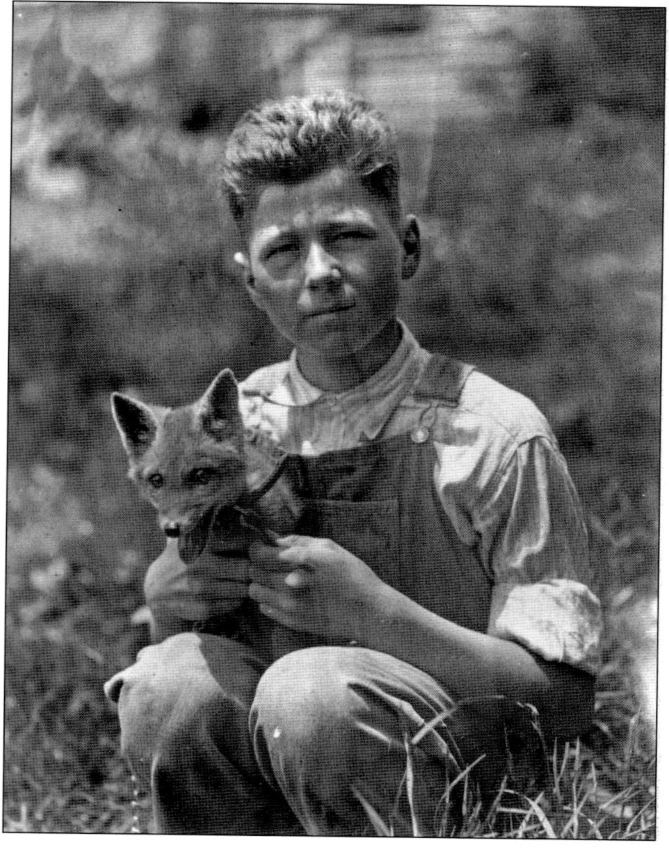

Stephen Morelock holds his pet fox in the early 1930s on the Morelock farm on Meadowbranch Road near Westminster. (Courtesy of Elinor Hull.)

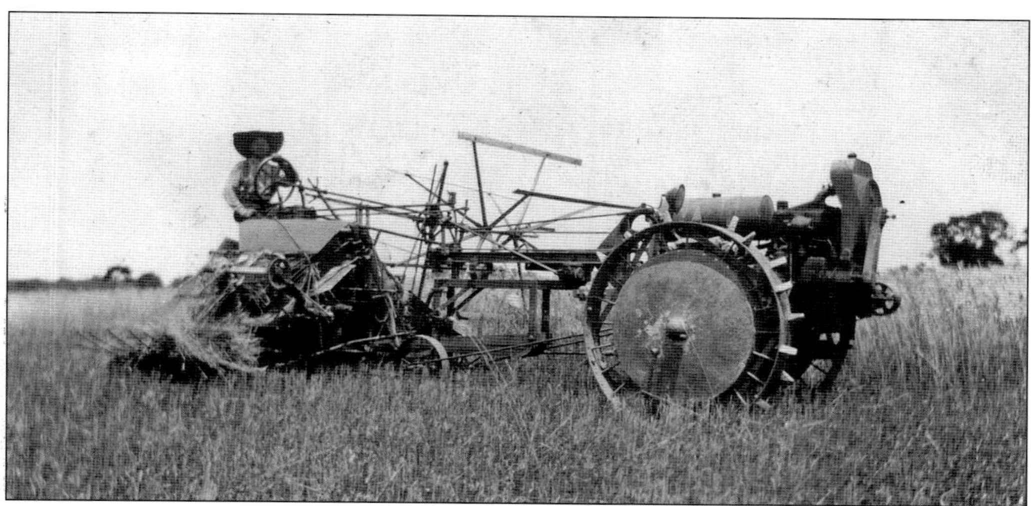

Grier Keilholtz is pictured riding a binder on his farm on Keysville Frederick County Road. The tractor was one of the first in the area. He sat on the wheat binder and steered the tractor. It was used both to cut the wheat and bind it in the 1920s. (Courtesy of Mildred Stine.)

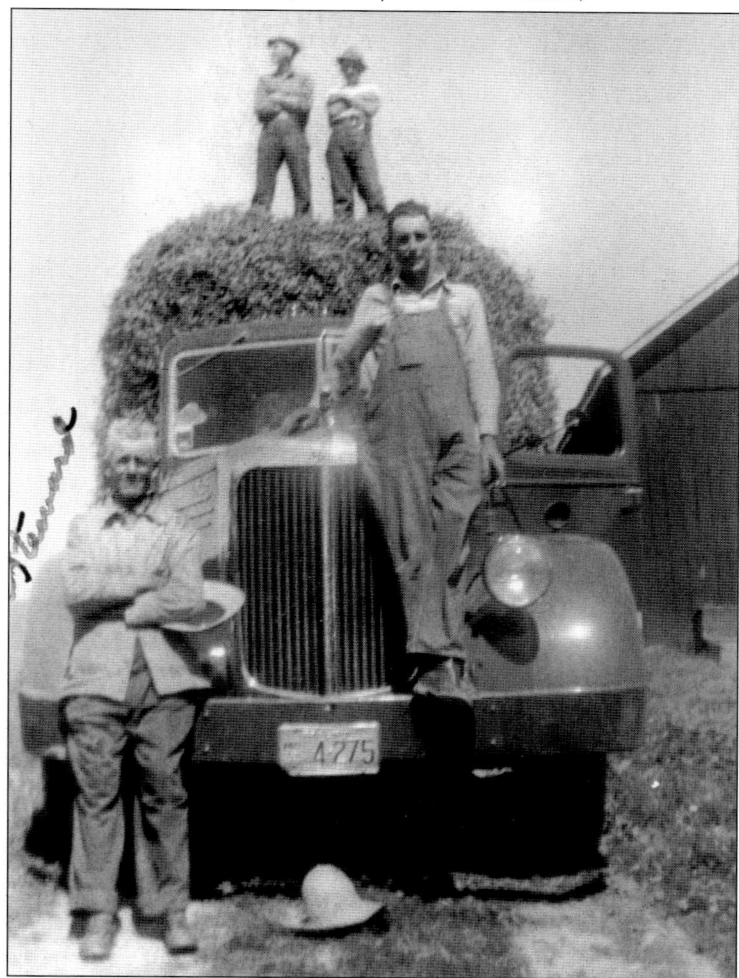

This is Harvey Shipley's new truck with a load of peas on the way to the cannery. Peas were a good cash crop for farmers. Herman Hoff sits on the grill of the truck. They are on the Francis Hoff farm in Gamber in June 1941. (Courtesy of Bonnie Fold.)

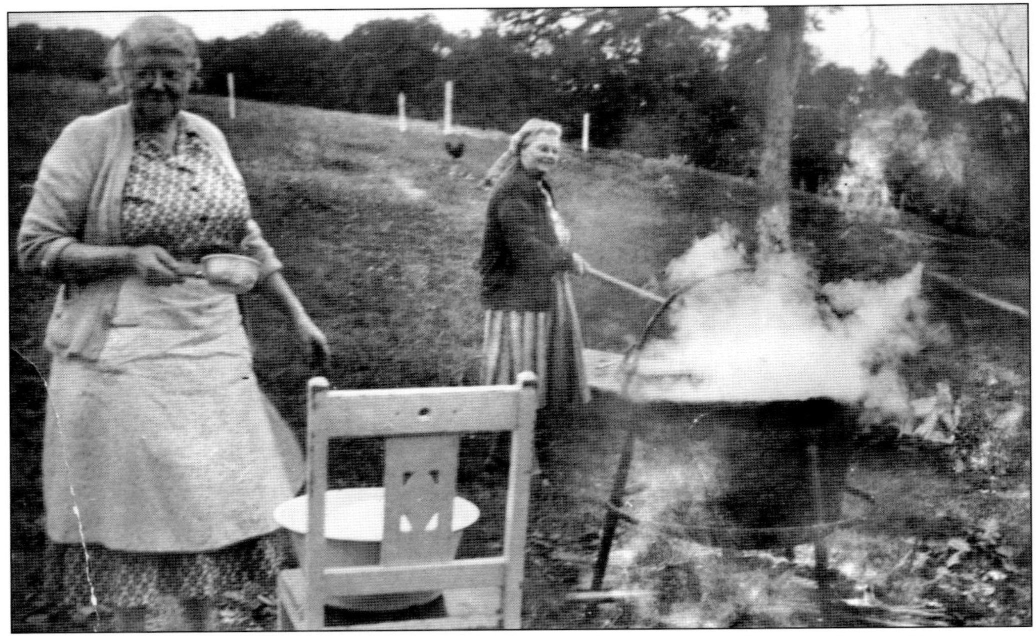

In November 1955, the Berrett Homemakers met on the Conaway farm in Sykesville to make apple butter. The women brought in 10 bushels of golden grimes apples from surrounding farms and pared them the night before. They began before dawn, cooking down apples in a copper kettle for hours with constant stirring. Only cinnamon was added. Katie Bennett is in front. (Courtesy of the Conaway family.)

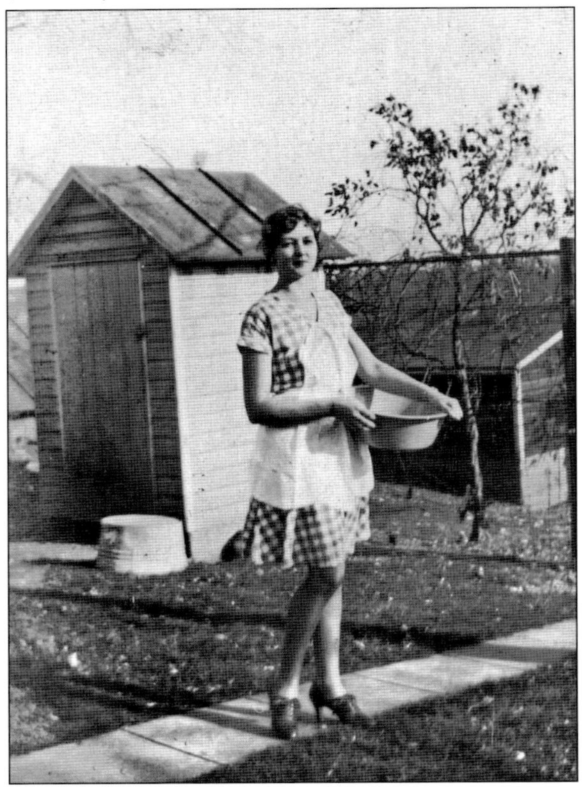

Evelyn Farver Lambert carries her wash pan on the Farver farm in Gypsy Hill on Route 27. Notice the outhouse behind her. Outhouses were on farms well into the 1960s, even near town. (Courtesy of Judy Naill.)

This is a late-1940s kitchen on the Null farm in Taneytown. Hubert Null's chair is to the left where he read his mail and farm magazines, and then fell asleep. The cook stove is still there in the old stone house on the farm. The stove was a gift to Hubert's wife, Gladys Zepp Null. George Daniel Null remembers it coming in crates and putting it together in the kitchen. (Courtesy of the Null family.)

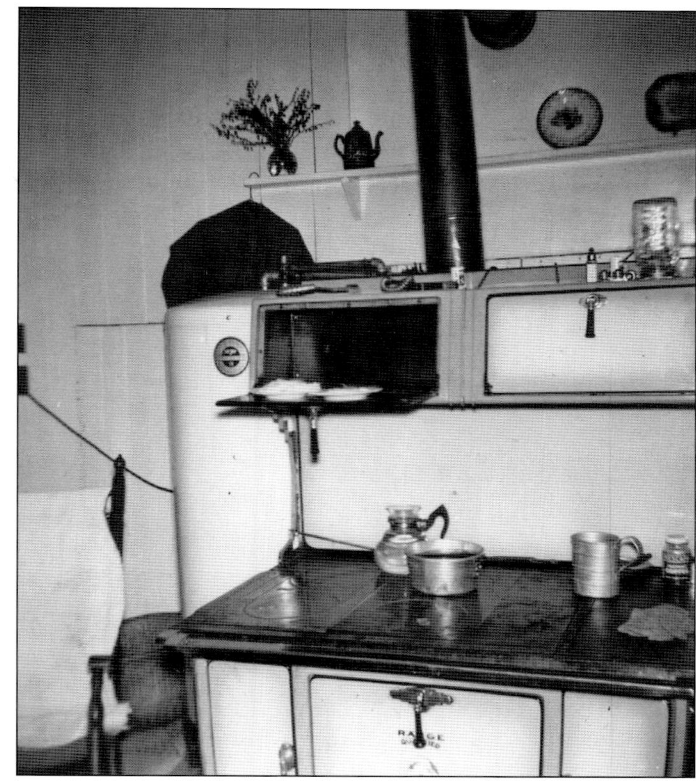

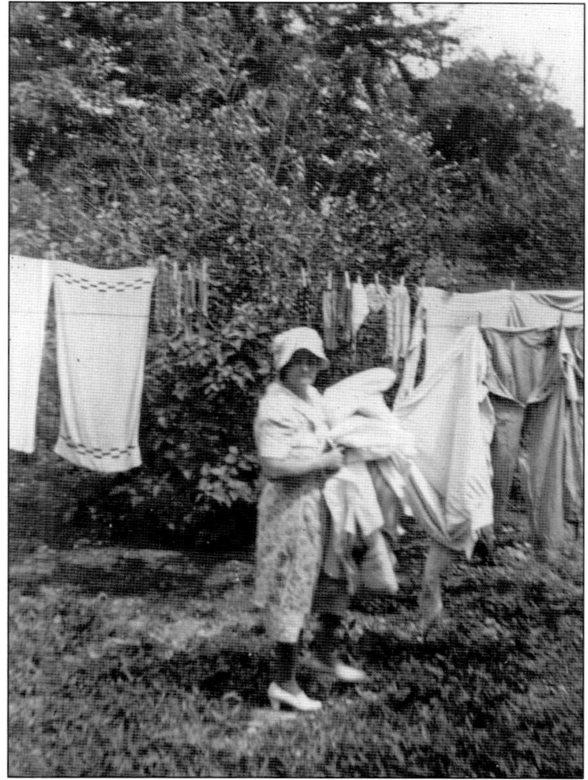

Ovie K. Miller Ecker washed every Monday using a Maytag wringer washer. She washed the clothes in the washer, ran them through the wringer by hand, and then put them in a tub of clear water. She used a wooden handled wash stick with three metal fingers to move them to another tub when that got soapy. The next tub took out that soap and the water became clearer. Then she hung the laundry on the lines. (Courtesy of Virginia Ecker Hierstetter.)

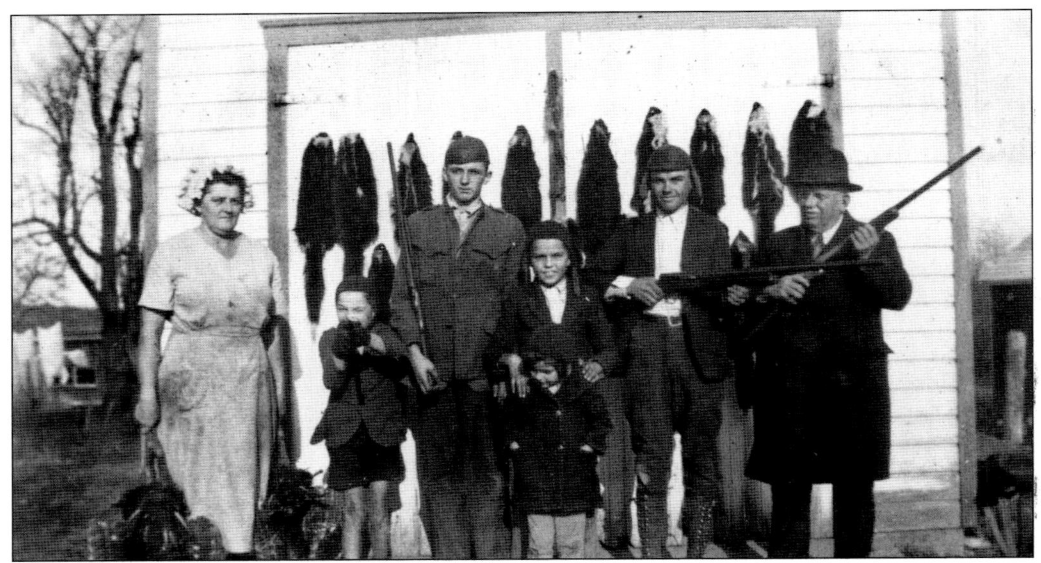

From left to right are Jeanette Bollinger and her children George Bollinger, Edward Bollinger Jr., Francis Bollinger, Stanley Bollinger, unidentified, and Audrey (in front) in January 1937, on the Bollinger farm at the corner of Bollinger and Deer Park Roads. Stanley trapped and sold skin pelts to earn spending money; note the skunk pelts. (Courtesy of Edna Bollinger.)

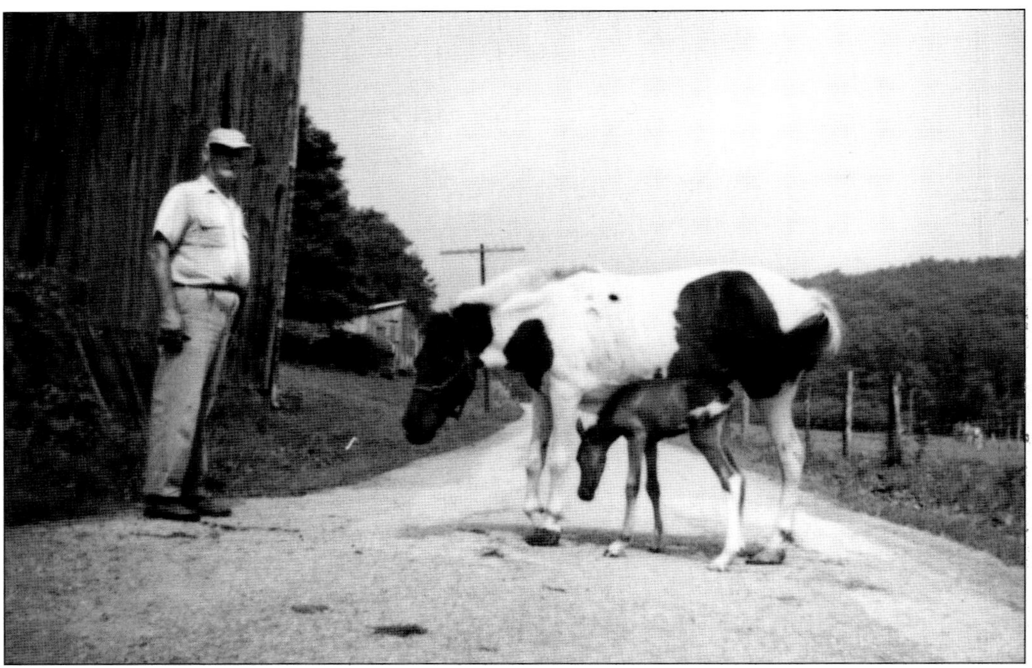

William Swartzbaugh is pictured on his farm on Hoffman Mill Road near Hampstead. Swartzbaugh bought and sold horses, including Clydesdales and Standards. He went to a horse show and bought a couple of horses, and he was hooked. All the pastures that did not have crops had horses on his farm. As farmers replaced their horses with tractors, he bought the horses and sold them to the Amish in New Holland, Pennsylvania. (Courtesy of Andrea Henderson.)

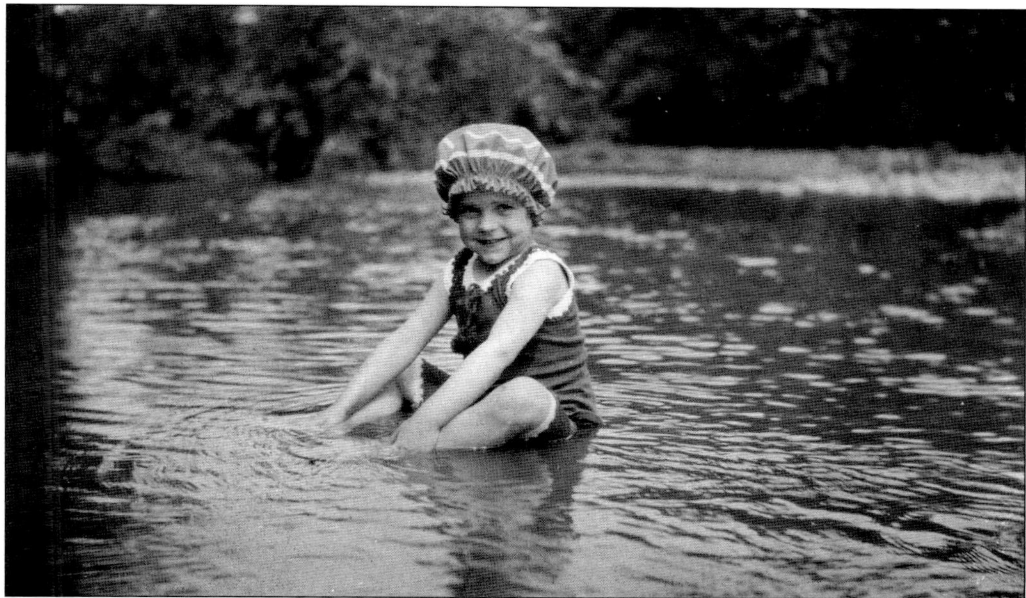

In 1922, Mildred Stull is swimming in the Monocacy River behind her home in Keysville on the Byron Stull farm. The river flooded as high as 65 inches in the basement of the house in 1972. It flooded the house three times in four years. (Courtesy of Mildred Stine.)

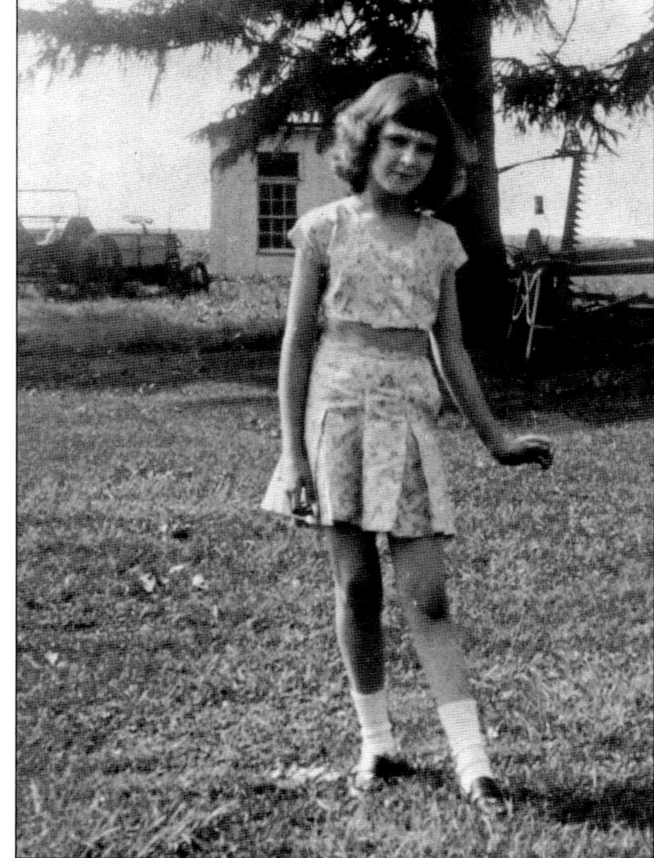

In 1948, ten-year-old Nancy Swartzbaugh Airing is pictured on a Shilling farm in Sandymount farmed by her grandparents Annie and William Blessing. She proudly wears a shorts set made by her grandmother from patterned hog or chicken feed bags, a common practice among farm families. Annie also made her own patterns, as farm wives often did. (Courtesy of Nancy Airing.)

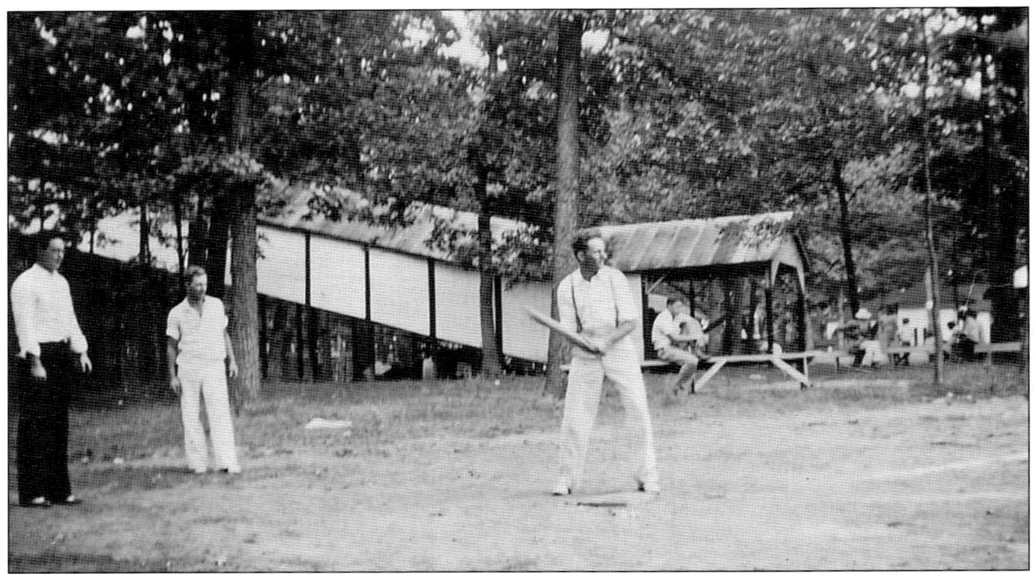

Playing baseball at Rocky Ridge Park and riding on the super large wooden sliding board has been a pastime for local people for the past 100 years. Clyde Wilhide is second from the left, and his brother Carroll is at bat. The park is not far from Keysville and is a favorite location for family reunions. (Courtesy of the Wilhide family.)

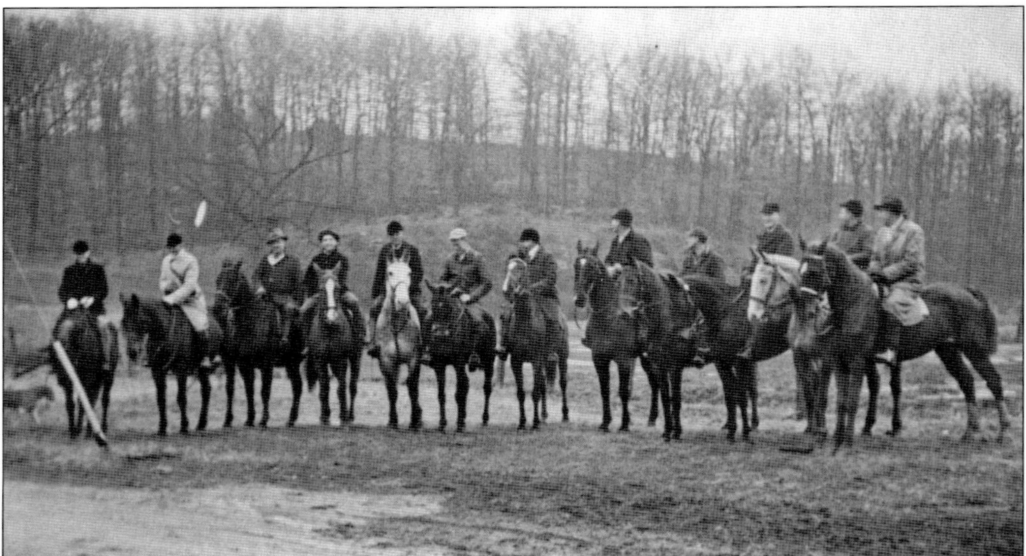

The Taylorsville Hunt Club gets ready to fox hunt in the 1940s. Gordon Conaway Sr. and Gordon Conaway Jr. of Berrett were members of the club and also participated in jousting tournaments, the Maryland state sport. In 1650, Col. Robert Brooke brought his hounds with him from Great Britain when he settled in Maryland and started the first hunting pack on this continent. The Dutch Picnic in Smallwood, established in 1877, has held a jousting tournament since the early 1900s. (Courtesy of the James C. Conaway Sr. family.)

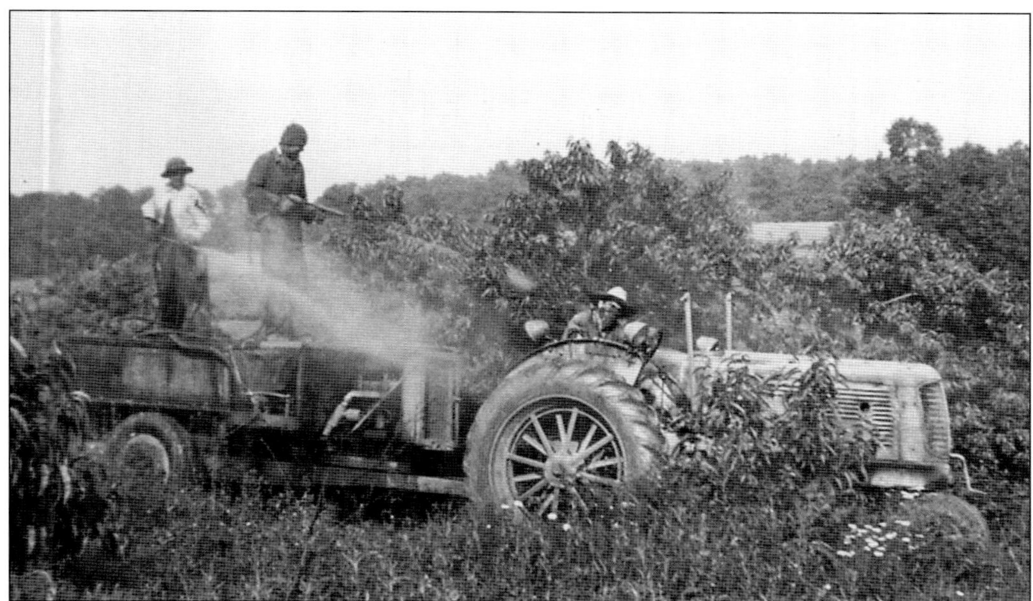

In this picture, the Bollingers spray their fruit trees with Edward Bollinger Sr. driving the tractor, on their Deer Park Road orchard. They have rags around their faces to protect themselves from the spray. The fruit was graded in the barn after it was picked. Fruits grown included peaches, a wide variety of apples, plums, cherries, and pears. (Courtesy of Edna Bollinger.)

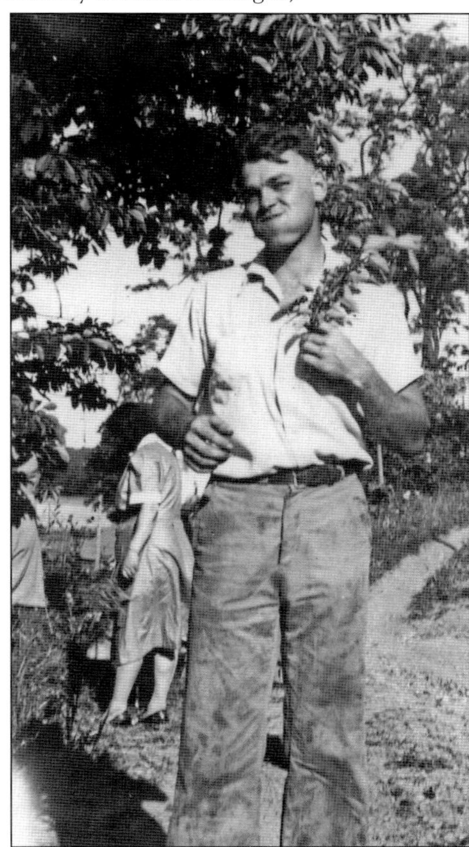

Stanley Bollinger grins with a mouthful of cherries he just pulled off one of the family orchard cherry trees on the Bollinger Deer Park Road farm. Sweet, sour, and yellow wax cherries were picked, sold, and canned. The fruits were also used for pies and jellies. (Courtesy of Edna Bollinger.)

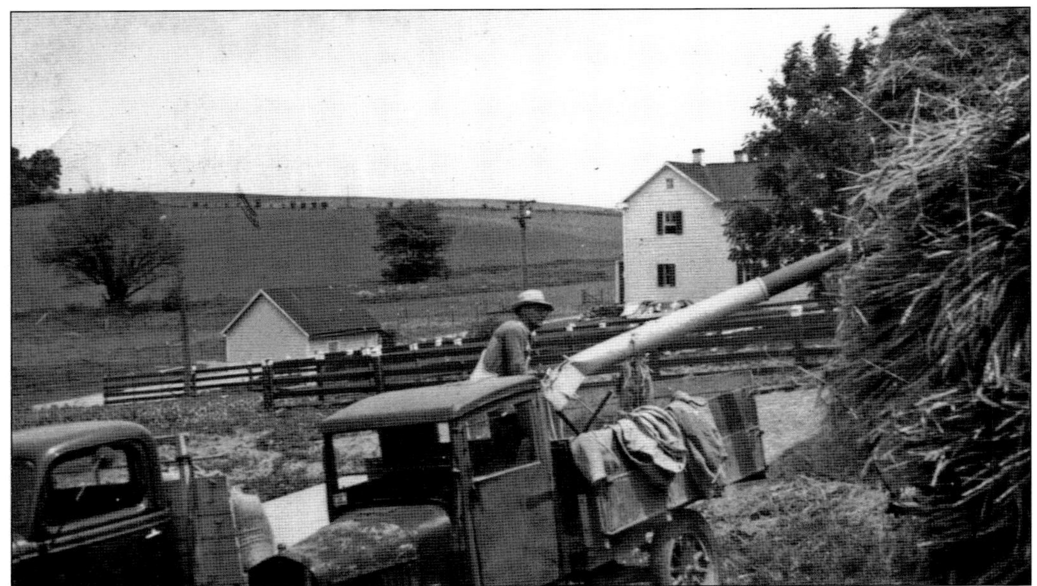

Wilbur Naill is pictured working on his farm in the 1930s in Dennings. Most farmers worked between 70 and 150 acres to feed their families and make a living. (Courtesy of Judy Naill.)

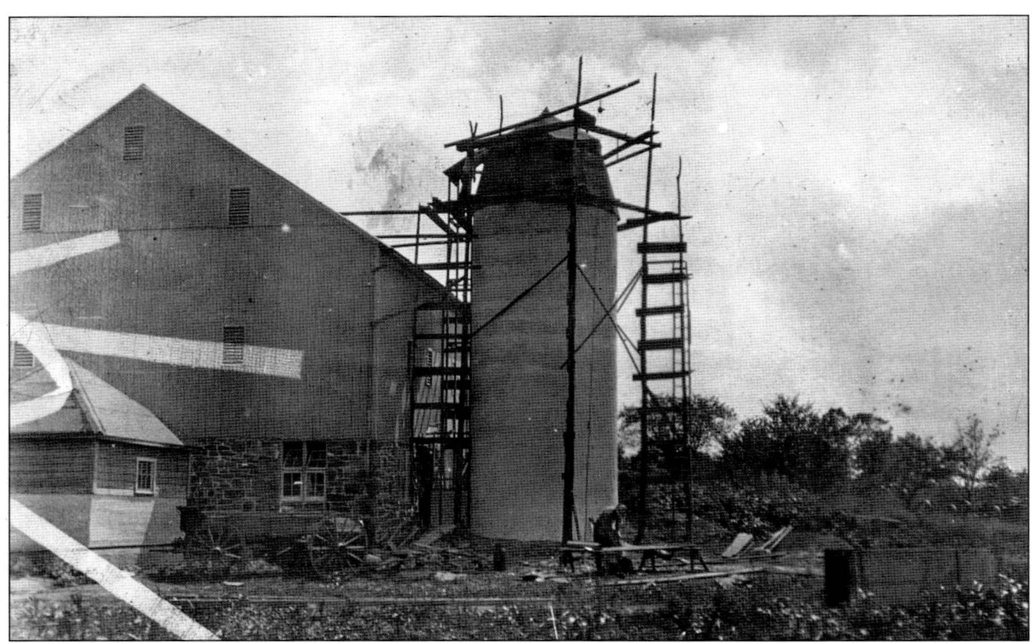

Building a silo was an important event on farms in the 1930s. This rare photograph shows the scaffolding used while the silo is being constructed on the Hubert Null farm in Taneytown. According to the 1924 county agent's report, the use of silos had increased 400 percent in the past 10 years. A silo allowed farmers to do year-round dairying since they were able to store silage in their silos for winter feed. (Courtesy of the Null family.)

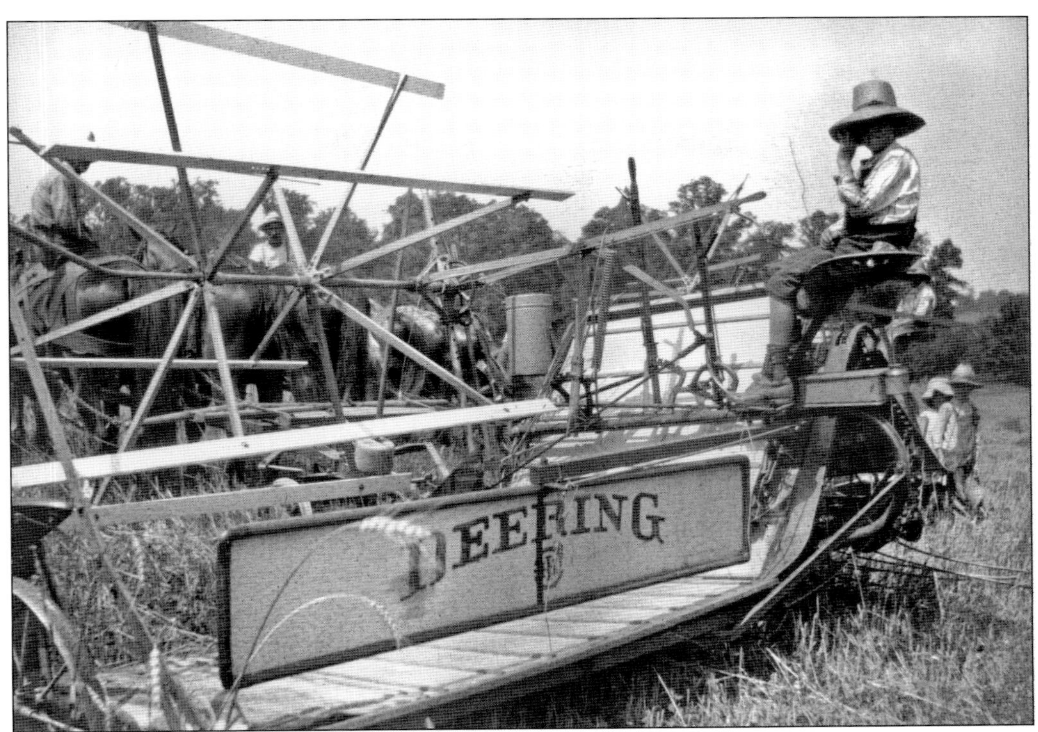

Known as the Katharine Hepburn of Taneytown, Mary Teeter Clingan sits on a wheat binder in Taneytown around 1940. (Courtesy of Rebecca Herrick.)

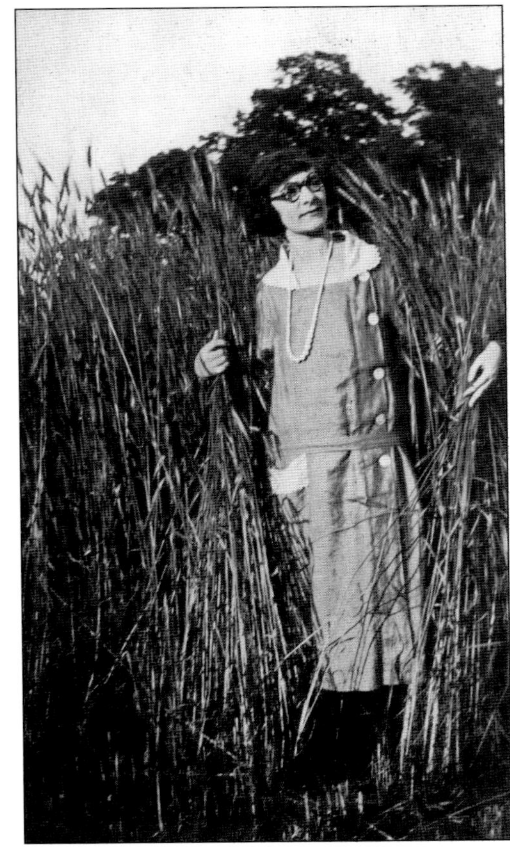

Helen Miller is standing in the wheat at the Miller farm in Miller's Station. (Courtesy of Virginia Ecker Hierstetter.)

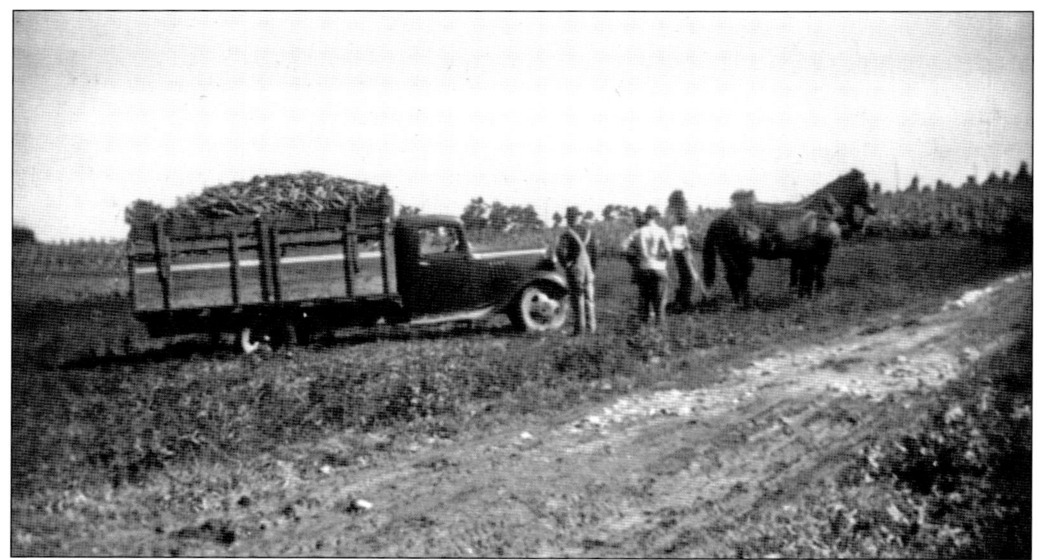

The Hoffs pull their farm truck out of the field on September 27, 1940, with the more reliable horses on the Francis Hoff farm in Gamber. (Courtesy of Bonnie Fold.)

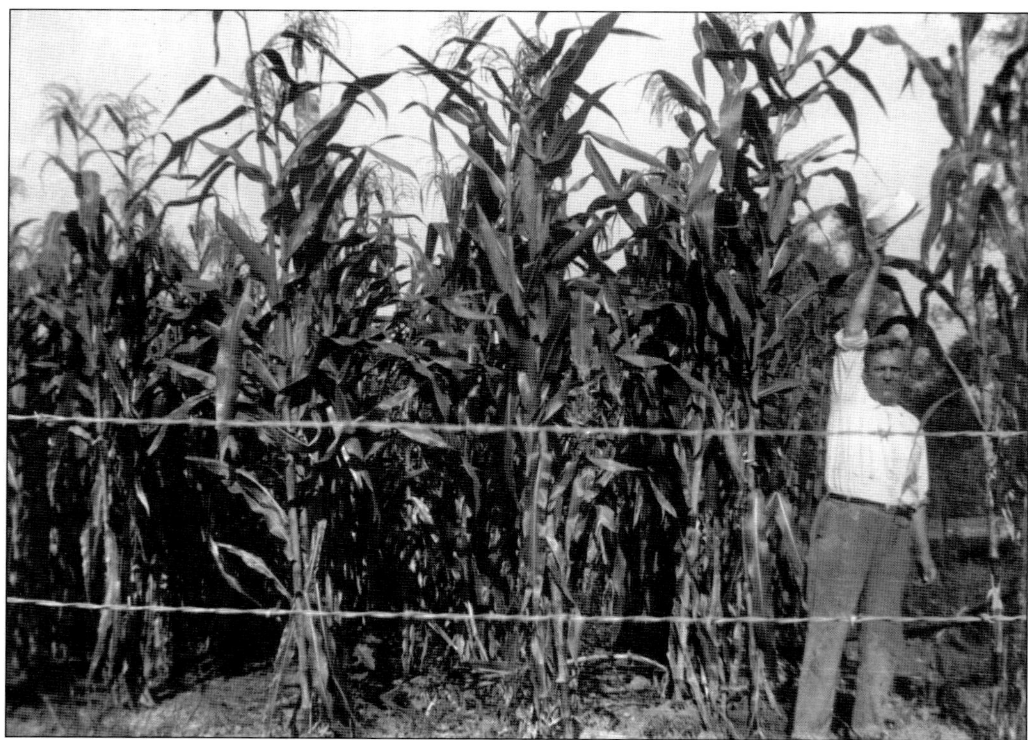

John S. Teeter is pictured in the mid-1940s holding up his hat to show how high his corn grew on Willow Brook Farm in Taneytown. Teeters farmed 900 acres in the area. (Courtesy of Rebecca Herrick.)

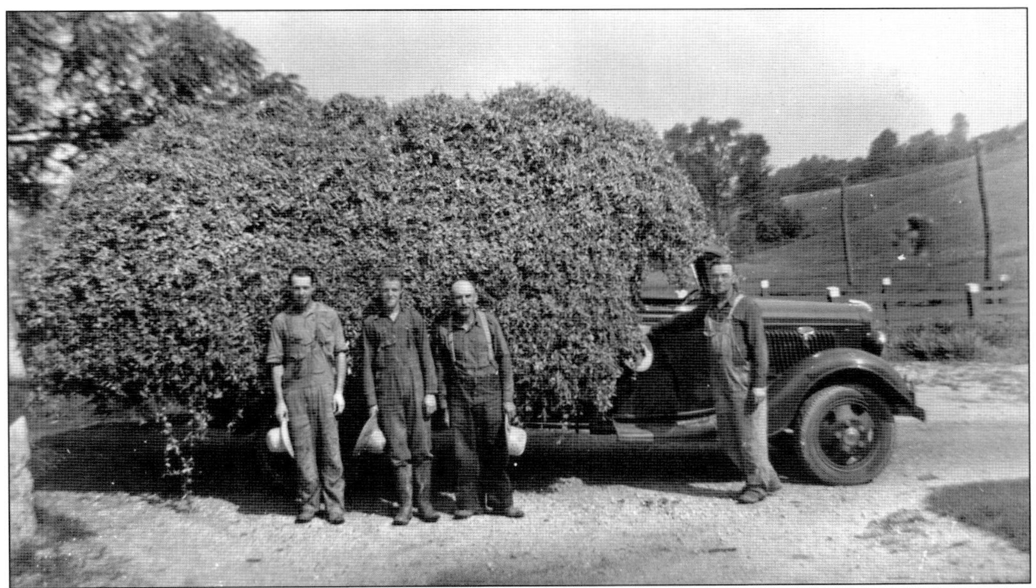

From left to right, Charles Frank, ? Bair, Jim Crumbacker, and Wilbur Naill are pictured with a truck of peas on the way to the B. F. Shriver Canning Company. (Courtesy of Judy Naill.)

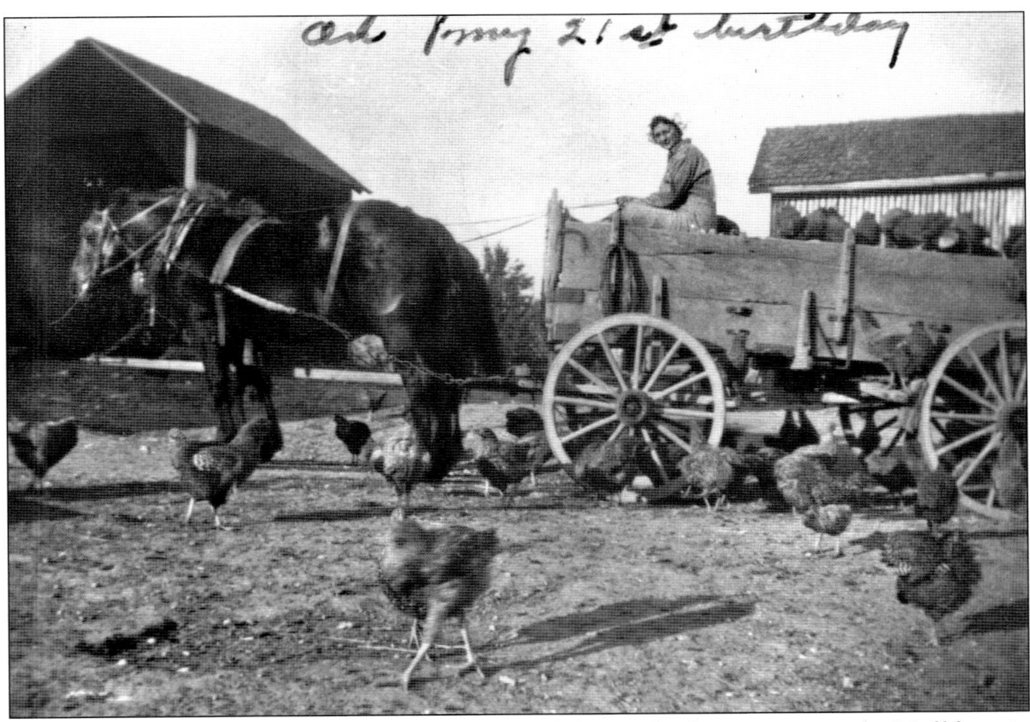

In the 1940s, Ruth Hoff is pictured on her 21st birthday on the farm wagon on the Hoff farm in Gamber. Francis and Ada Hoff bought the farm in the early 1920s. They sold it to their son and his wife, Herman and Ruth Hoff. The Hoffs raised wheat, corn, sweet corn, and hay on their 125-acre farm. (Courtesy of Bonnie Fold.)

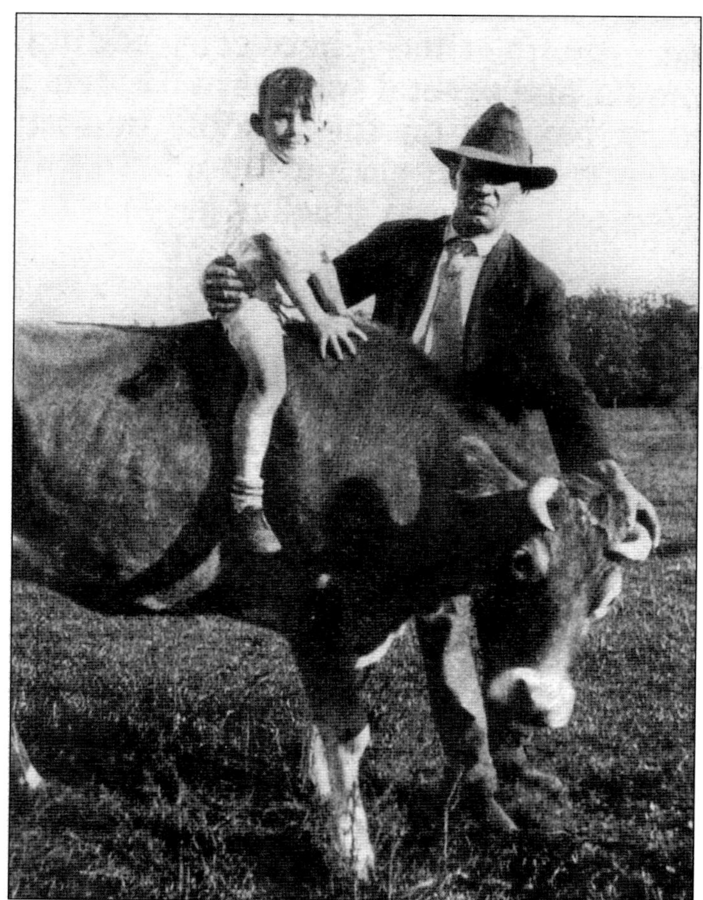

Guy Myers and his son Roger are shown with their pet cow on the Del-Mar Farm on Kate Wagner Road in 1931. Guy bought the 159-acre farm in 1925. They bought milkers in 1940. The Myers family had a small dairy herd and raised sweet corn, peas, and tomatoes. They sold peas and corn to the B. F. Shriver Canning Company in Westminster. Today Roger's son, Jason Myers, has won national recognition as a progressive dairyman and breeder on his Windsor Manor Farm in New Windsor. (Courtesy of Roger Myers.)

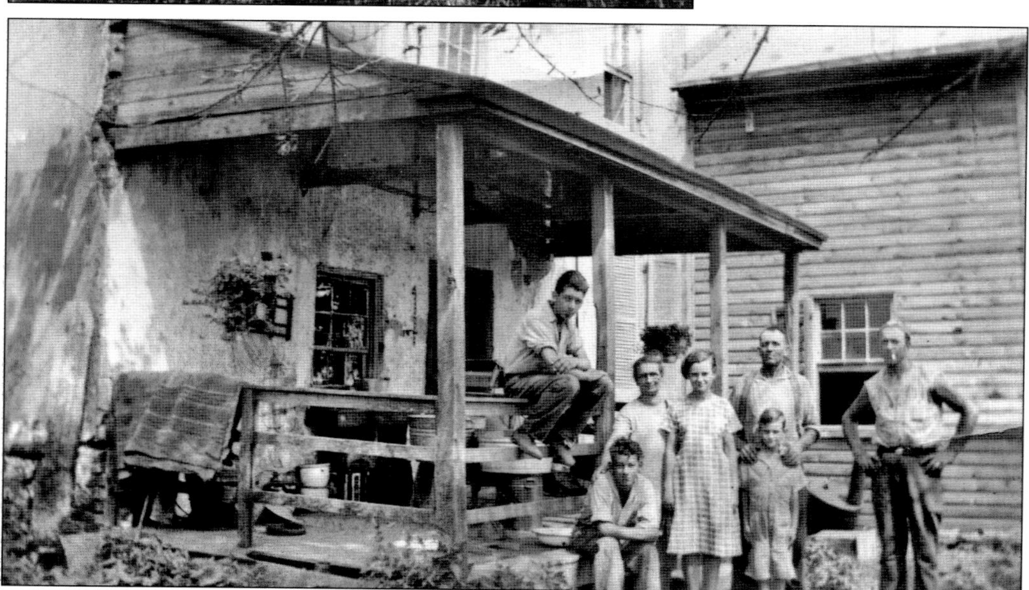

From left to right, Dennis, Ralph, Bessie, Marietta, Roger, and Guy Myers and Carroll Green (a Myers cousin) are pictured in front of the Myers homestead on Kate Wagner Road near Westminster. The house was built before 1837. (Courtesy of Roger Myers.)

Marguerite Wells Hampshire is pictured driving a steel-wheeled tractor on the Hampshire farm in Hampstead during World War II, when rubber for tires was scarce. German prisoners helped on their farm. They were treated well and ate dinner with the family. The prisoners stayed at the B. F. Shriver Canning Company. The Hampshires raised corn, tomatoes, and peas for the Bankerts Canning Company in Hampstead. (Courtesy of the Hampshire family.)

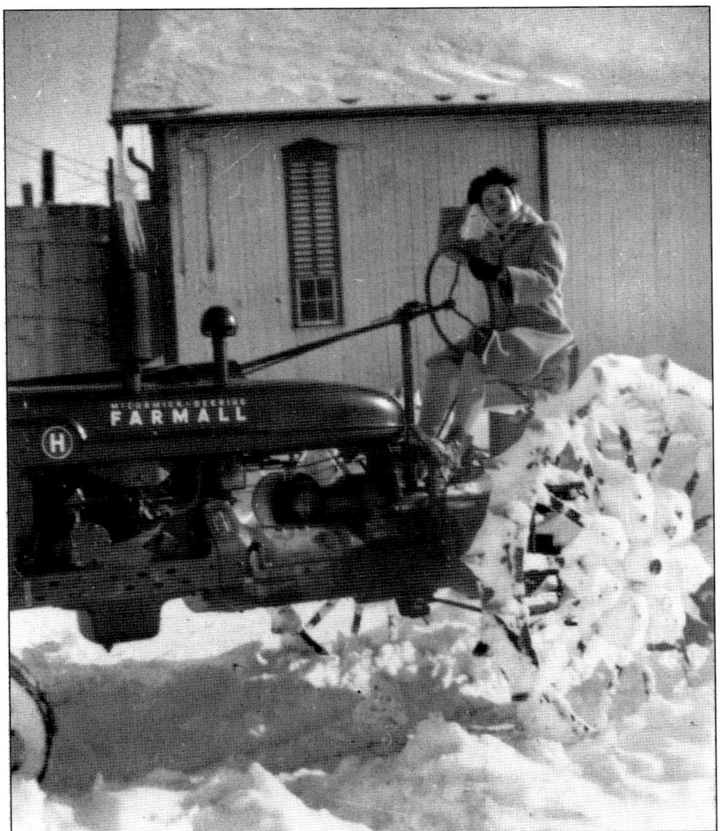

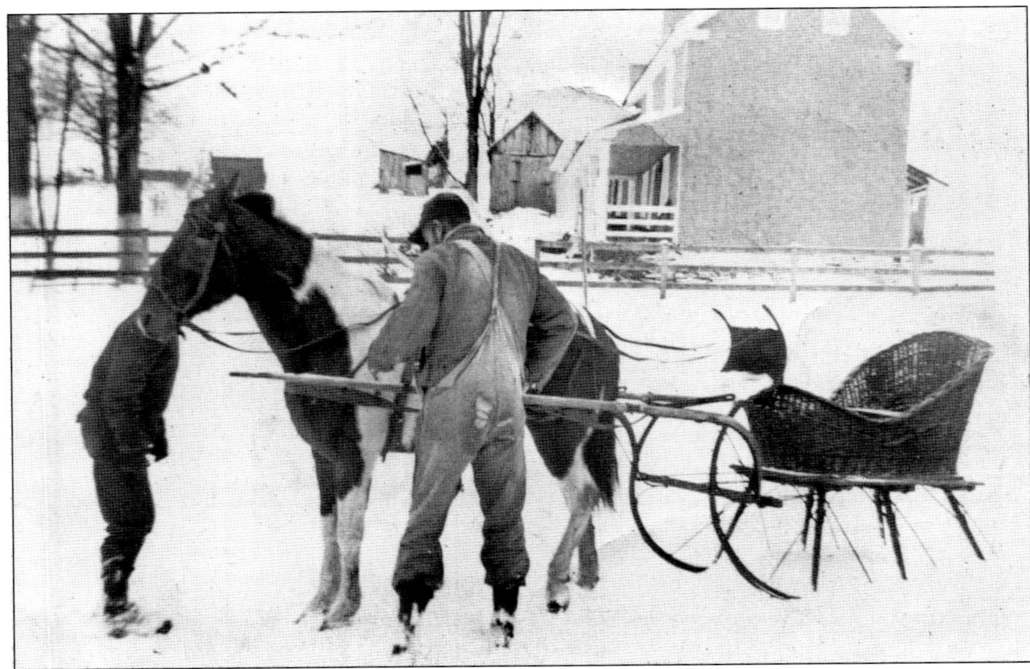

Gordon Conaway Sr. and Gordon "Bill" Conaway Jr. are shown hooking up Nellie to the sleigh on the Conaway farm in Berrett around 1952. (Courtesy of the James C. Conaway Sr. family.)

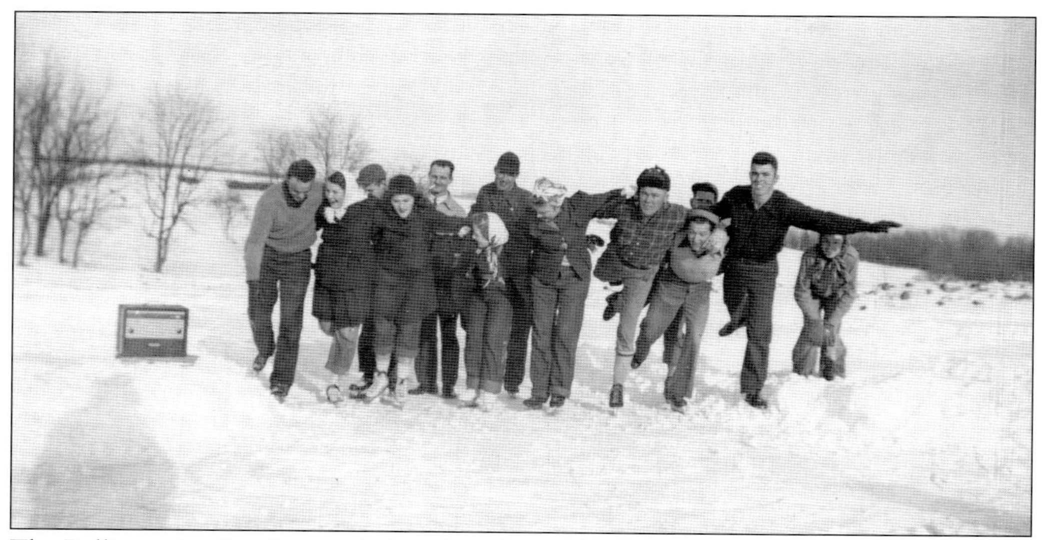

The Bollinger family, along with friends and neighbors, ice-skate on the Bollinger Pond on Bollinger Road in January 1948. From left to right are Francis Bollinger, Carolyn Nightingale, David Brauning, Audrey Bollinger, N. Gist, T. Jones, Jonah Kibler, Edna Bollinger, Stanley Bollinger, Gordon Bellson, Albert Bellson, George Bollinger, and Jim Beard. Notice the radio beside them. (Courtesy of Edna Bollinger.)

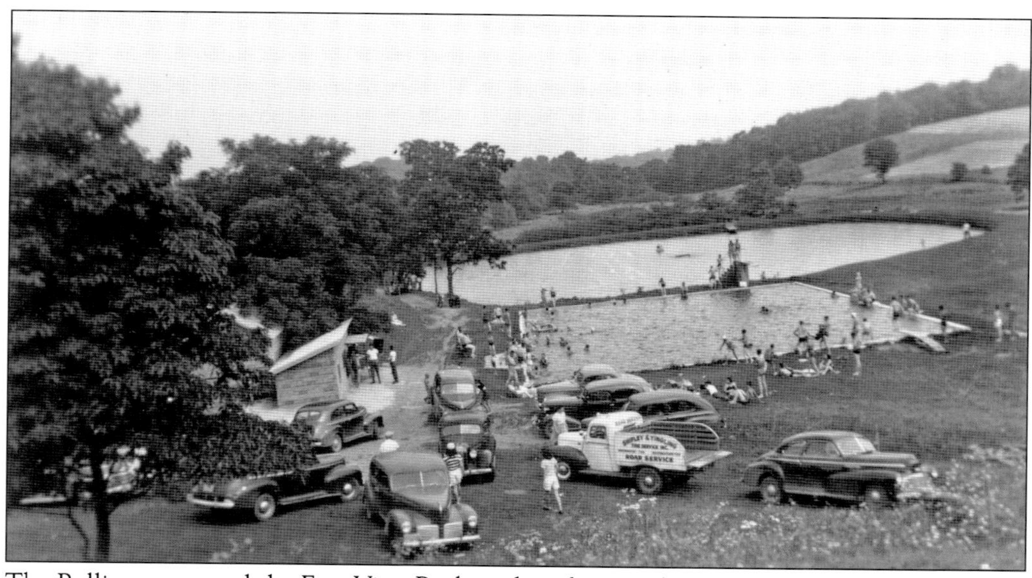

The Bollingers opened the East View Pool on their farm to the public in the late 1940s. There was a concession stand, a bathhouse, cabins, a fireplace for grilling, and a picnic area. The water was ice cold from the spring that fed it. The Red Dog cabin with its big stone fireplace was used for playing cards and to host fishing parties. (Courtesy of Edna Bollinger.)

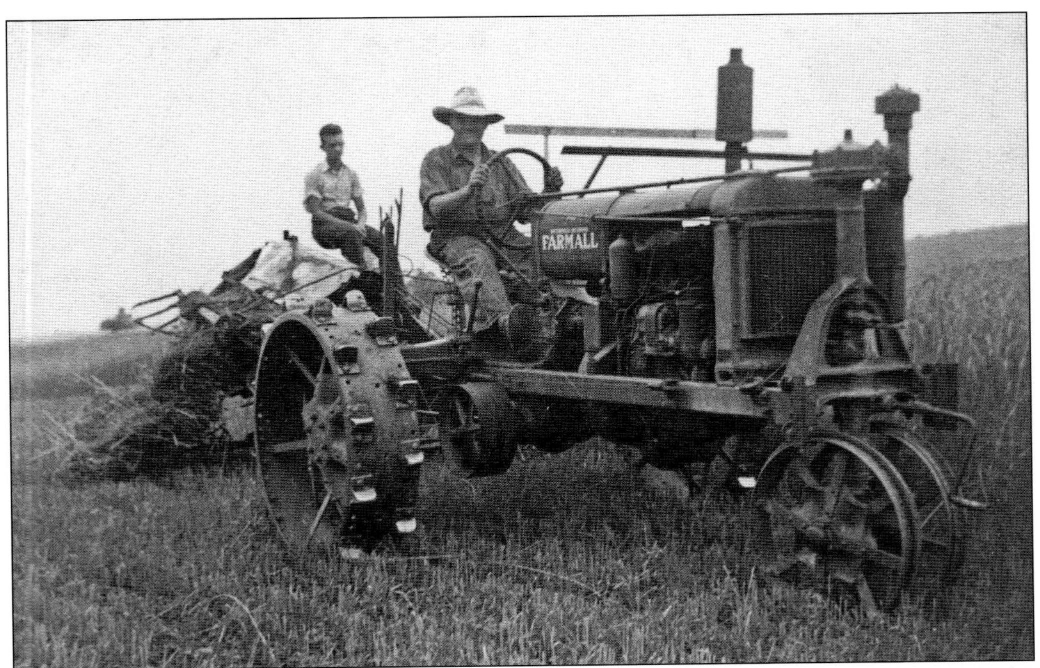

George Tracy is pictured in 1939 or 1940 riding his first Farmall tractor that he bought with the money the government gave him for serving in the army in World War I. Fred Brown, a cousin from Baltimore who came to the farm in Bachmans Valley for the summer, is riding on the back of the wheat binder. (Courtesy of Helen Tracy Totura.)

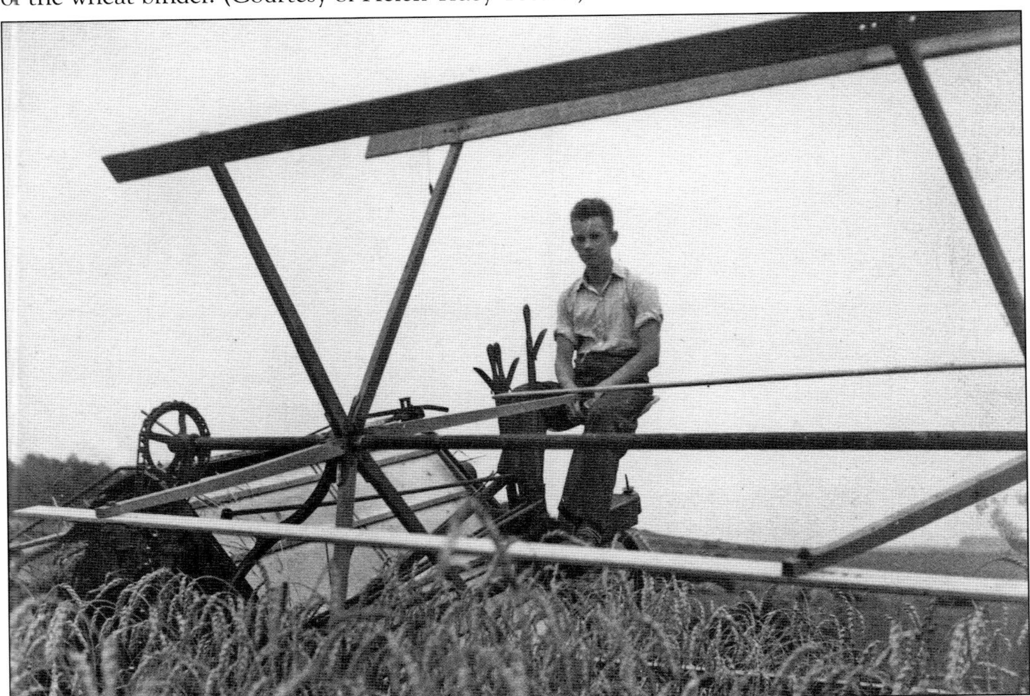

Fred Brown came to work on the Schaeffer farm, owned by relatives George and Lela Tracy, around 1940. Here he sits on a wheat binder. The wheat binder cuts the wheat and ties it into a sheaf. Then the wheat is stacked and taken to the thresher. (Courtesy of Helen Totura Tracy.)

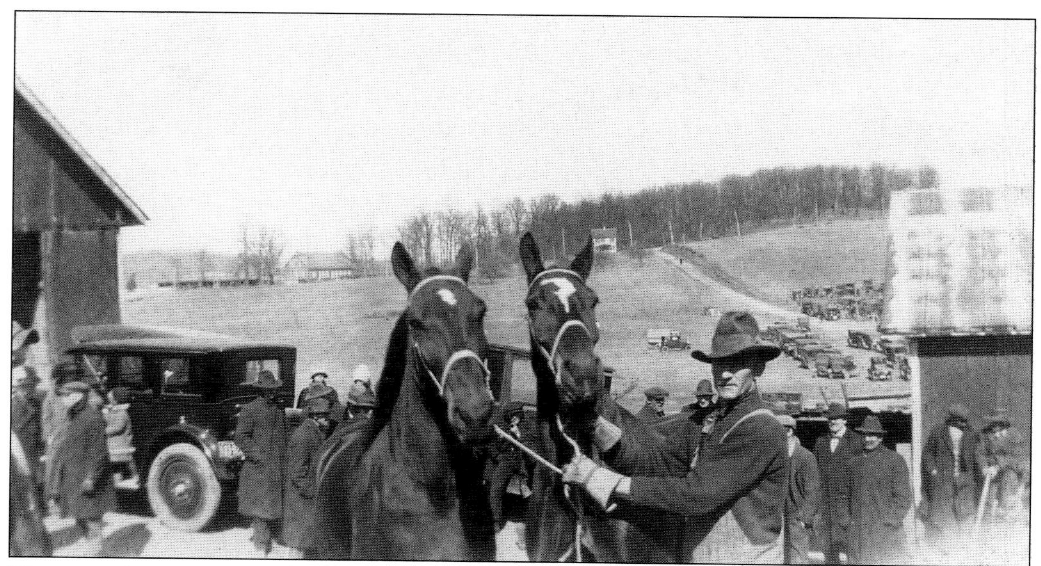

Horses are being auctioned off on the Royer Farm in this photograph. (Courtesy of the Historical Society of Carroll County.)

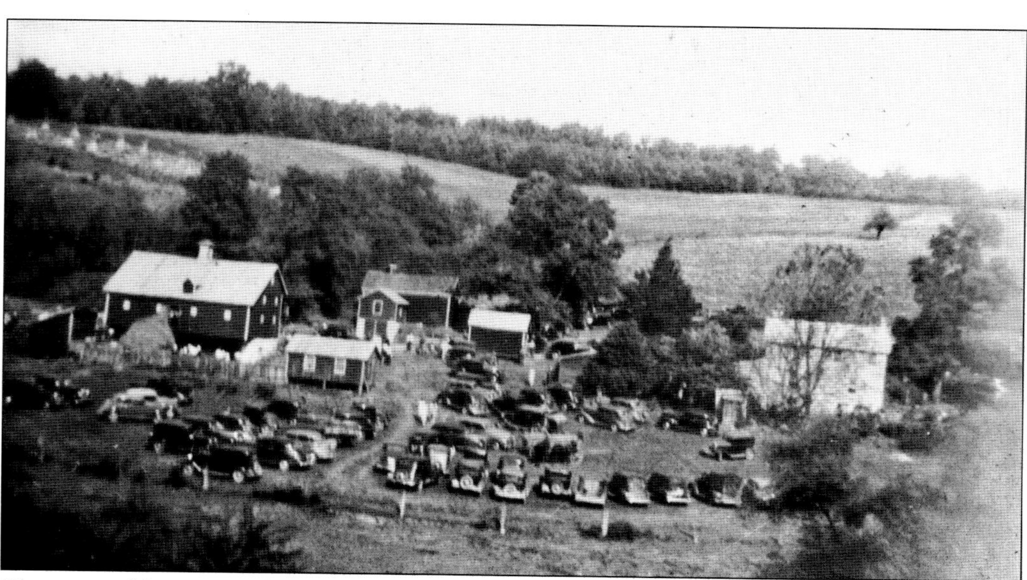

This is a public auction held on October 4, 1941, on the William Barber farm after his death. Automobiles filled the fields for the auction. When farm families retired or passed away, the farm and its contents were sold at auction. Farmers came from all over to buy equipment and household goods. (Courtesy of Bonnie Fold.)

TRUSTEE'S SALE OF A VALUABLE FARM!

Near Uniontown, Carroll County, Maryland.

By virtue of a decree of the Circuit Court for Carroll County, wherein Alfred Stevenson, next friend, &c., is complainant and Alice E. Billmyer infant, et al., are defendants, it being No. 4186 Equity, the undersigned trustee will offer at Public Sale, on the premises, on the afternoon of

THURSDAY, DECEMBER 15th,

1904, at 1 o'clock, P. M., the following Property, viz: All the farm containing

68¾ ACRES

of Land, more or less, situate, lying and being near the public road leading from Uniontown to Taneytown, adjoining the properties of Theo. Ecker, Josiah C. Bankert and others, that was owned by the late Scott H. Billmyer, deceased. This property is improved by a good

Dwelling House,

of 8 or 9 Rooms, Barn, Dairy, Wash House, Corn House, Wagon Shed and all necessary outbuildings. It has an excellent Apple Orchard and crops unusually well. There is running Water at house and Barn, and about 10 Acres of good Meadow Land. A sufficient quantity of this farm is Wood Land, and the rest is tillable. This sale will present a rare opportunity for persons desiring a place of its size.

TERMS OF SALE.—One-third cash on the day of sale, or upon the ratification thereof by the court, and the residue in two equal payments, one to be paid in one year, and the other in two years from the day of sale, with interest, to be secured by the notes of the purchaser or purchasers, with approved security, or all cash at the option of the purchaser, or purchasers.

ALFRED STEVENSON, Trustee.

Guy W. Steele, Solicitor. J. Thos. Roop, Auctioneer.

SENTINEL STEAM JOB PRINT, WESTMINSTER, MD.

This 1904 farm auction poster is typical of the kind printed to advertise farm sales. Alfred Stevenson is the trustee on this farm auction poster, Gary W. Steel is the solicitor, and J. Thomas Roop is the auctioneer. (Courtesy of Lyndi McNulty.)

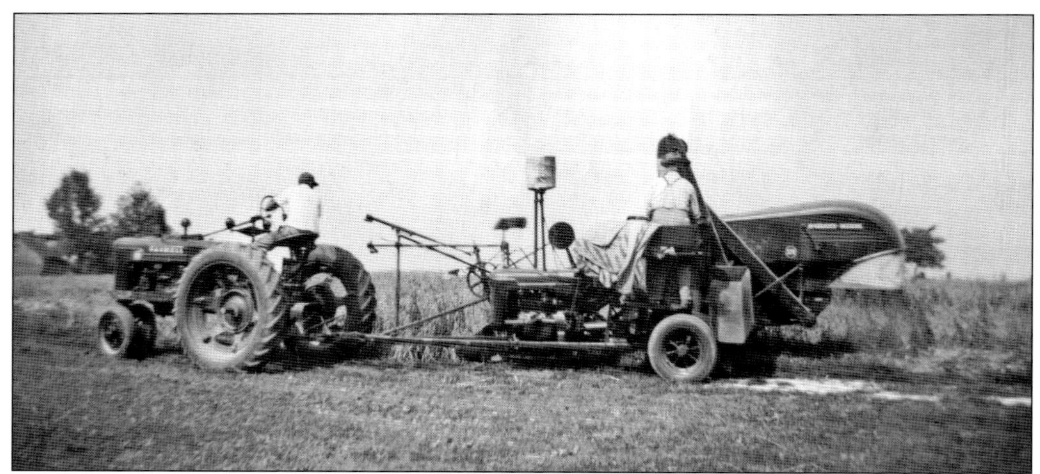

In 1947, the Hampshires purchased this new combine. The Clarence E. and Edna Stuller/Hampshire dairy farm in Hampstead was purchased from John H. Hampshire in 1918. They put their milk cans at the end of road to be picked up and taken to Greenspring Dairy in Baltimore. The Hampshires raised 500 to 600 turkeys, ducks, capons, and pheasants. They also butchered hogs and steers for their own use and had a huckster route on Saturday. Pictured are Maurice Hampshire on the tractor and his father, Clarence Hampshire, on the combine. (Courtesy of the Hampshire family.)

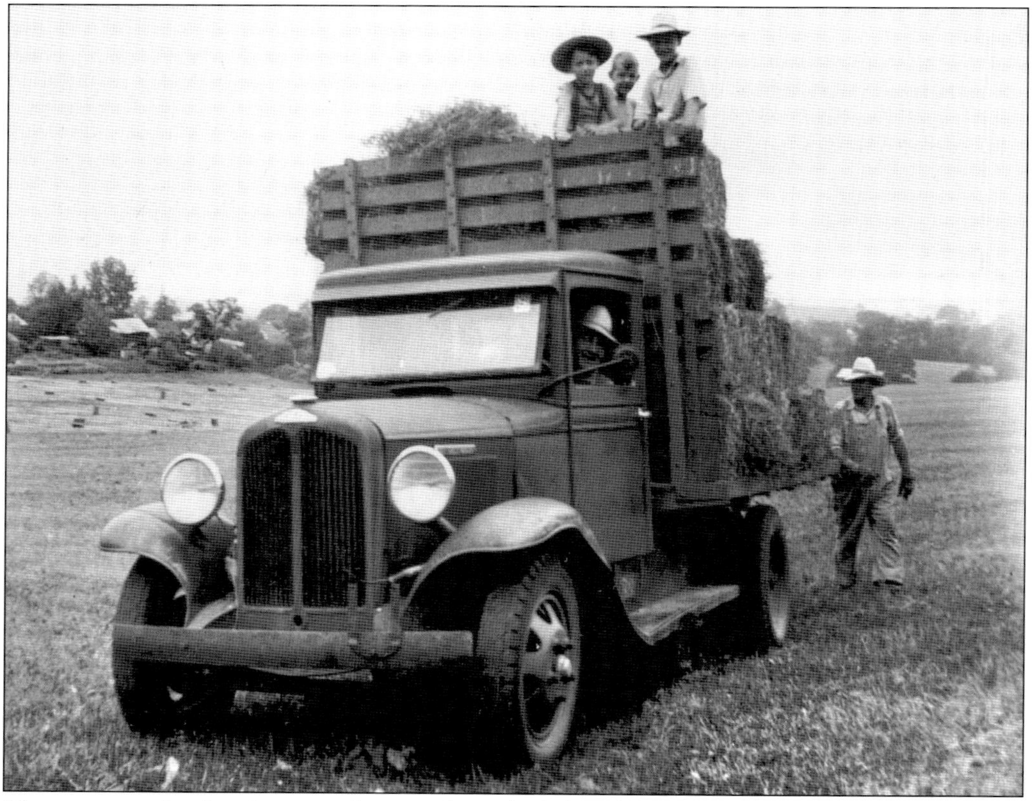

These men are hauling hay on a farm truck on the Edward C. Myers farm in Uniontown. Notice the windshield is pushed out in the front of the truck to let in air, an early form of air-conditioning. (Courtesy of Lisa Monthly.)

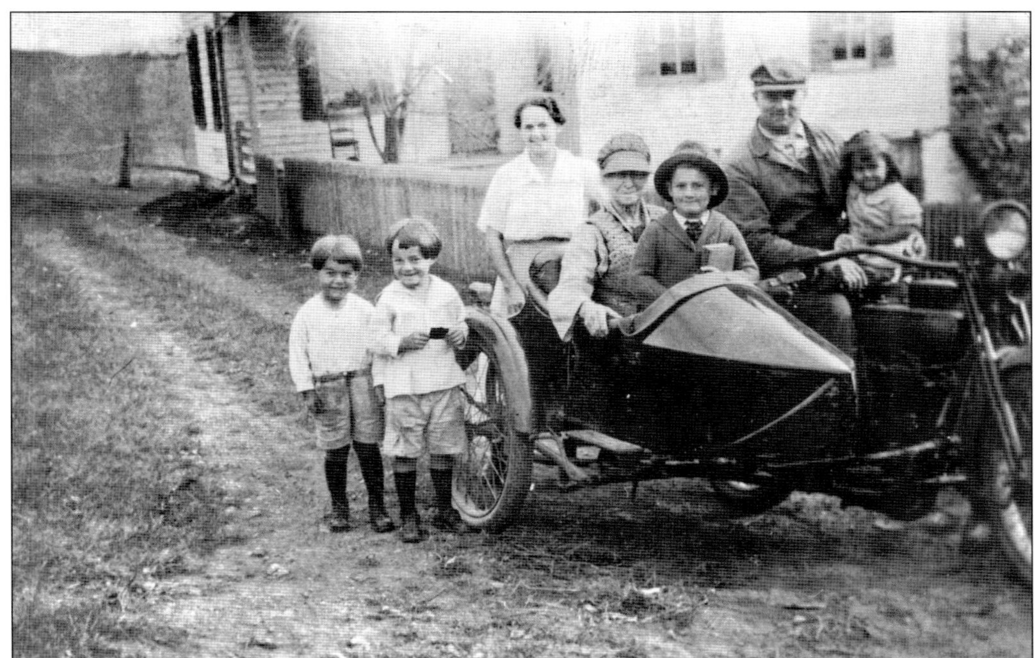

The Ecker family moved from Tyrone to a farm in Manchester. In addition to farming, Clyde R. Ecker bought the Harley-Davidson dealership in Westminster. He rented a room in Charlie Klee's garage on Railroad Avenue. Here he is taking his aunt, Jane Ecker (in the side car), to teach school. From left to right are Chester M. Ecker, K. Monroe Ecker, Ovie K. Ecker (standing), M. Jane Ecker, (on her lap) Vernon R. Ecker, and Clyde R. Ecker (driving) holding his daughter, Erma L. Ecker. (Courtesy of Virginia Ecker Hierstetter.)

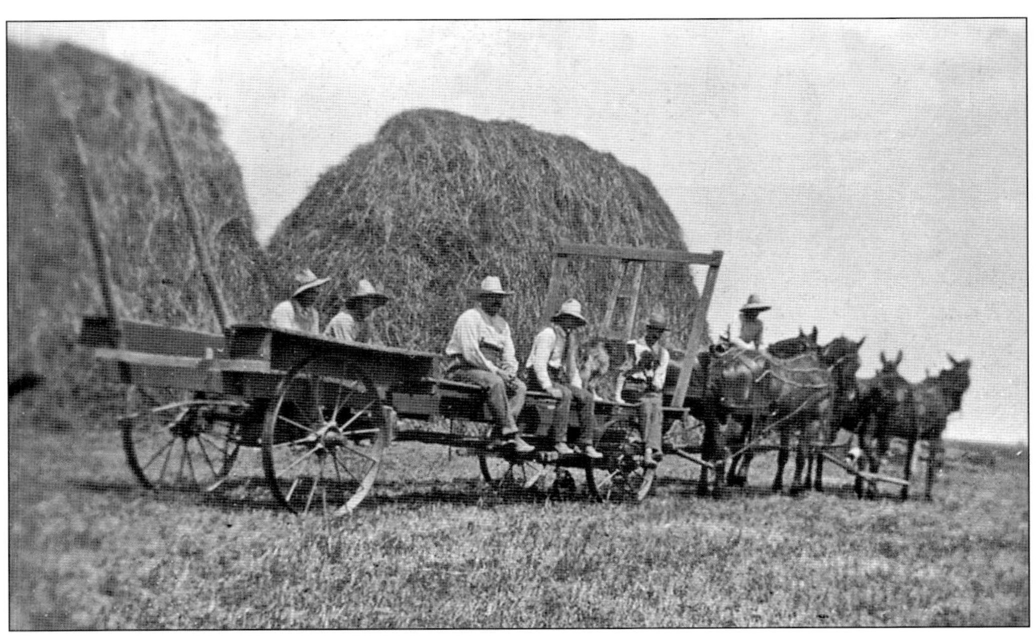

Men sit on a hay wagon on the Royer farm. (Courtesy of the Historical Society of Carroll County.)

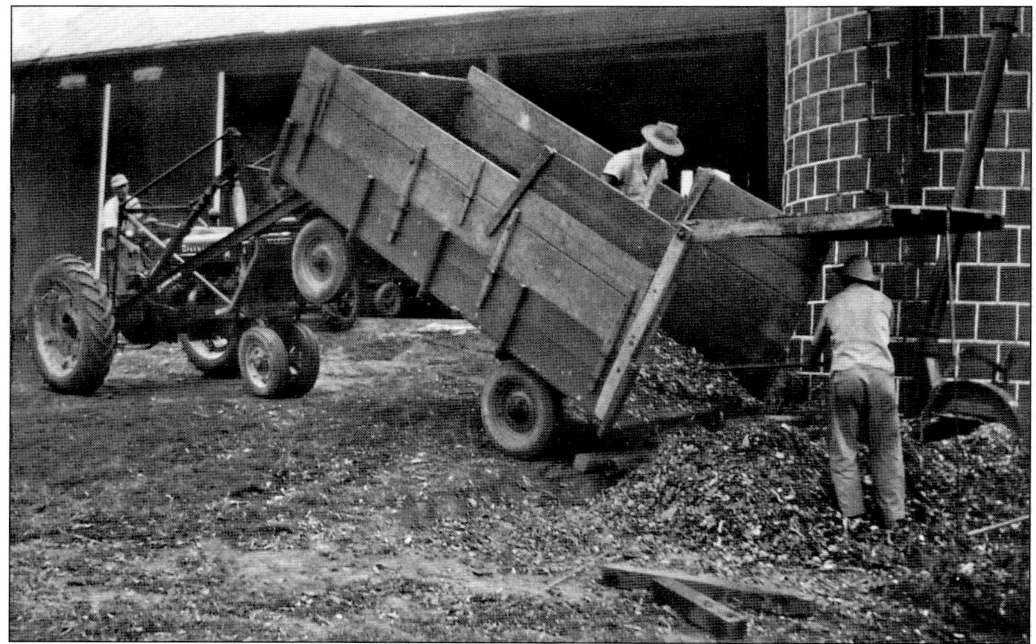

In 1950 in Keysville, the Wilhides are unloading chopped corn silage. They are using a bucket loader on their tractor, their own invention, instead of unloading it by hand. The silage is then poured into a hopper and blown into the silo. (Courtesy of the Wilhide family.)

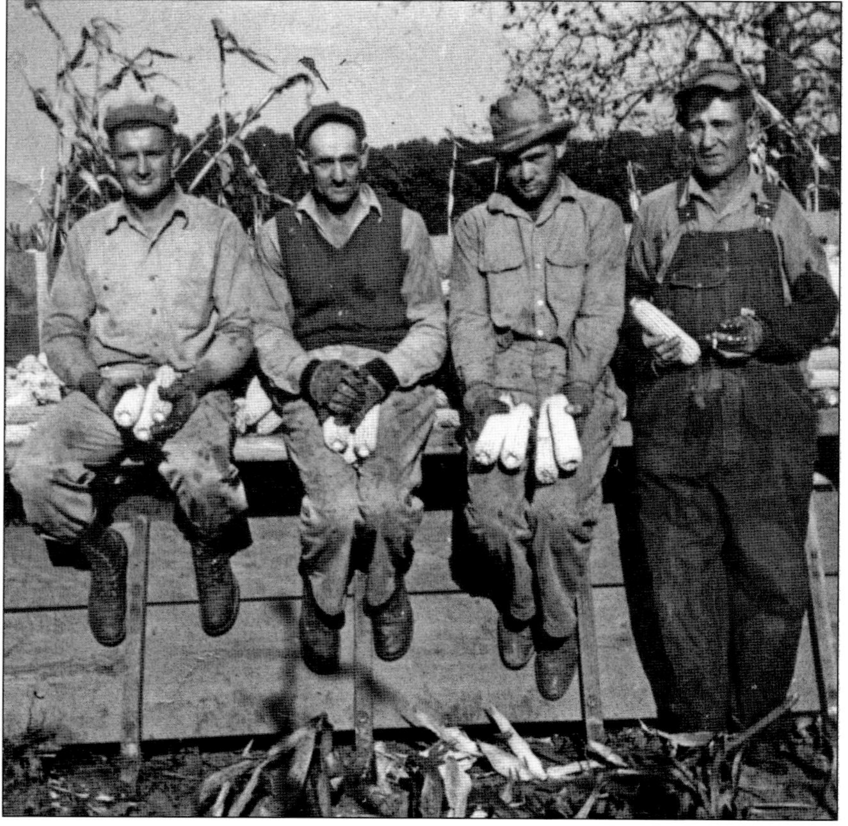

Showing off a good corn crop in the early 1950s on the Hubert Null farm in Taneytown are, from left to right, George Null, Hubert Null, Charlie Null, and Ed Harvey, a hobo farmhand. (Courtesy of Edward Null.)

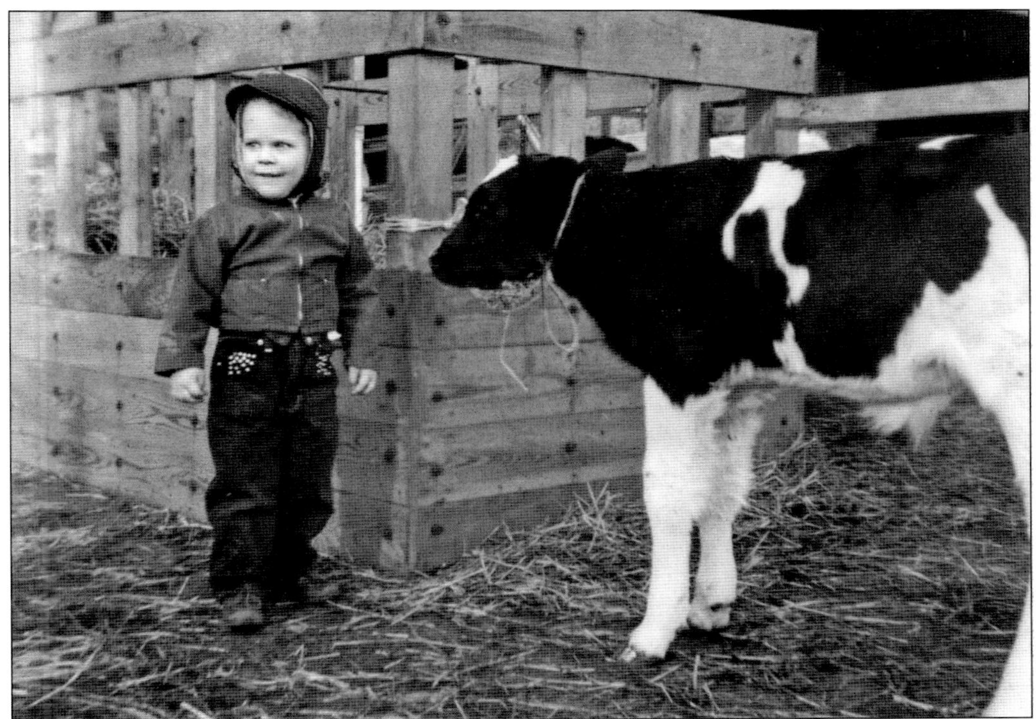

In 1955, Fred Teeter Jr. and a calf are on the Willow Brook Farm, owned by the Teeter family, in Taneytown. (Courtesy of Rebecca Herrick.)

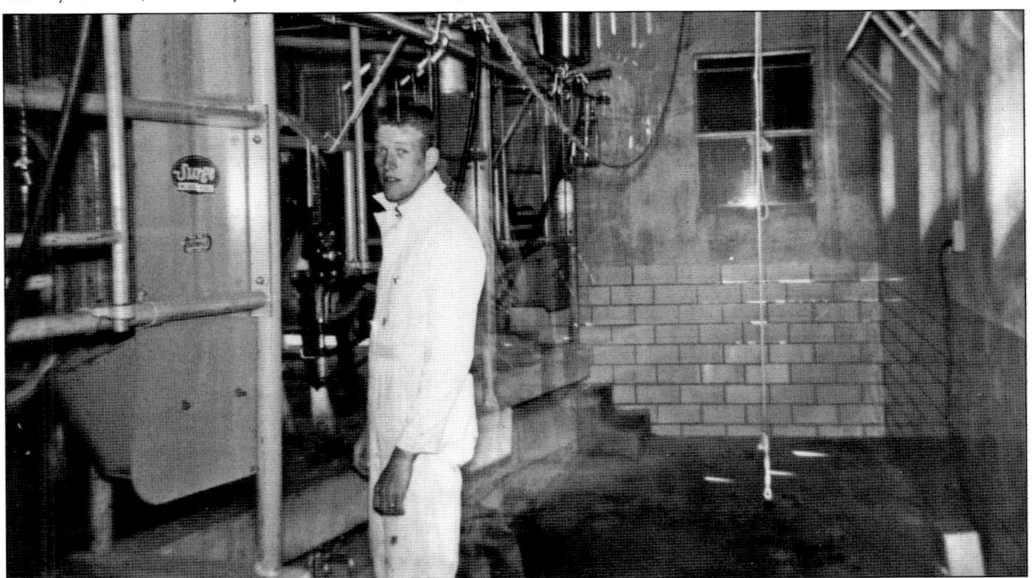

Having never farmed before, Evelyn Peterson of Washington, D.C., purchased her first farm in the early 1940s. In 1955, Peterson purchased her third farm, which was located on Walnut Grove Road near Taneytown. She had one of the first easy-to-clean ceramic milking parlors in the area, costing $20,000. Stuart Peterson, her son, is pictured standing in the pit so he did not have to stoop over to milk the cows. Maurice Zentz picked the milk up in his tank truck and transported it to the Baltimore Milk Market. They milked 60 cows a day, three at a time, at 4:00 a.m. and 4:00 p.m. (Courtesy of the Peterson family.)

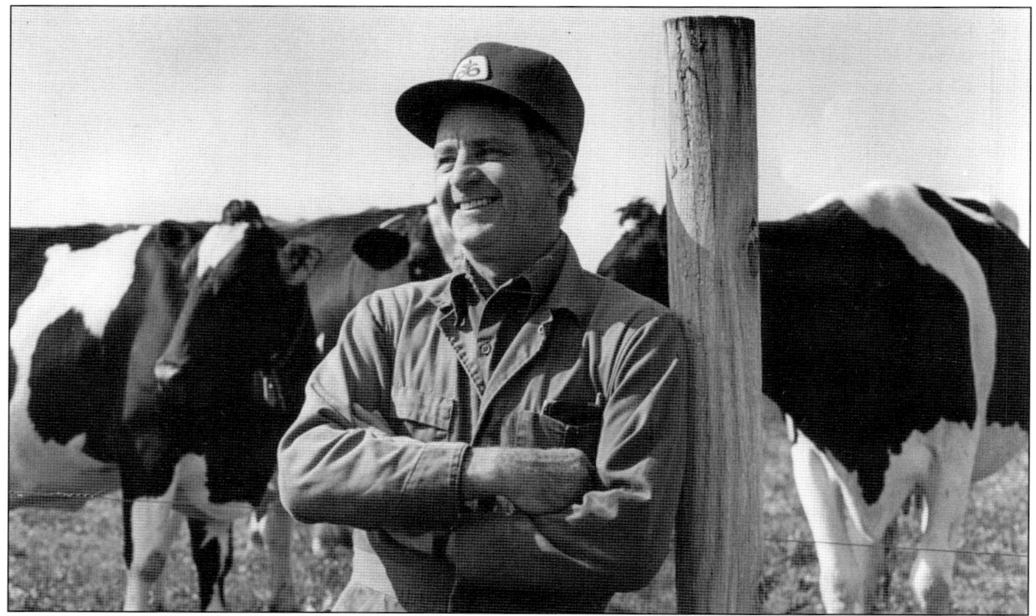

Donald Dell leans on the fence on his farm near Manchester in the 1970s. When Dell grew up in Gamber, his family used the milk from their six cows to make butter. They put it in a crock in the stream to keep it cold. His mother, Elsie Dell, packed the butter into a wooden butter mold with a flower on it that pressed the shape into the butter and then wrapped the butter in wax paper. Dell carried butter to homes in Gamber from 1935 to 1937 and sold it for 25¢. He carried 8 pounds of butter at a time. The Dells sold butter until 1943. Milk sold for $3.49 for 100 pounds of milk or 30¢ a gallon. (Courtesy of the Dell family.)

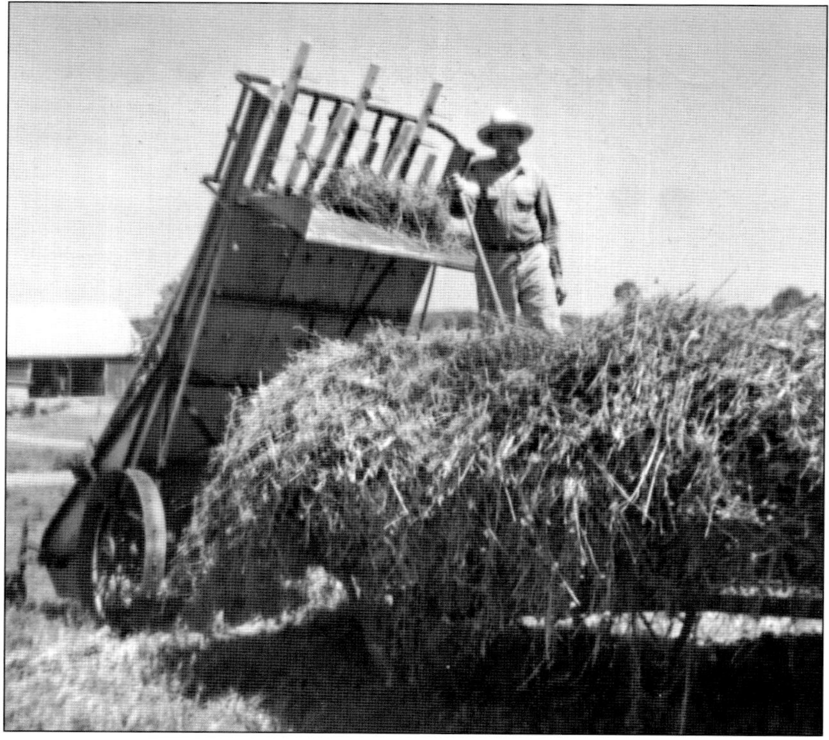

Francis B. Nelson is pictured taking in loose hay in 1964 on his farm on Route 32. (Courtesy of Robert Nelson.)

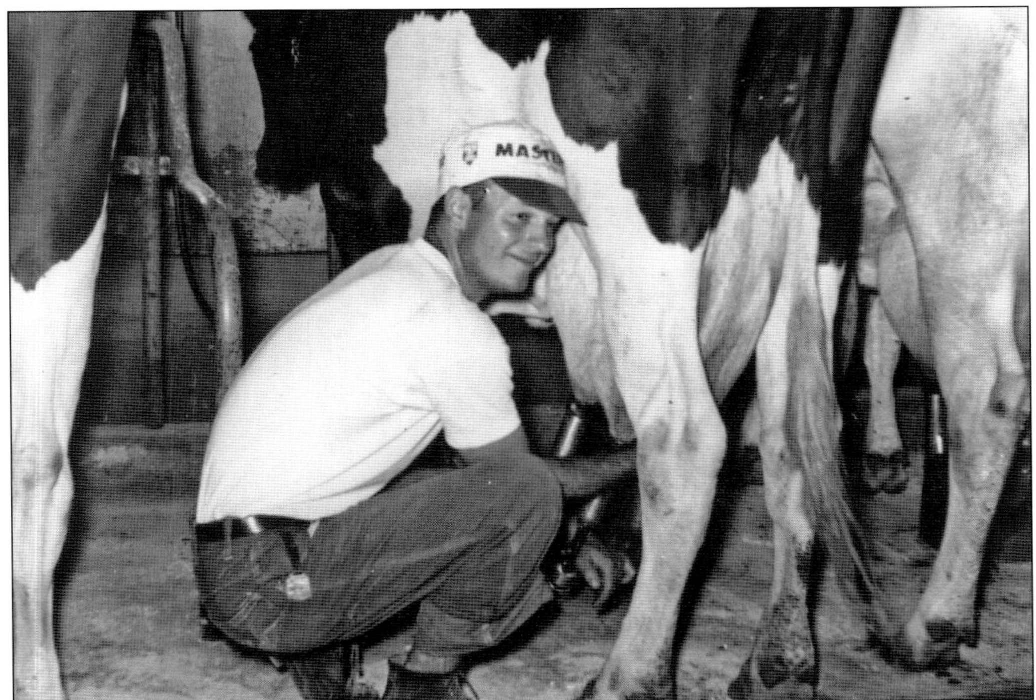

Frederick Keller Teeter is pictured milking a cow in 1954 on John S. Teeter's Willow Brook Farm in Taneytown. The farm was a Holstein dairy operation. When the farm was sold, it was one of the premier sales in the county, with people coming from as far as New York. (Courtesy of Willow Brook Farm.)

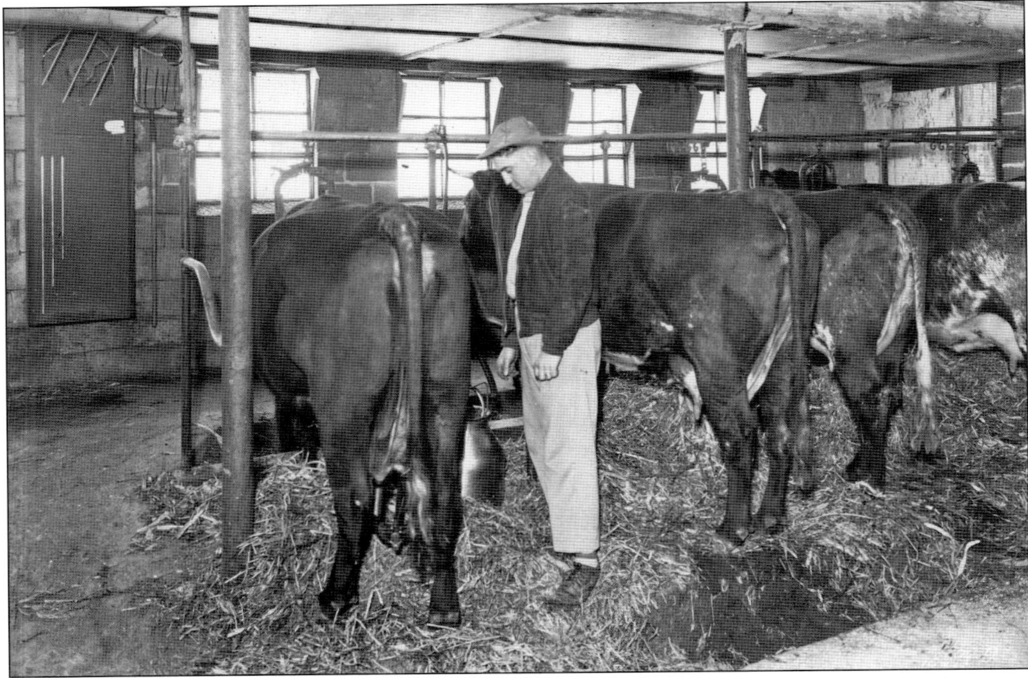

This milking barn was on the Vernon Mathias Hillcrest farm in the 1940s. The family raised prize-winning milking shorthorns. (Courtesy of the Mathias family.)

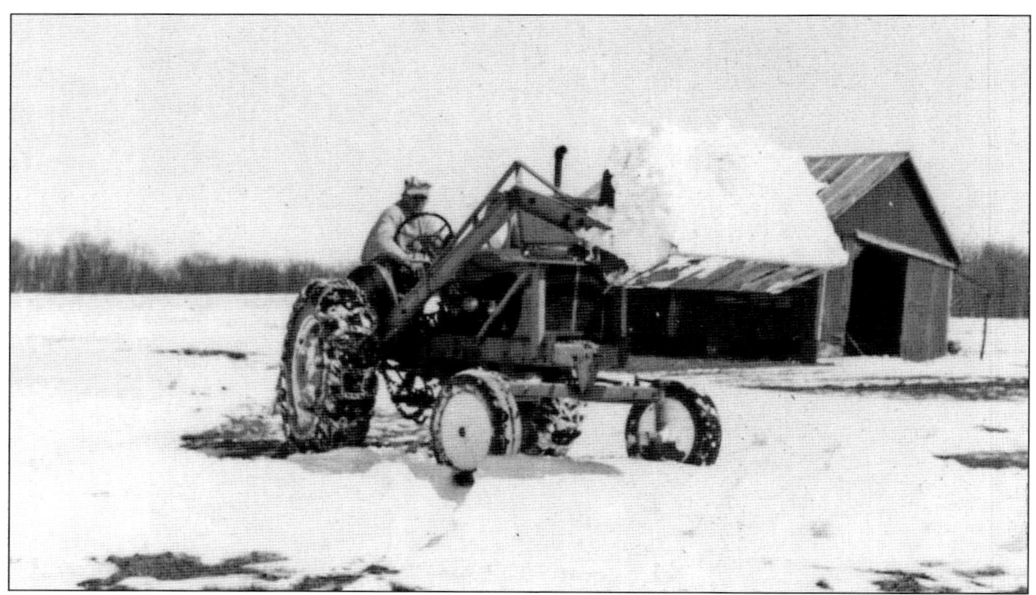

Daniel Shipley is pictured scooping the snow out of the half-mile lane in the 1950s on the Daniel and Eleanor Shipley farm on Old Bachman Valley Road so the milk truck could get in. (Courtesy of the Shipley family.)

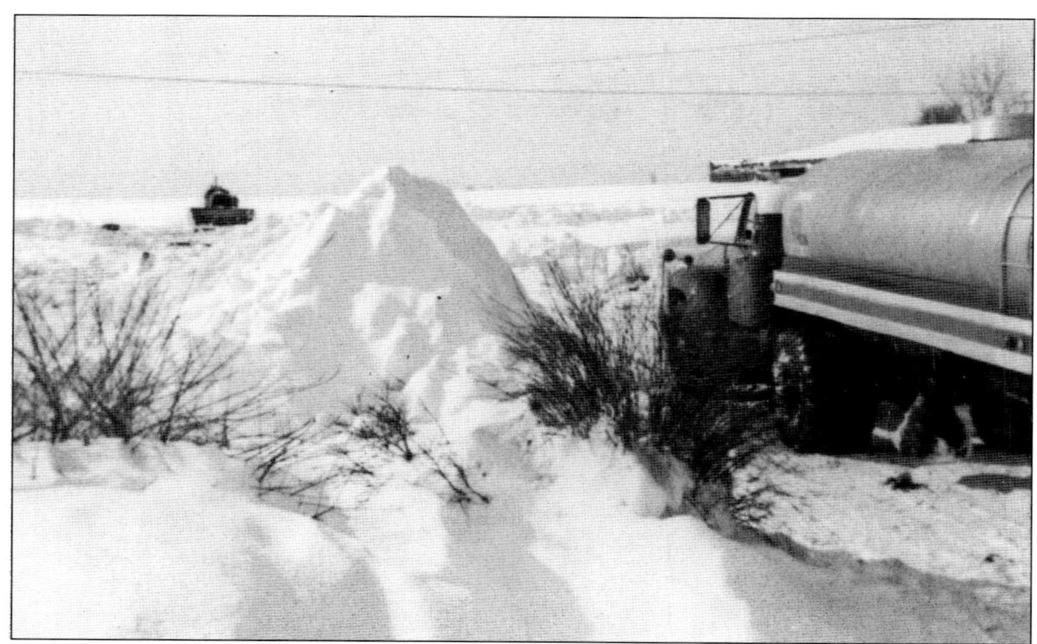

During the 1966 blizzard, the enterprising Wilhides in Keysville were able to get a tank truck to their farm from nearby Detour so they could save three days' worth of milk. Other farmers were not so lucky. (Courtesy of the Wilhide family.)

Henry Dodrer is pictured taking silage off the wagon and filling the silo on the Nicodemus Farm. As with most farm children, Dodrer got up at 4:00 a.m. and milked cows before he went to school. When he finished his work at home, he worked for neighbor Walter Cook, earning $1 an hour in 1958. They served three meats for lunch: ham, beef, and chicken. Dodrer worked there as much for the food as for the pay. (Courtesy of Henry Dodrer.)

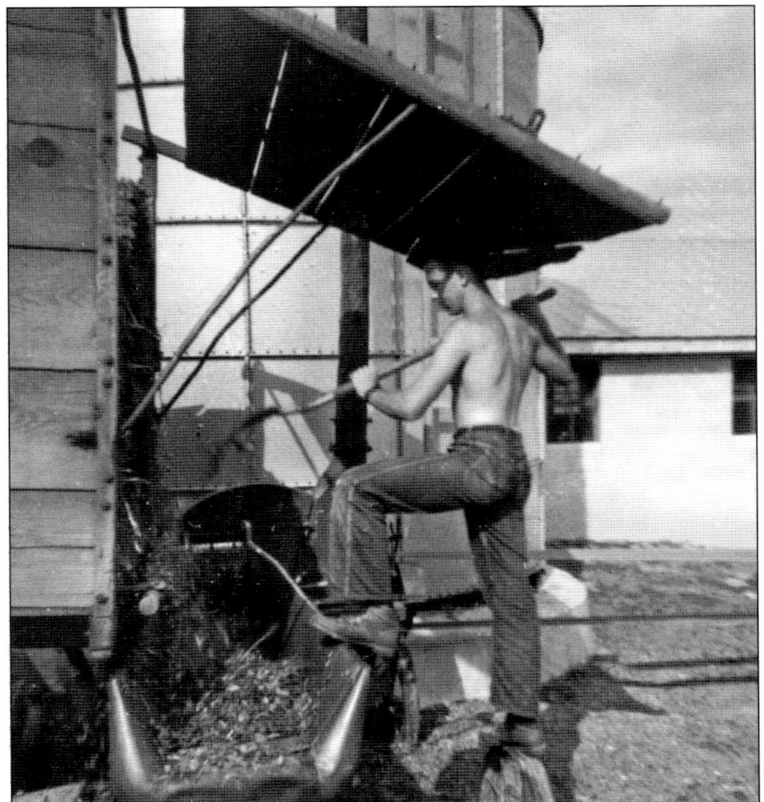

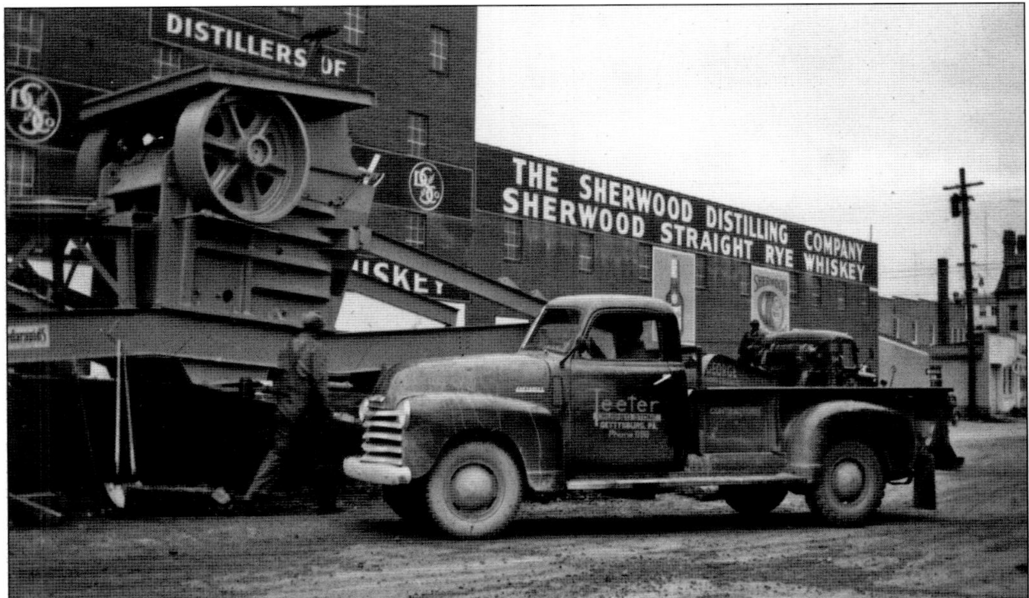

A Teeter Quarry truck from the Willow Brook Farm in Taneytown stops by the Sherwood distillery in Westminster in 1954. Sherwood distilleries were one of Maryland's best-known rye distilleries. The distillery had a structure constructed during World War II with large glass windows that served as a mash-drying house, producing feed for cattle from the mash used in the whiskey production. (Courtesy of Rebecca Herrick.)

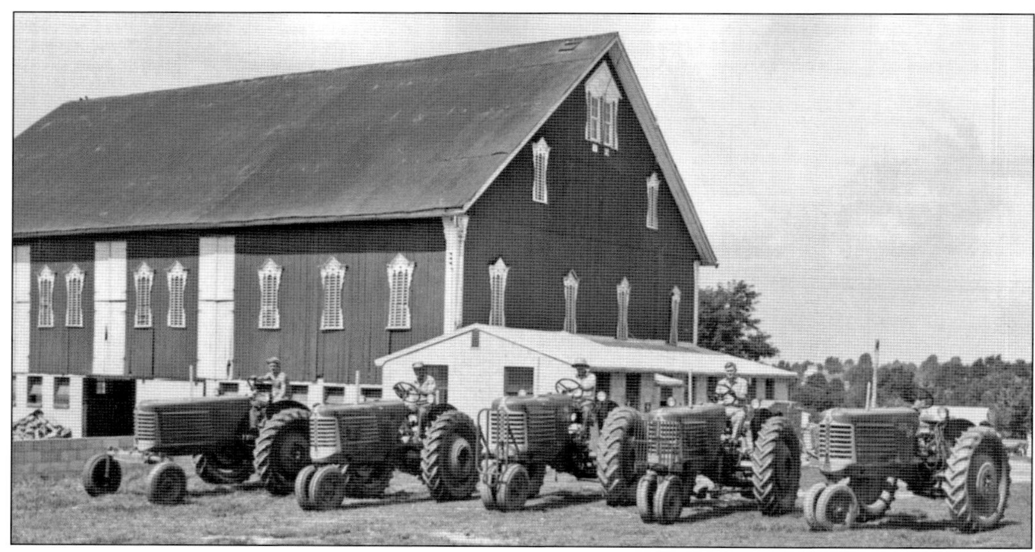

Sitting on tractors on the Paul and Ruth Hoff farm are, from left to right, Donald Hoff, Wilfred Hoff, Paul Hoff, and Carl Hoff. In 1932, Paul H. and Ruth Hoff bought their 145-acre dairy farm on Old Westminster Pike. They raised hogs and chickens, and sold eggs and milk. In the 1940s, there was a little landing strip on the farm that was used by airplanes. In addition, a Mr. Hunter rented a building on the property and ran the Hunter Canning Factory there. A baseball field was also on the farm. (Courtesy of Dora Lee Eyler Hoff.)

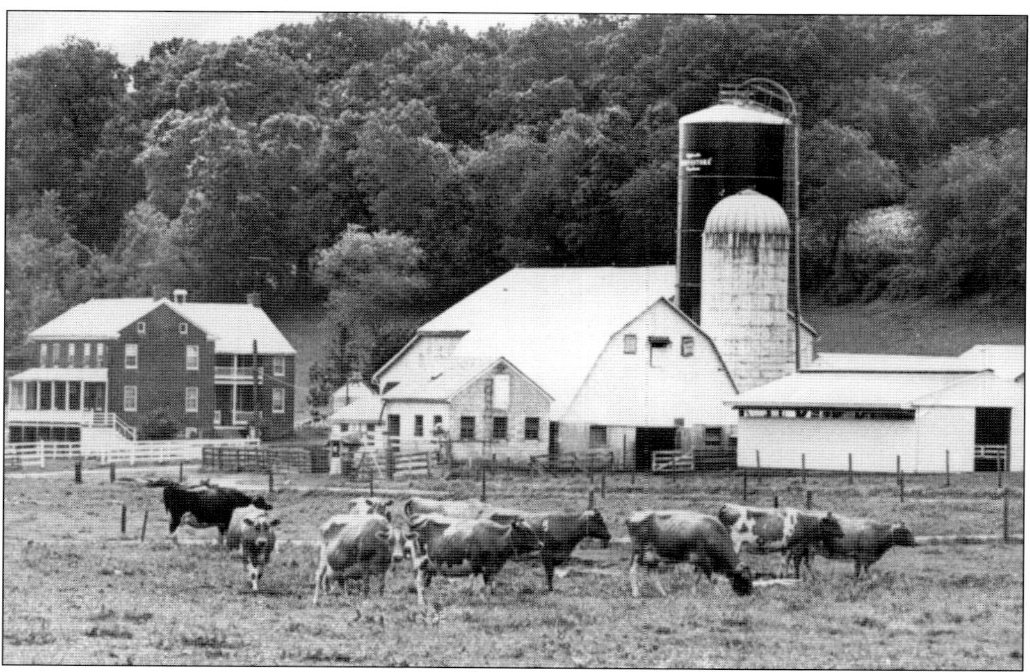

The Hullside Farm on Sullivan Road, shown in the 1970s, was purchased by Eli Hull in 1856. The brick farmhouse was built in 1871. Hull was an insurance agent, shoe cobbler, and farmer. From 1936 to 1974, John Hull Sr. ran this small dairy farm and farmed another through 1996. During World War II, German prisoners worked on the farm, as they did on many others, and were treated as family and fed at the dinner table. (Courtesy of the Hull family.)

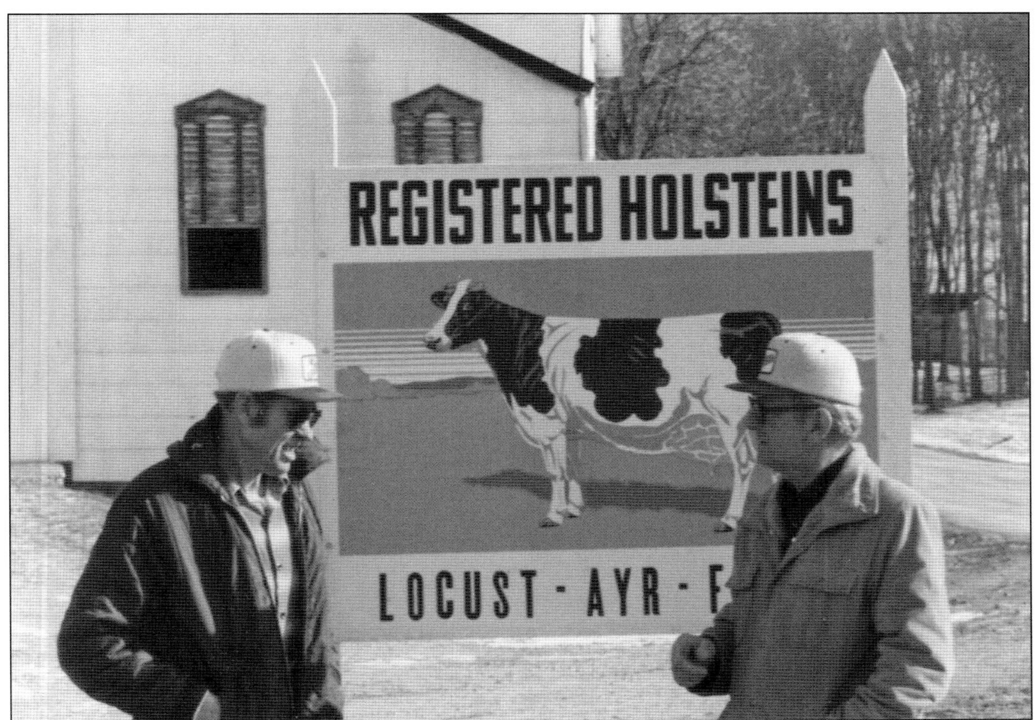

Ray Haines (left) and Bob Myers share local news at the Haines farm on Black's Schoolhouse Road. (Courtesy of the Carroll Soil Conservation District.)

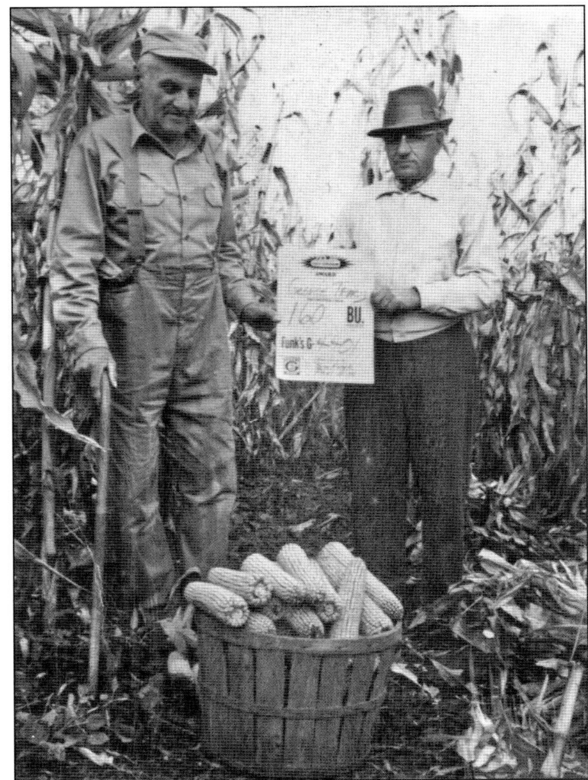

Pictured are George Tracy (left) and Paul Wine, a seed corn salesman who came and evaluated the corn. Tracy received an award for outstanding crop production one year in the late 1960s. (Courtesy of Helen Tracy Totura.)

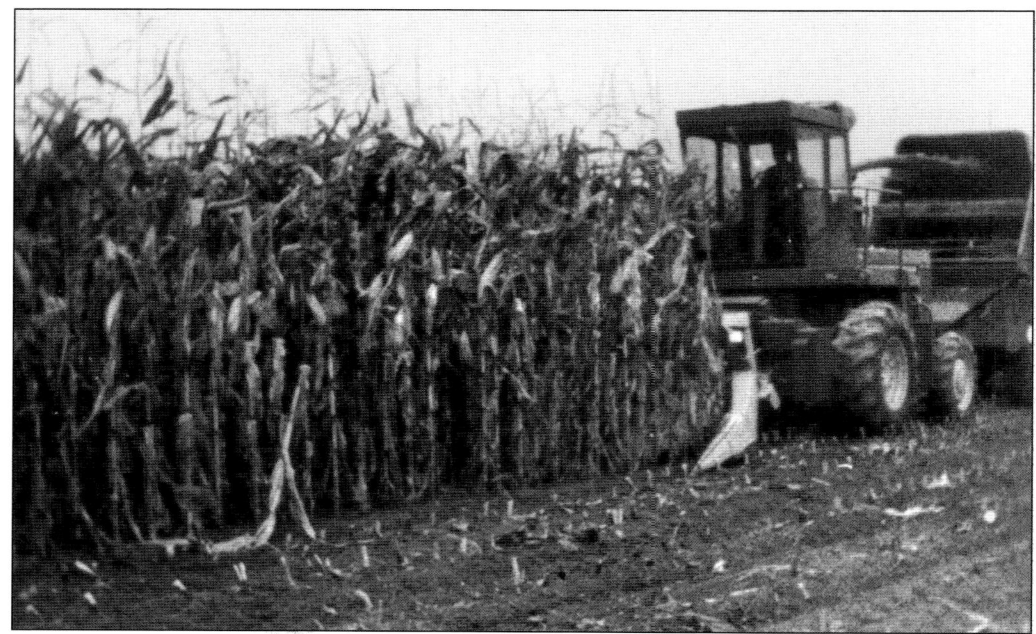

Todd Weant is driving a John Deere forage harvester that is chopping field corn for silage on the 117-acre Weant-Haven farm in the Harney suburbs in the 1980s. Carl and Grace Weant, in partnership with their son and his wife, have 100 milk cows and 50 young livestock. Grace Weant sells brown eggs laid by her 125 chickens. Even today, she puts her eggs on the porch and neighbors leave money, recycling their used egg boxes. The rest she sends to auction. (Courtesy of the Weant family.)

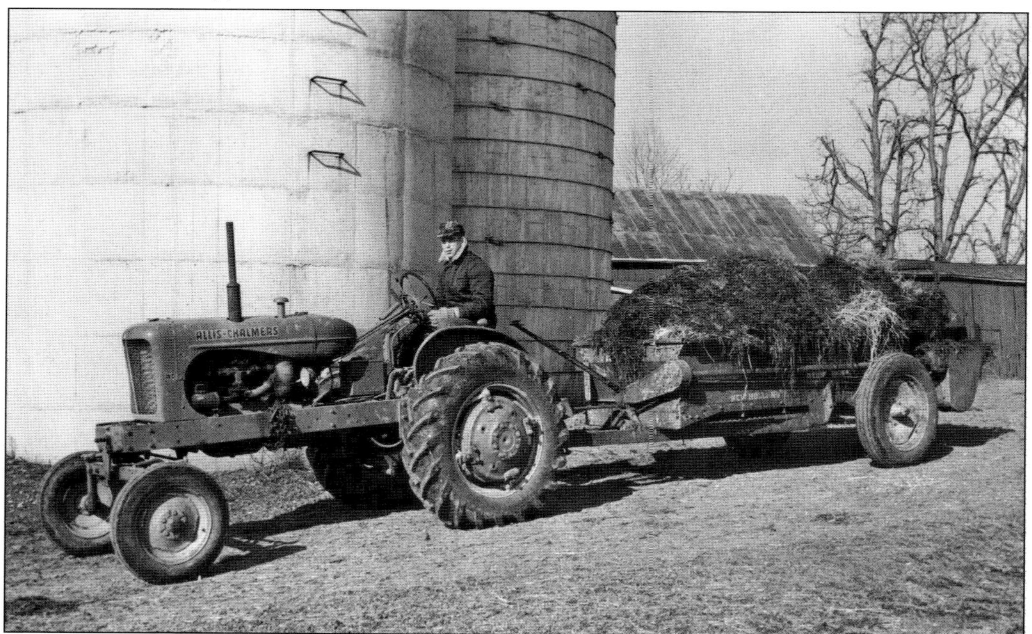

In 1952, twenty-year-old Donald Essich drives an Allis Chalmers tractor pulling a manure spreader. A front-end loader was used to load manure onto the spreader. A power take-off from the tractor drags a chain that moves the load toward the back. The beaters spread it out in the field. It had different settings for heavier or lighter loads. (Courtesy of the Essich family.)

Two

Leading the Way

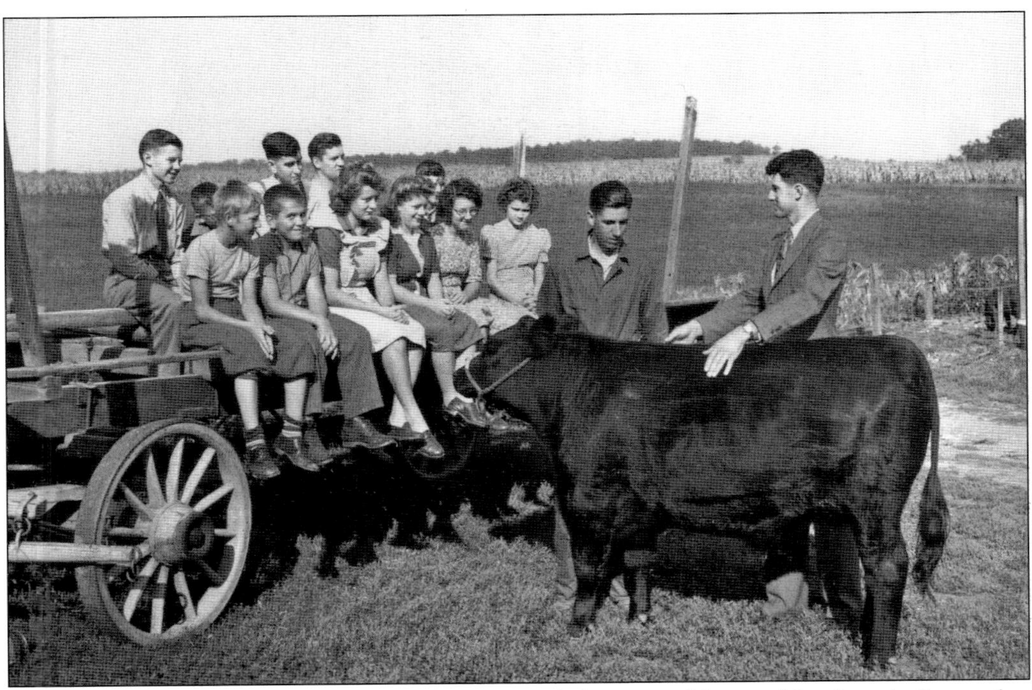

The Pig Club holds a demonstration of fitting and showing of fattened beef cattle for market and sale at the Timonium State Fair in 1944. From left to right are (first row) John Ed Grove, ? Fisher, Florence Hoke, Mildred Arbaugh, Kathryn Arbaugh, and Fannie Hoke; (in front by steer) Vernon Wolfe; (with steer) John Hull; (second row) Paul Frock, unidentified, John Victor Bixler, Solomon Hoke, and unidentified. (Courtesy of the University of Maryland Cooperative Extension, Carroll County.)

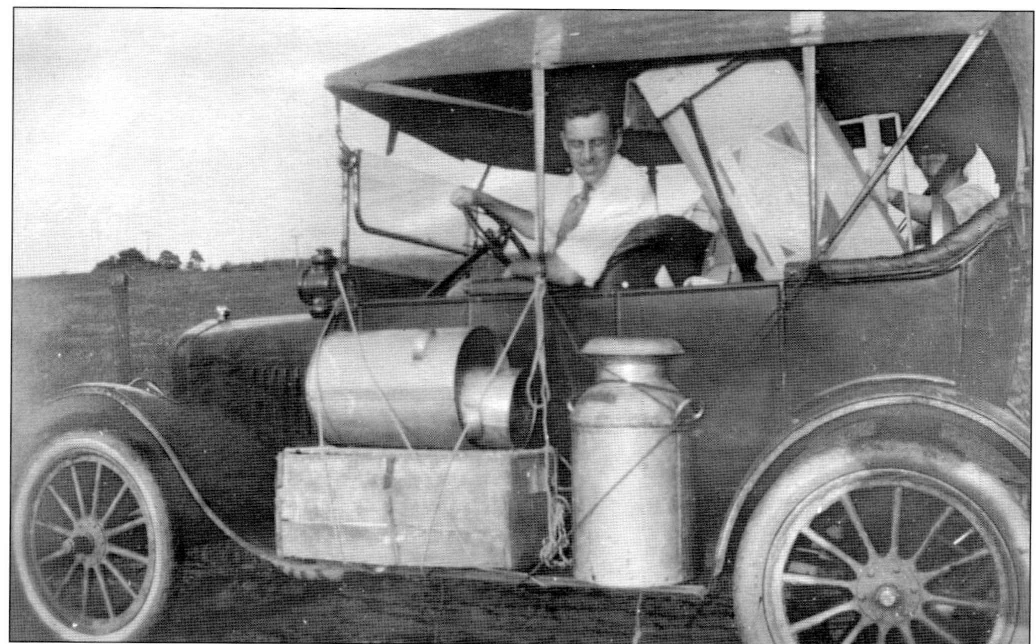

County agent Frederick Fuller is pictured in his loaded car in 1920 in Carroll County. During his first years, Fuller traveled 69 miles by team and 300 miles by train. (Courtesy of the University of Maryland Cooperative Extension, Carroll County.)

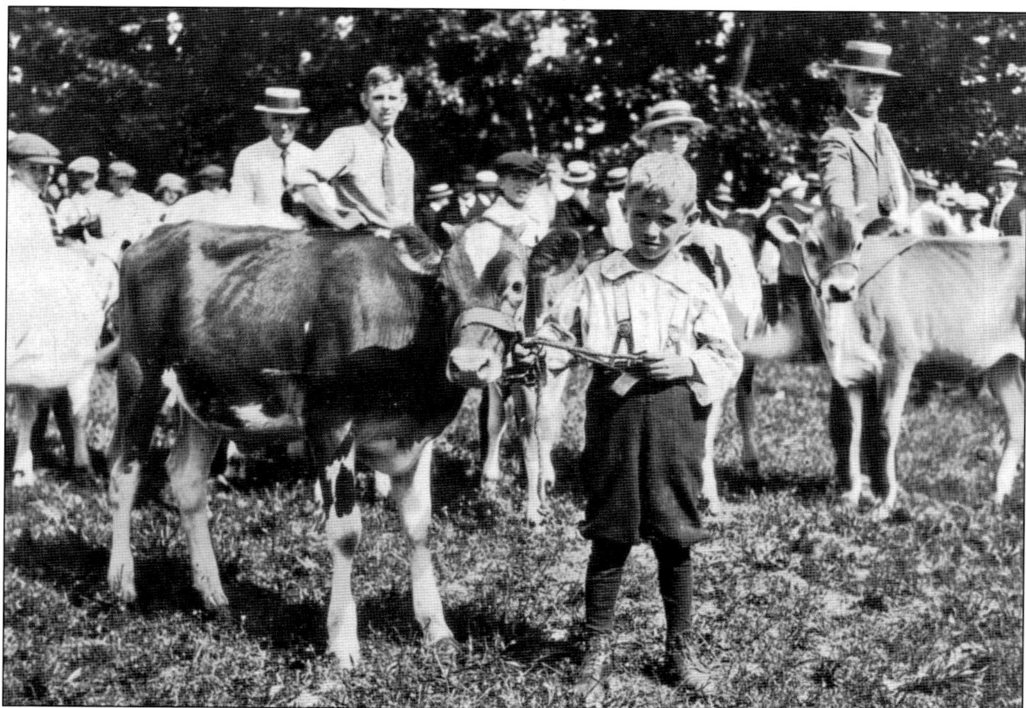

This 1925 photograph of a farm boy at a dairy cow field day in Carroll County was captioned, "Too young to be a calf member practicing a grade." Farm boys and girls learned to breed, raise, and show cattle as part of their participation in 4-H and other boys and girls clubs throughout the county. (Courtesy of the University of Maryland Cooperative Extension, Carroll County.)

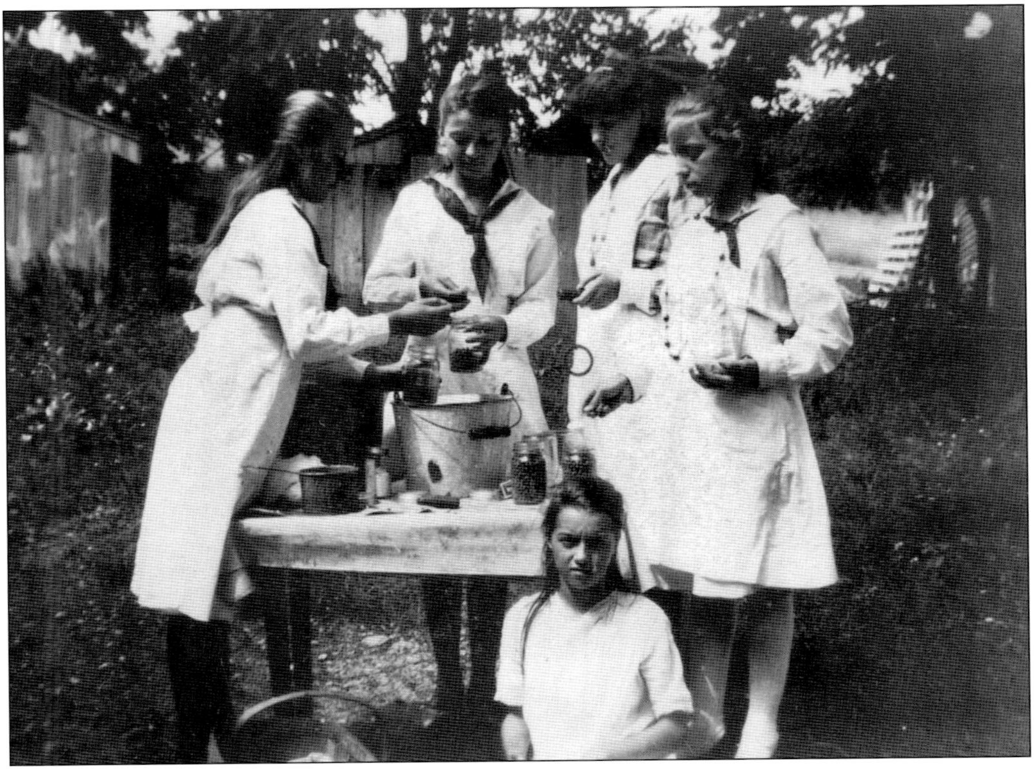

The home demonstration agent in Carroll County reported that teaching canning was the most important project of her office and the introduction of the pressure cooker was the most important improvement over methods used at that time. The Girls Club (above) is canning peas. Below, a county nurse demonstrates canning. Both images were taken in 1919. (Both courtesy of the University of Maryland Cooperative Extension, Carroll County.)

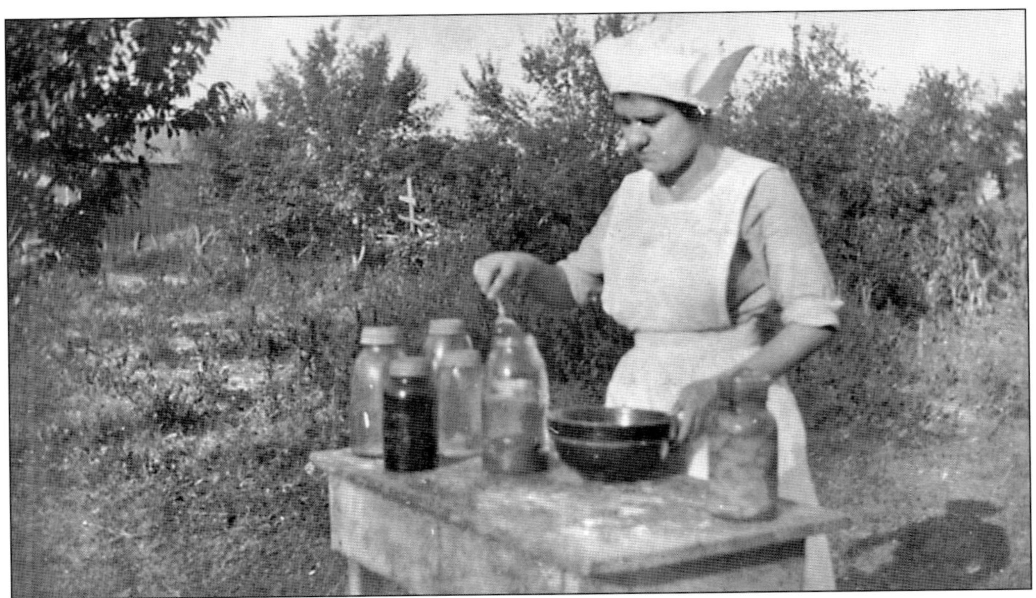

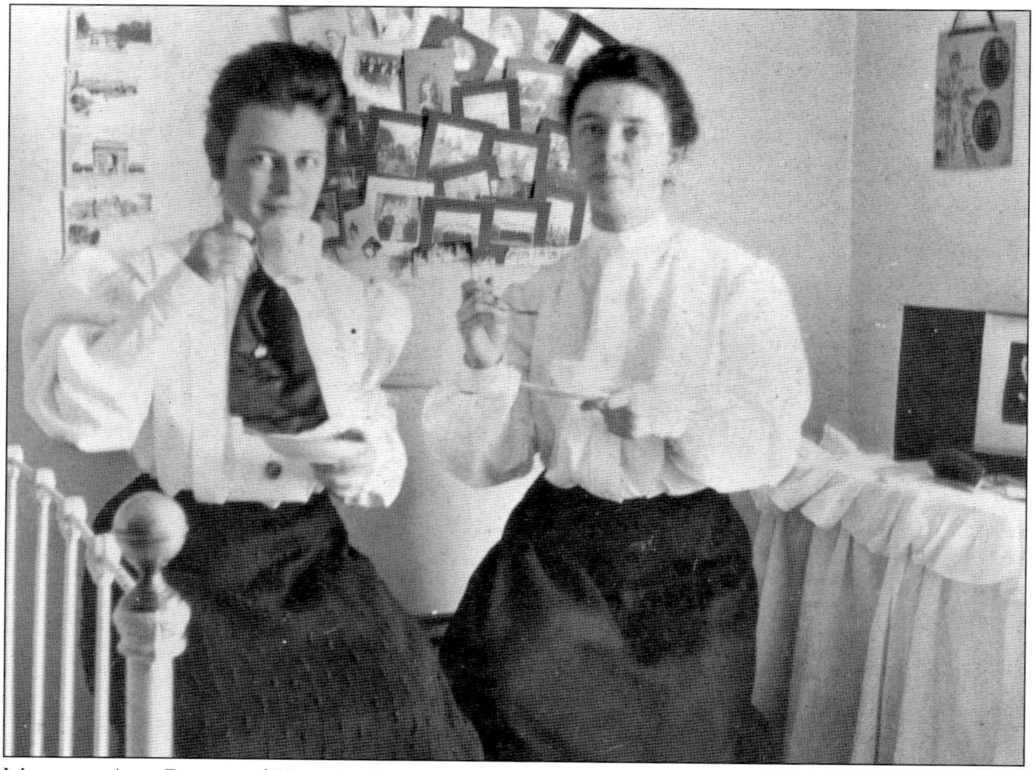

Margaret Ann Roop and Katie Miller John are shown in the dormitory when they attended the Maryland Collegiate Institute, later Blue Ridge College, in New Windsor. Roop lived on the farm owned by her grandparents John and Margaret Utz on Teeter Road in Taneytown. Margaret married John S. Teeter on December 25, 1907. (Courtesy of Rebecca Herrick.)

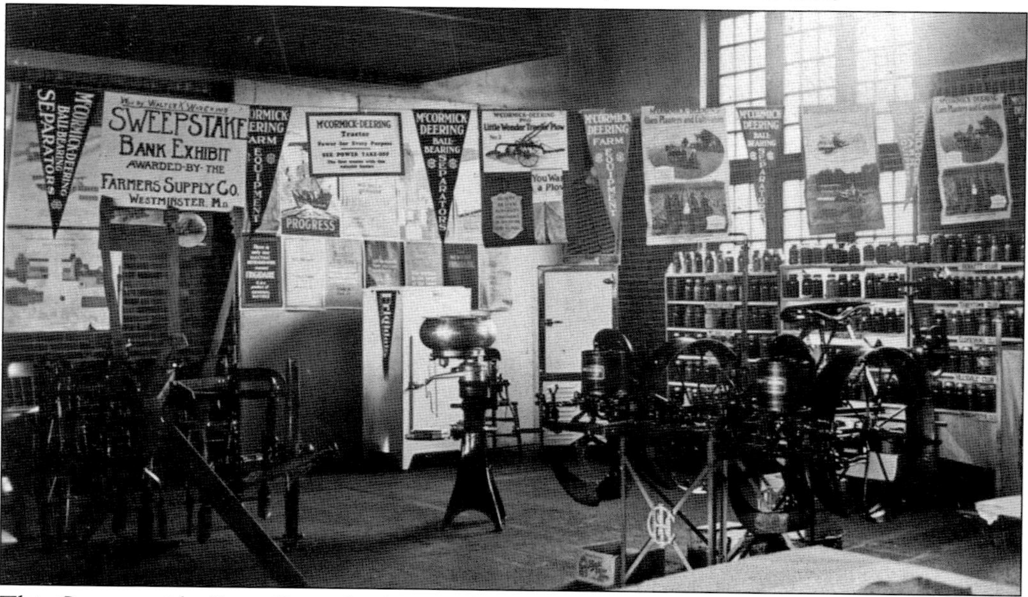

This County-wide Corn Show display was held in the Westminster Armory building in 1927. Equipment on exhibit and canned vegetables to be judged are in this photograph. (Courtesy of the University of Maryland Cooperative Extension, Carroll County.)

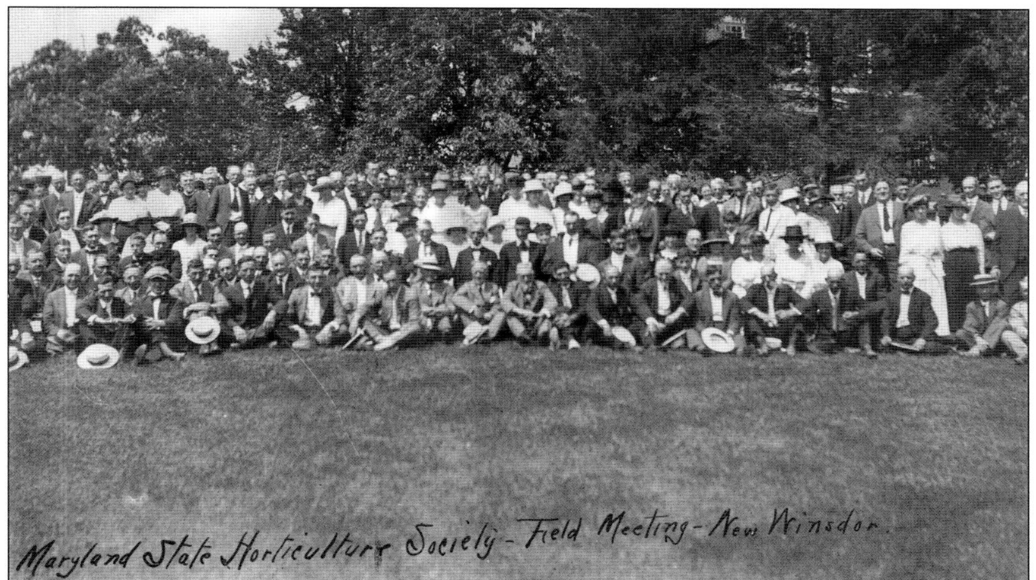

In 1920, the Maryland State Horticultural Society held its first field meeting in New Windsor at Blue Ridge College. According to the county agent's report, there was a demonstration in growing fruit with fertilizer treatments at the Mount Olivet orchard. Dr. T. B. Symons and Dr. F. B. Bomberger led the tour. (Courtesy of the University of Maryland Cooperative Extension, Carroll County.)

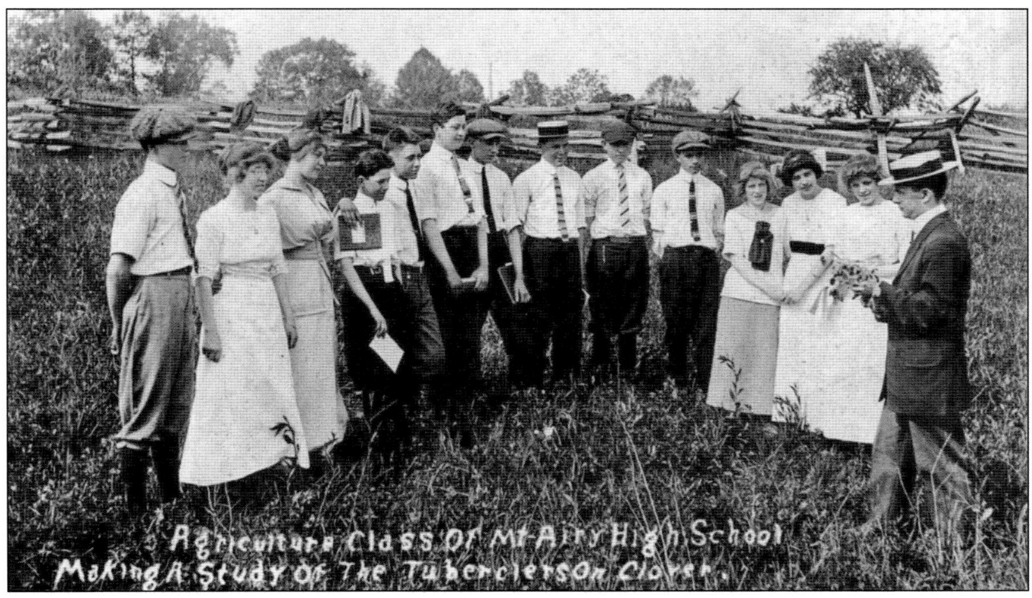

The agricultural class of Mount Airy High School is pictured making a study of the *Tuberclerson* clover. In 1921, it was believed that alfalfa and clover juices aided in destroying the tuberculosis germ, according to Dr. Hyman Lischner of San Diego, California, at the convention of the American Institute of Homeopathy. (Photograph by Hoffecker's Photo Studio, Mount Airy; courtesy of the Historical Society of Mount Airy, Maryland.)

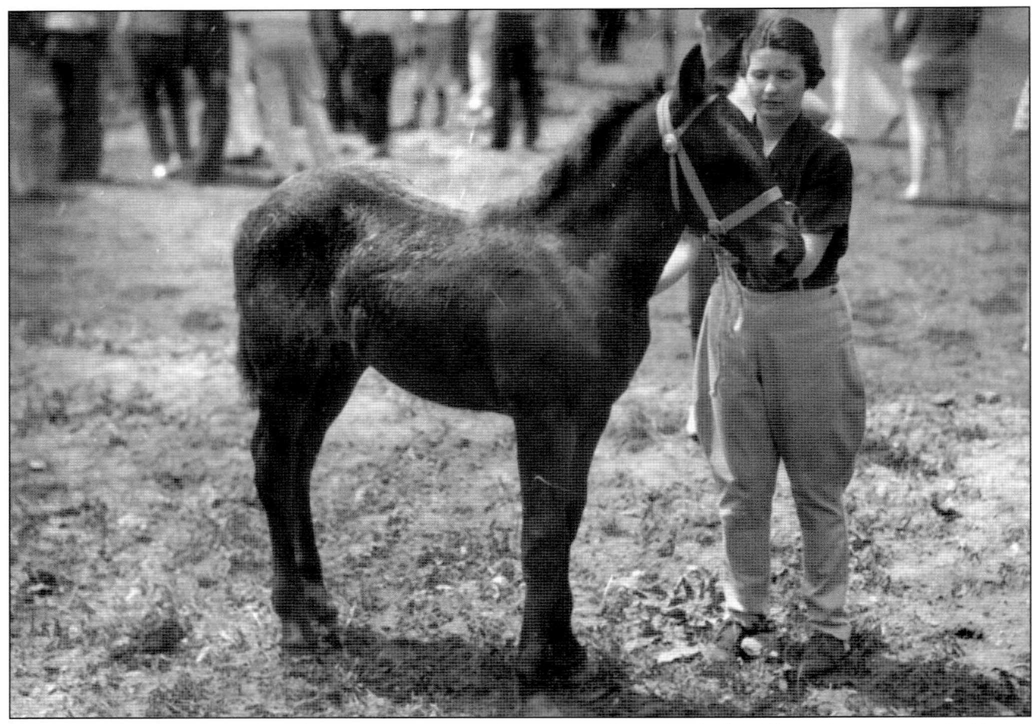

Leticia, a Percheron colt, is being shown by Elinor Ruth Morelock (Hull) at the county field day on the family farm on Meadowbranch Road near Westminster. (Courtesy of the Hull family.)

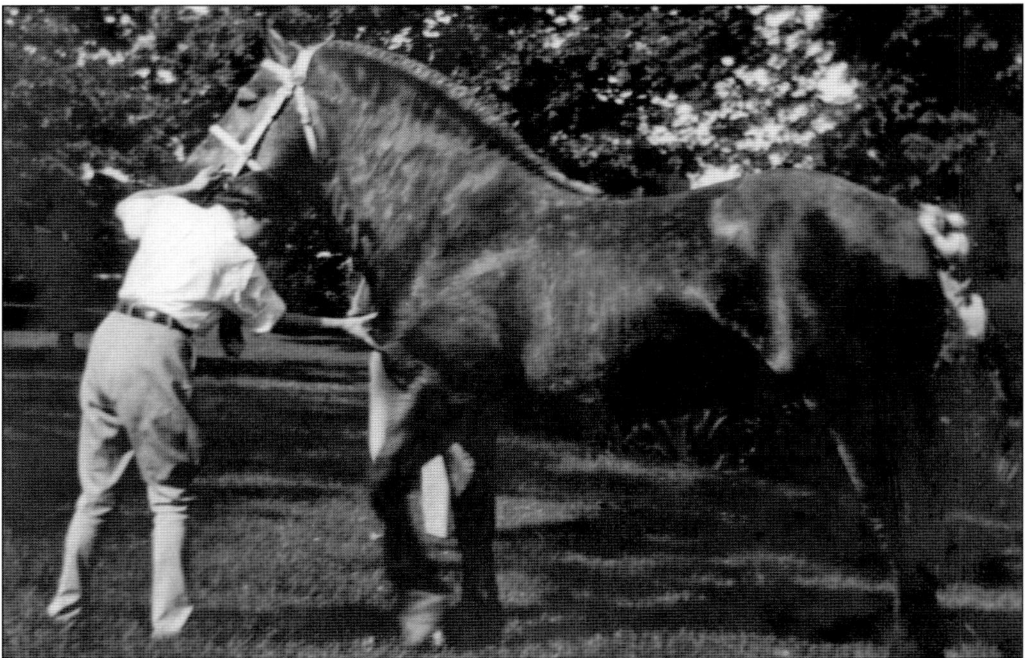

In 1939, Elinor Ruth Morelock (Hull) is pictured with Charlemane, a 3-year-old stallion, practicing for a Carroll County field day. Harry Paul Morelock, her father, raised Percherons. The farm was deeded by Rebecca Roop to Andrew Reese in 1842, and then David Reese inherited it. There have been six generations that lived on the farm. (Courtesy of the Hull family.)

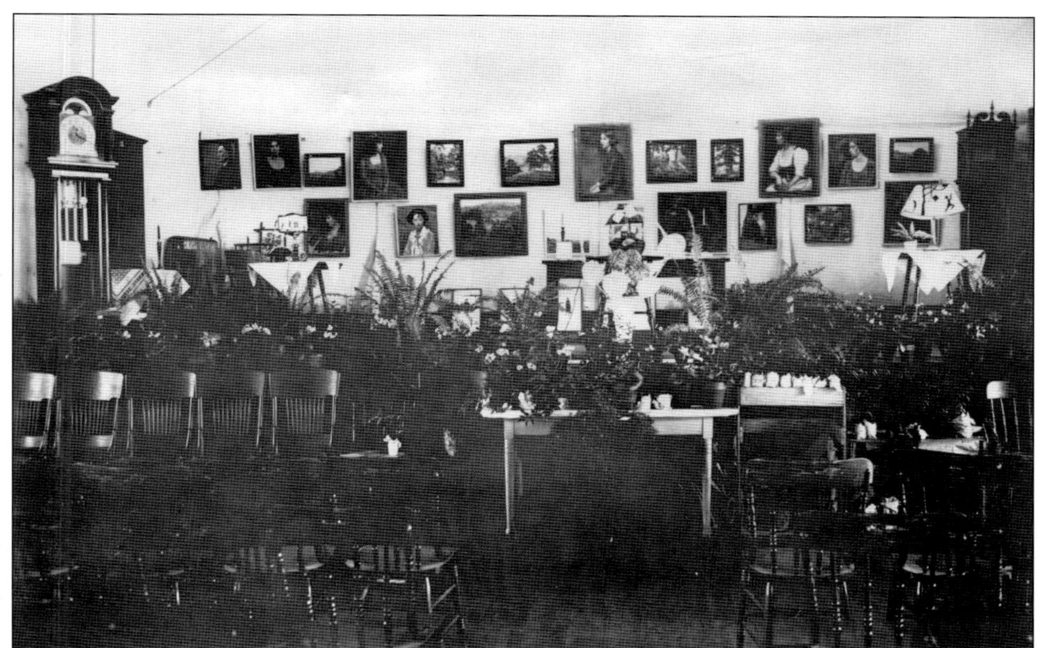

In this 1922 photograph, taken at the Armory in Westminster, there is an art show held as part of the county fair. Since the trip to Baltimore and Washington, D.C., was long, one of the only ways most Carroll Countians were able to see art was at these fairs. (Courtesy of the University of Maryland Cooperative Extension, Carroll County.)

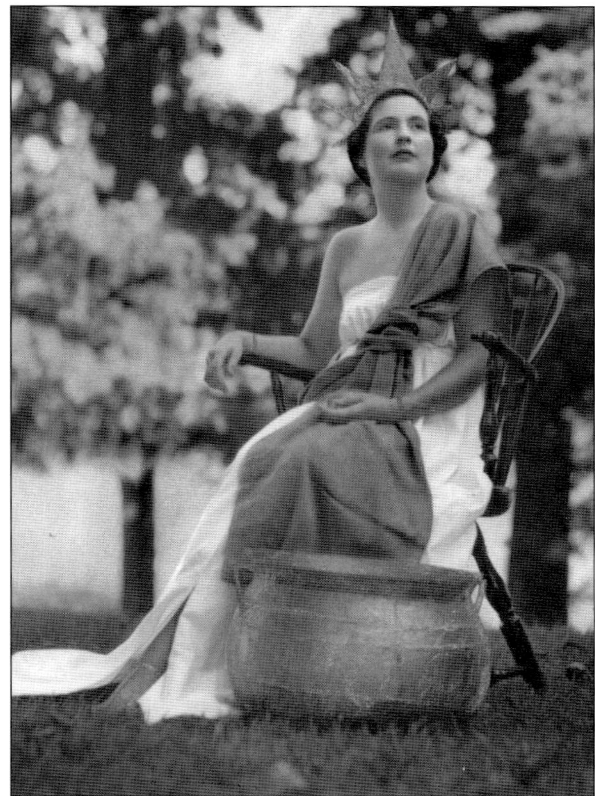

Elinor Morelock Hull is dressed as Miss Liberty with her pot of gold ready for the county fair held in Taneytown in the early 1930s. She had to stand for an hour holding a light. The photograph was taken of her sitting in an old Windsor chair in her yard on the family farm on Meadow Branch Road near Westminster. (Courtesy of the Hull family.)

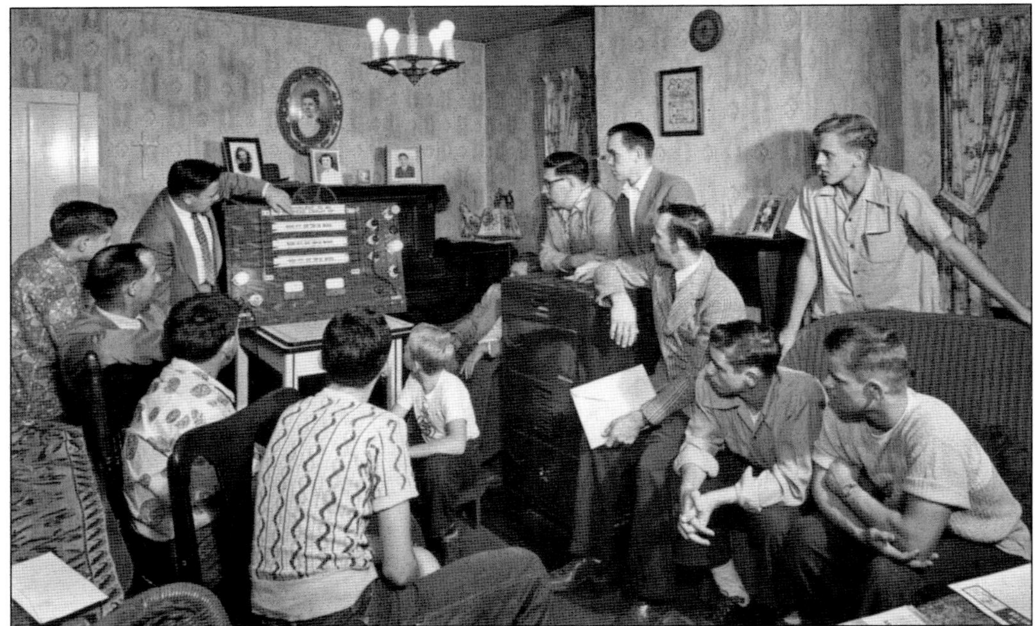

As a result of the county agent's cooperative extension work in agriculture in Carroll County, farm boys belonging to a 4-H Club received "Electrification Training" in 1950. In 1948, some 87 percent of farms in the Baltimore and Carroll County areas were electrified as compared to 68 percent nationally. (Courtesy of the University of Maryland Cooperative Extension Office, Carroll County.)

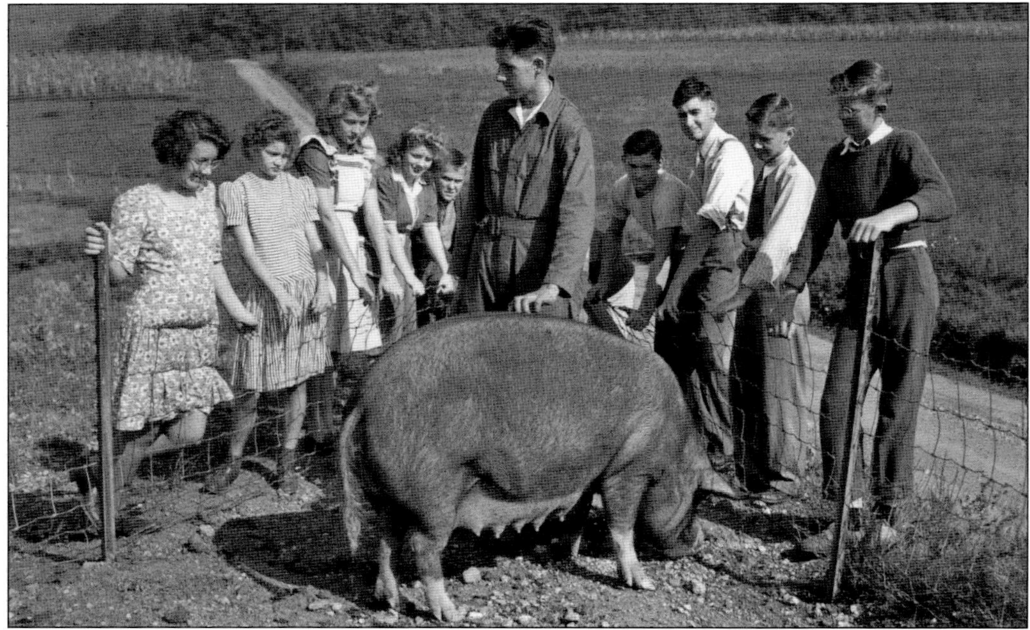

In 1944, the Pig Club holds a demonstration on how to properly feed a mother sow. Pictured from left to right are Kathryn Arbaugh, Fannie Hoke, Florence Hoke, Mildred Arbaugh, ? Fisher, Vernon Wolfe (touching pig), unidentified, Solomon Hoke, Victor Bixler, Paul Frock, and John Ed Grove. Formed in 1937, it was the first club to be integrated in the 1940s. (Courtesy of the University of Maryland Cooperative Extension, Carroll County.)

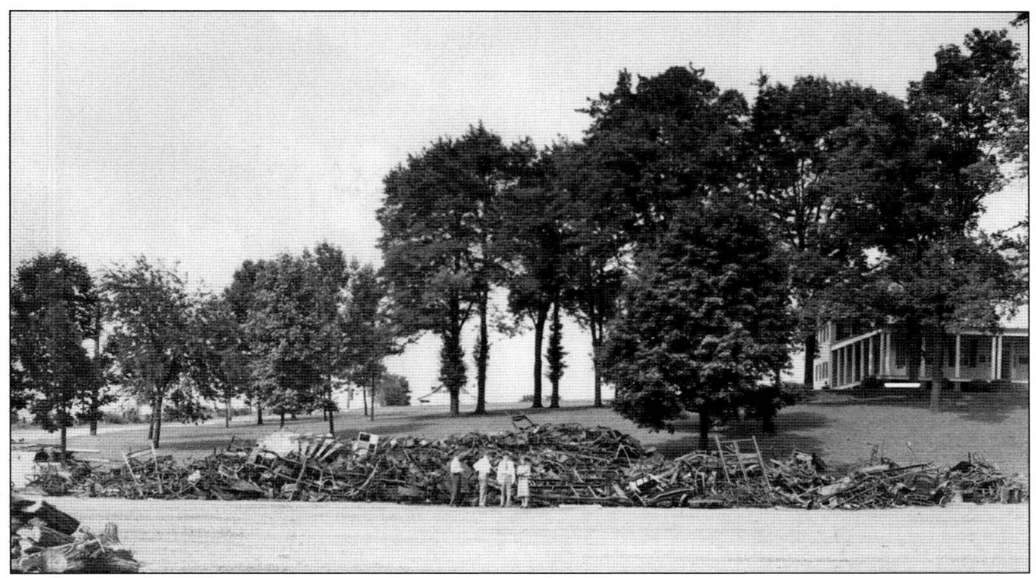

In 1942, Carroll County led all counties in the state in assembling scrap that was needed by the war effort. The International Harvester Company, in cooperation with the county agent, ran a three-week contest in scrap collection and brought in 250 tons. Defense bonds were offered as prizes by different feed businesses in the community. (Courtesy of the University of Maryland Cooperative Extension, Carroll County.)

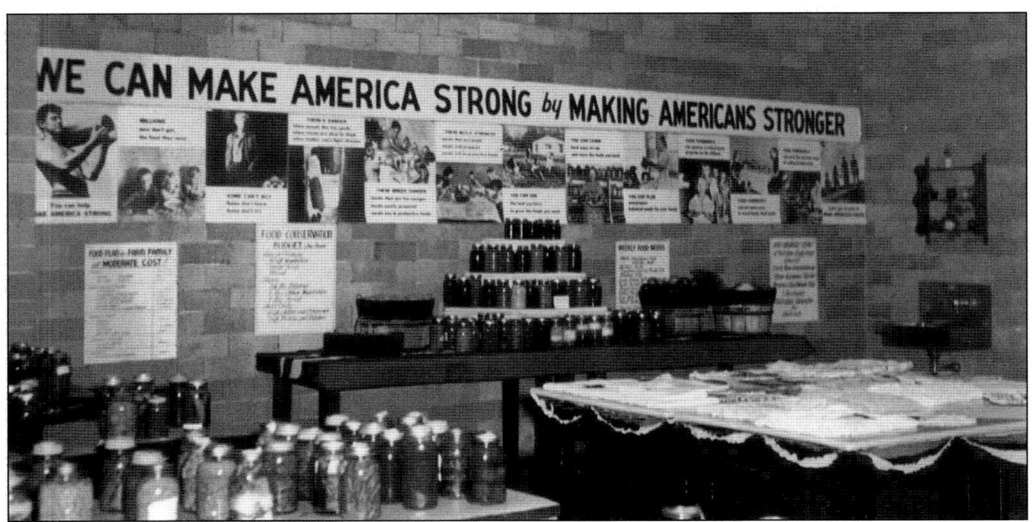

In the county agent's report of 1941, farmers were encouraged to be more efficient in their production of food for the war efforts. Every family was encouraged to plant a victory garden. In 1942, he reported, "Food Will Win the War and Write the Peace." (Courtesy of the University of Maryland Cooperative Extension, Carroll County.)

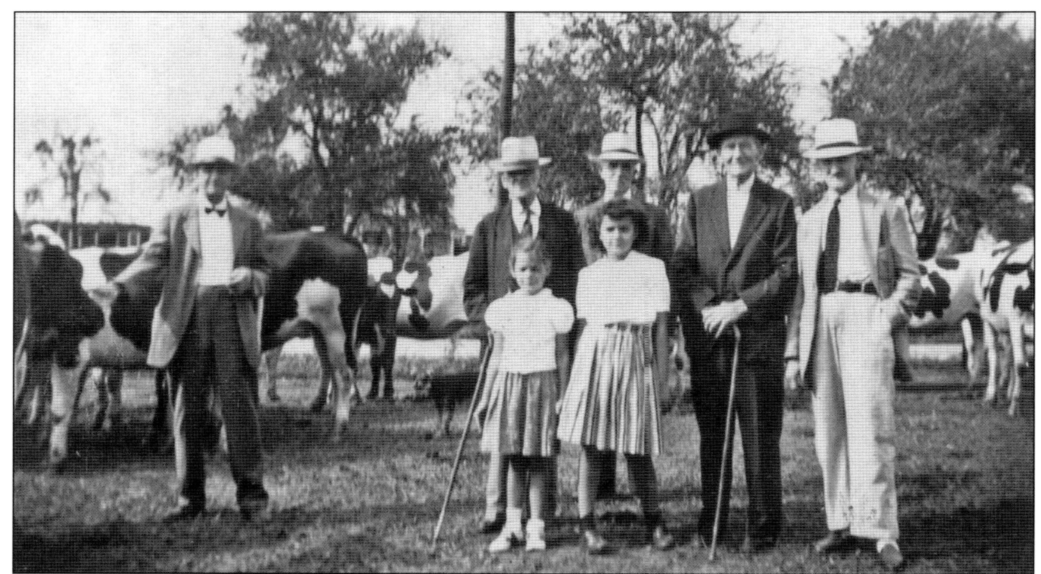

After World War II, the W. Roger and Olive V. Roop dairy farm on Middleburg Road in Union Bridge, Maryland, became the gathering place for the Heifer Project, a vision of the Church of the Brethren to restock farms after World War II. Heifers were donated and delivered to the farm from all over the United States between 1945 and 1948. They were shipped from the port of Baltimore to war-torn countries as a result of World War II. In the center, from left to right, the two girls are Patricia Roop (Robinson) and Shirley Roop (Kirkwood). (Courtesy of Patricia Roop Robinson.)

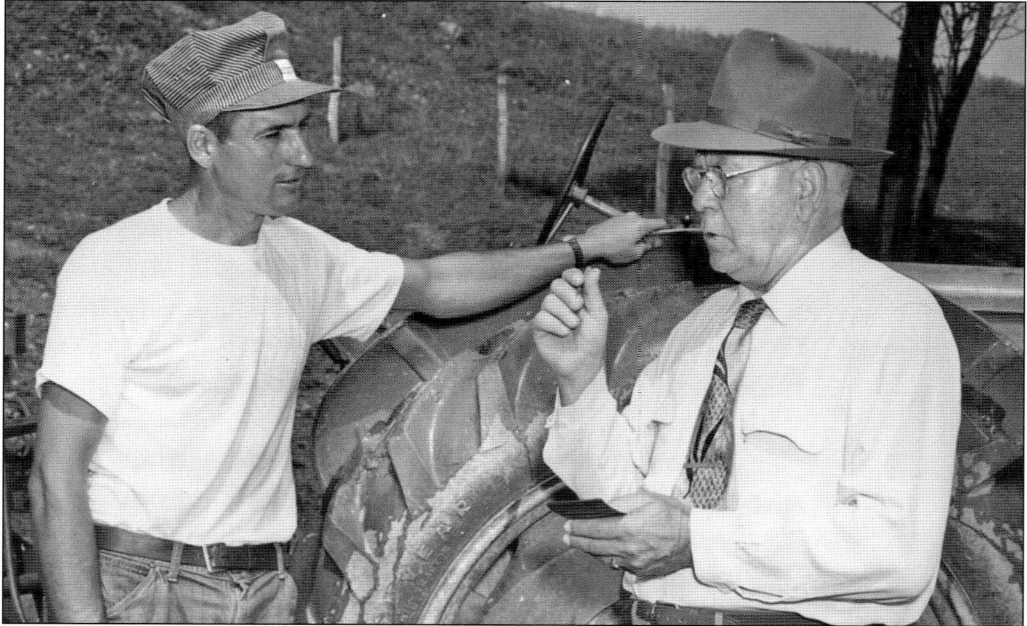

In 1957, John Harbaugh (left), farm owner, is pictured with Raymond P. Buchman, Soil Conservation District supervisor. Buchman enlists Harbaugh as a district cooperator. Farmers working with the Soil Conservation Agencies has a signed Soil Conservation and Water Quality Plan where they agreed to install and implement best management practices on their farms to decrease soil erosion and improve water quality. (Courtesy of the Carroll Soil Conservation District.)

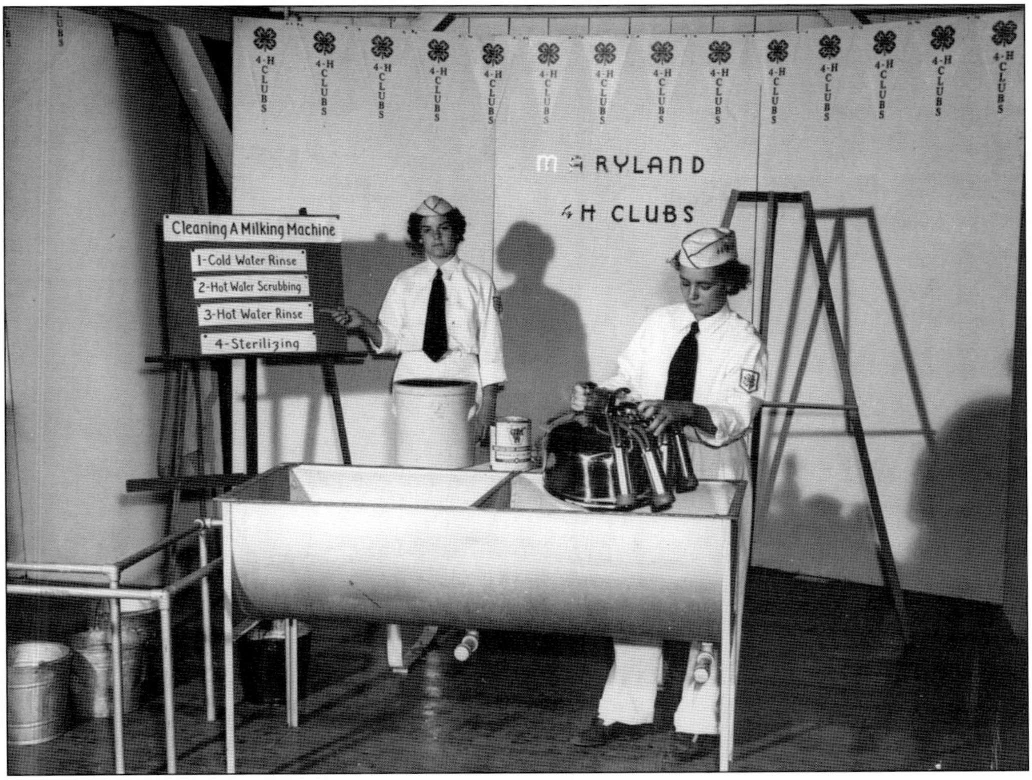

The Taneytown Agricultural 4-H Club Dairy Team was the first prize winner in 1950 for the demonstration of cleaning a milking machine. Pictured are Marion Miller (left) and Mary Null. (Courtesy of Peggy Soper.)

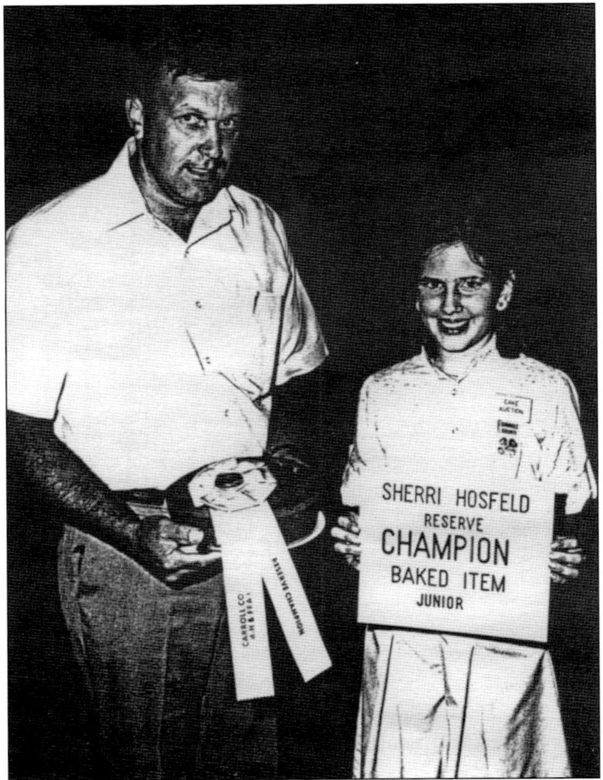

This picture was taken of Sherri Hosfeld Joseph, age 11, in 1982 at the Carroll County 4-H Fair. She received the Reserve Junior Champion Baked Item for her sour cream pound cake. It was purchased by John D. Myers Jr. of Old Bachman's Valley Road, Westminster. (Courtesy of Peggy Soper.)

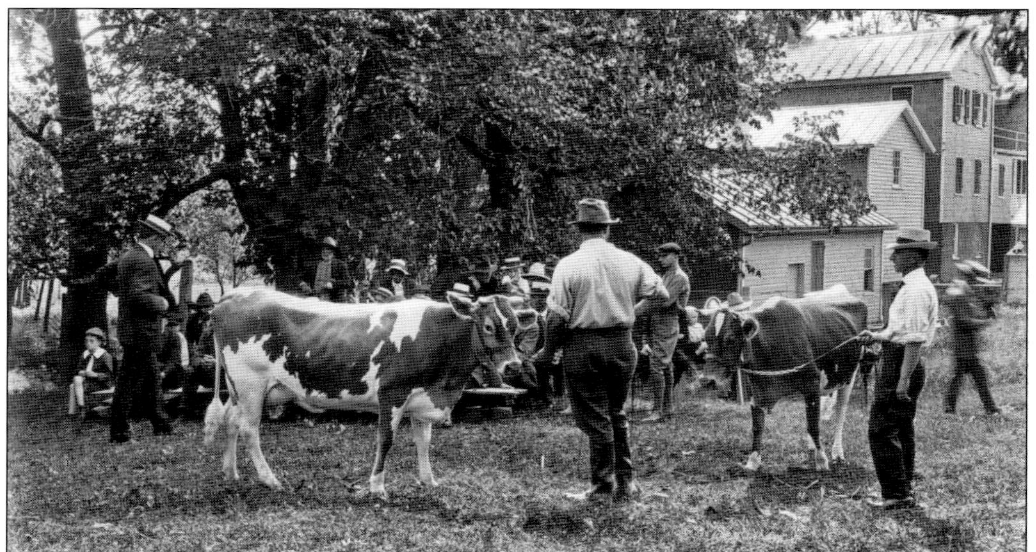

Granville Hibberd (left) judges Guernsey cows on the Getty farm in New Windsor at the Maryland Guernsey Field Day in 1939. Hibberd inherited the Mill Dale Farm in New Windsor in 1917 from his father, Charles Hibberd. He raised Guernsey dairy cows, which are known for the high butterfat content of their milk. (Courtesy of G. Hibberd.)

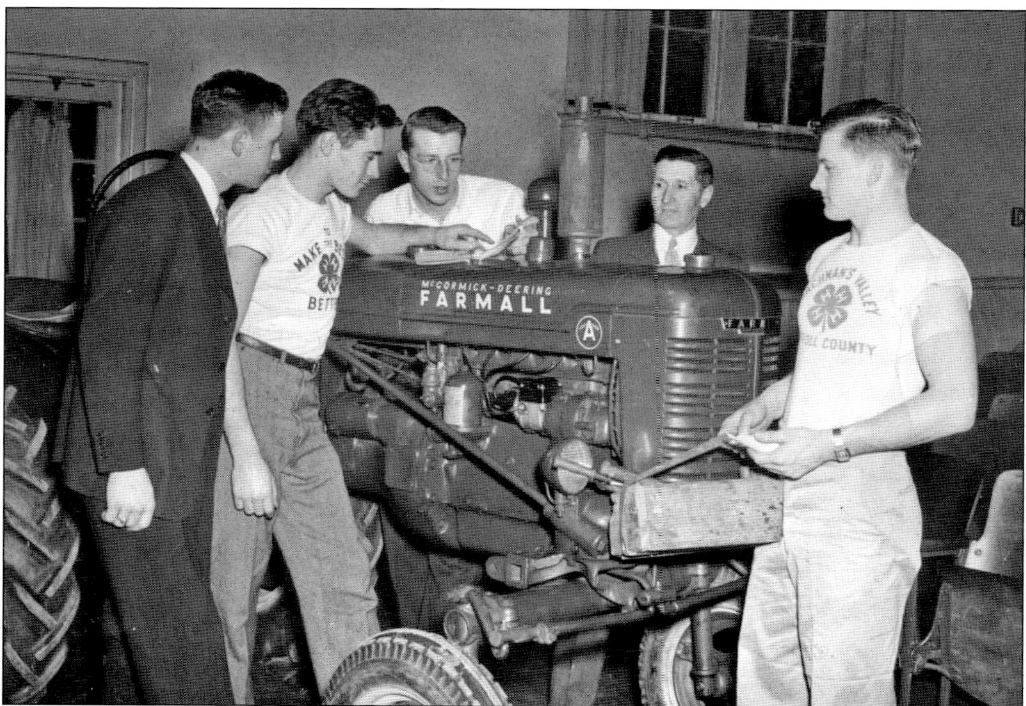

This picture shows the 4-H Tractor Maintenance Club review of their activities in 1947. About 250 people came to the meeting exhibiting the only tractor ever put in Westminster High School to learn about safety, maintenance, and rubber on tractors. The war was over, so they learned how to get the best out of their equipment. From left to right are Stewart Young, Gary Brauning, Charlie Brehm, John Young, and Solomon N. Hoke, holding a handmade toolbox. "Don't be a hammer, pliers, and screwdriver mechanic," they were taught. (Courtesy of the Hoke family.)

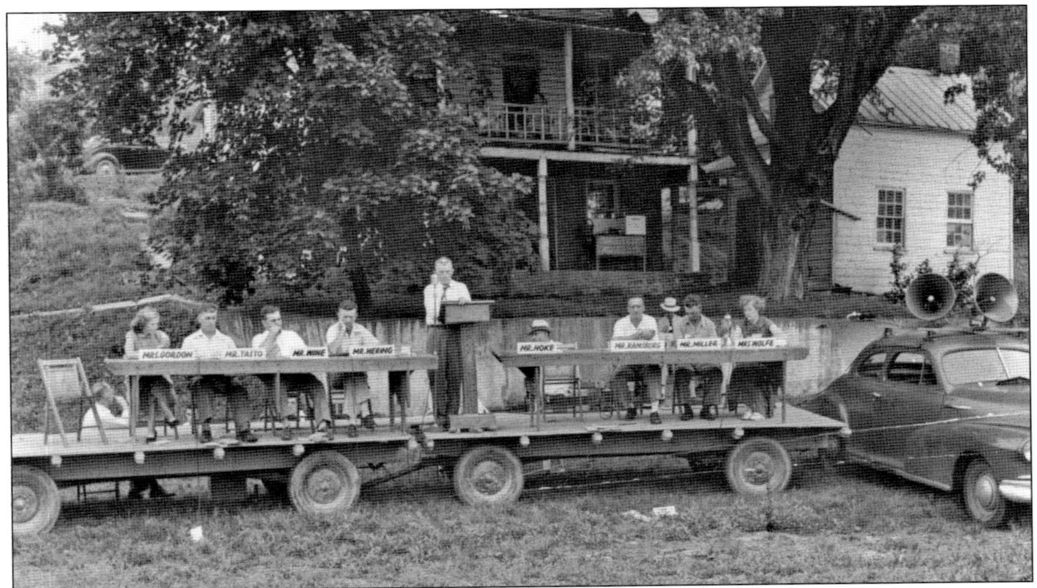

This meeting was held on the Jim Shriver Sr. farm in 1947 to discuss the Pipe Creek Water Shed Project. Seated from left to right are Landon Burns, ? Gordon (Fridinger Mill Road), ? Tasto, Guy Wine (Tracey Mill Road), ? Hering, Jim Shriver Sr., Solomon Hoke, ? Ramsburg (shop teacher), ? Miller, and Florence Wolfe. (Courtesy Carroll Farm Service Agency.)

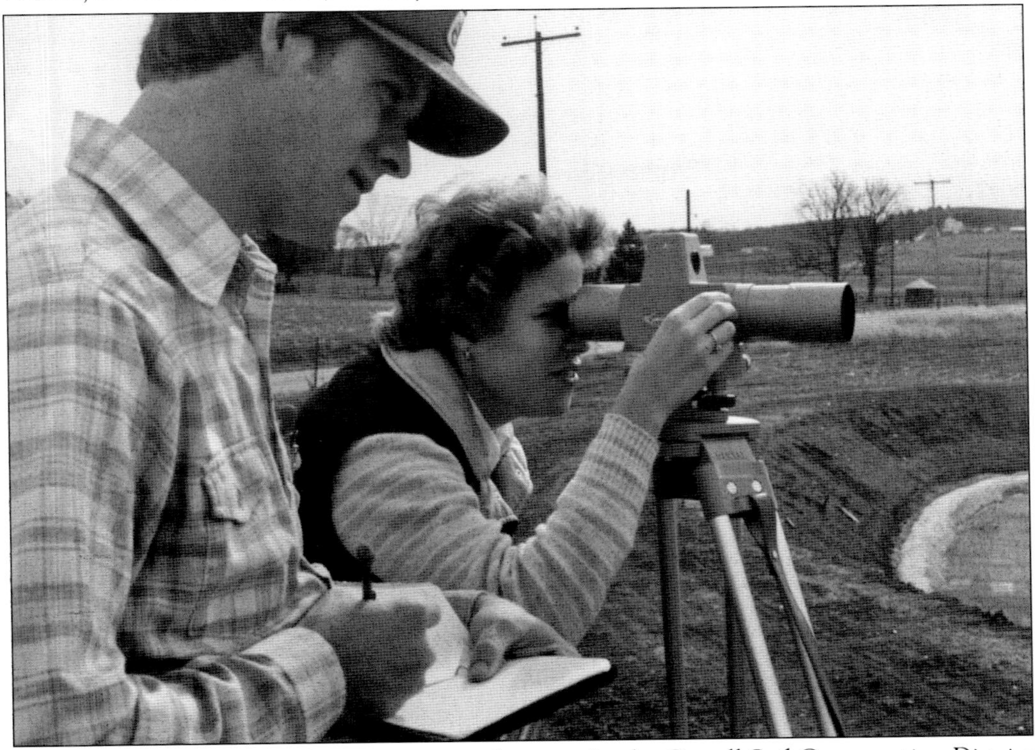

Jan Roop Stambaugh, a soil conservation technician for the Carroll Soil Conservation District Office in Westminster, is using a transit to make measurements for the grading of a pond in 1982. To her left stands Randy Bachtel, a soil conservationist. (Courtesy of the Carroll Soil Conservation District.)

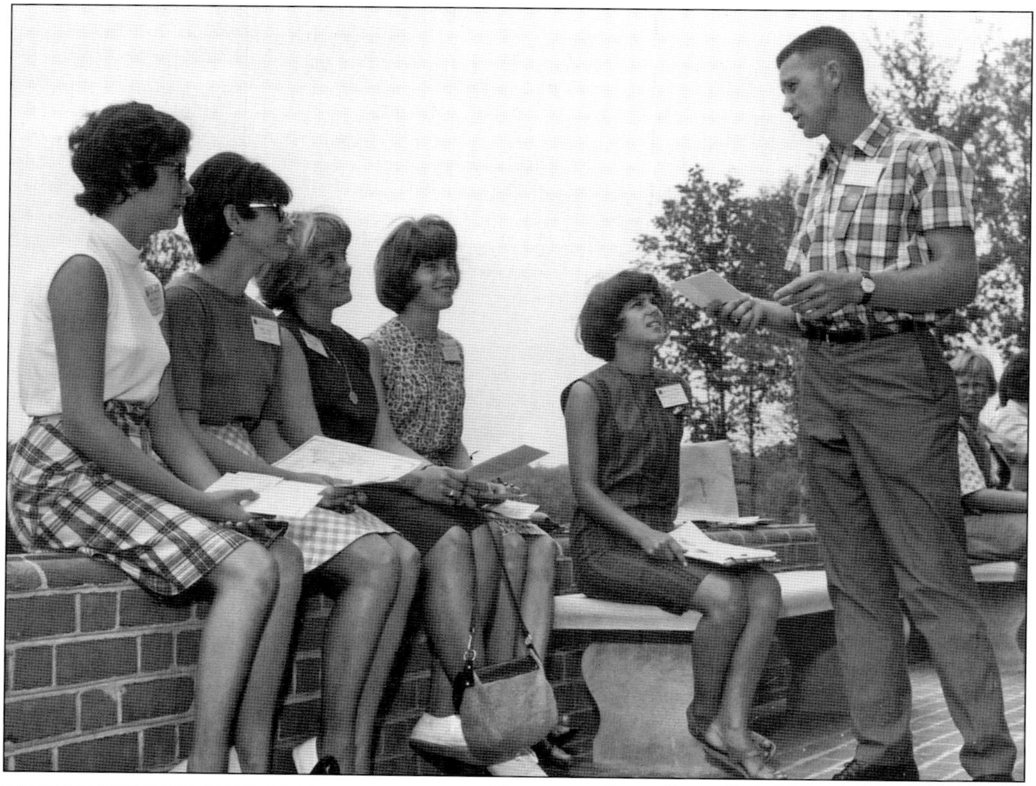

Teenagers from Carroll County discuss the first 4-H Conference held by the University of Maryland on the College Park campus in August 1966. The 4-H members attending from Carroll County were, from left to right, Debra Bowman, 15; Sandy Boyd, 15; Peggy Born, 14 (all three of Westminster; Barbara Davidson, 14; and Marian Metcalfe, 15, from New Windsor; and Ken Stonesifer, 19, from Taneytown. (Courtesy of the Historical Society of Carroll County.)

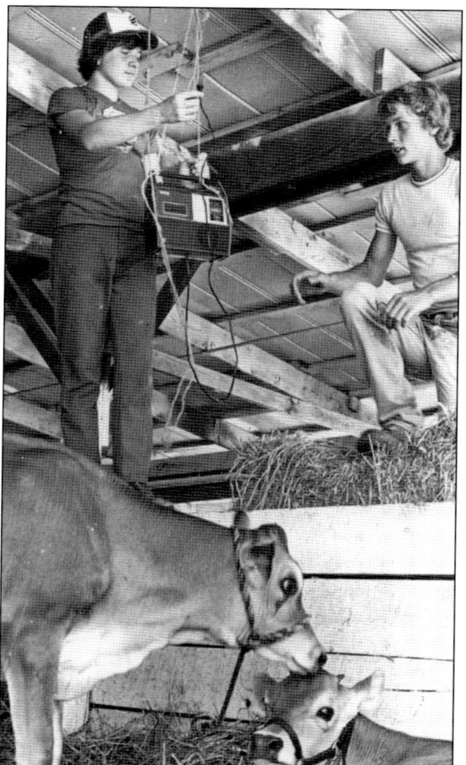

These 4-H boys are setting up to stay all week at the c. 1985 county fair in Westminster. They are going to stay all night, so they are plugging in their radio. Girls were not allowed to spend the night at the fair. (Courtesy of Peggy Soper.)

Three

The Business of Agriculture

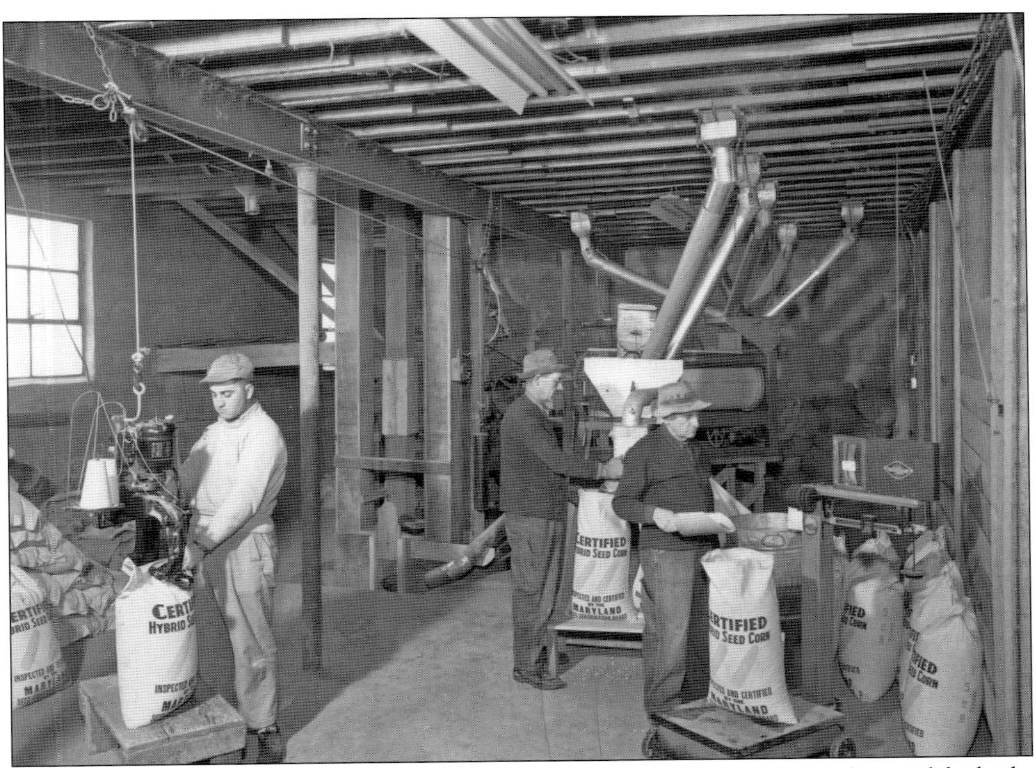

As farms changed from subsistence farming to producing crops as a business, the need for high-quality corn was recognized. Vernon Mathias raised Maryland certified seed corn on his farm near Westminster. This is the seed corn building on Hillcrest Farm outside Westminster. The men in this 1940 photograph bagging seed corn are, from left to right, Malcolm Mathias sewing a bag of seed corn shut, ? Baile filling the bags with 56 pounds of seed (bushel), and Vernon Mathias weighing the corn. Chutes come from the ceiling and bring corn down from the second floor. (Courtesy of the Mathias family.)

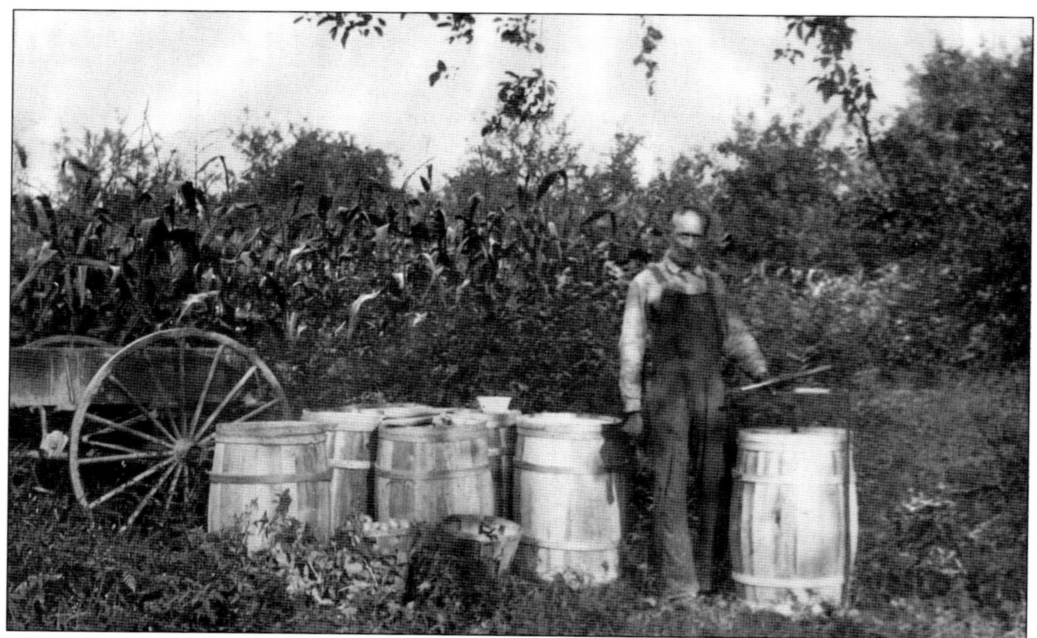

J. M. Myers is pictured packing early apples in the 1920s. (Courtesy of the University of Maryland Extension, Carroll County.)

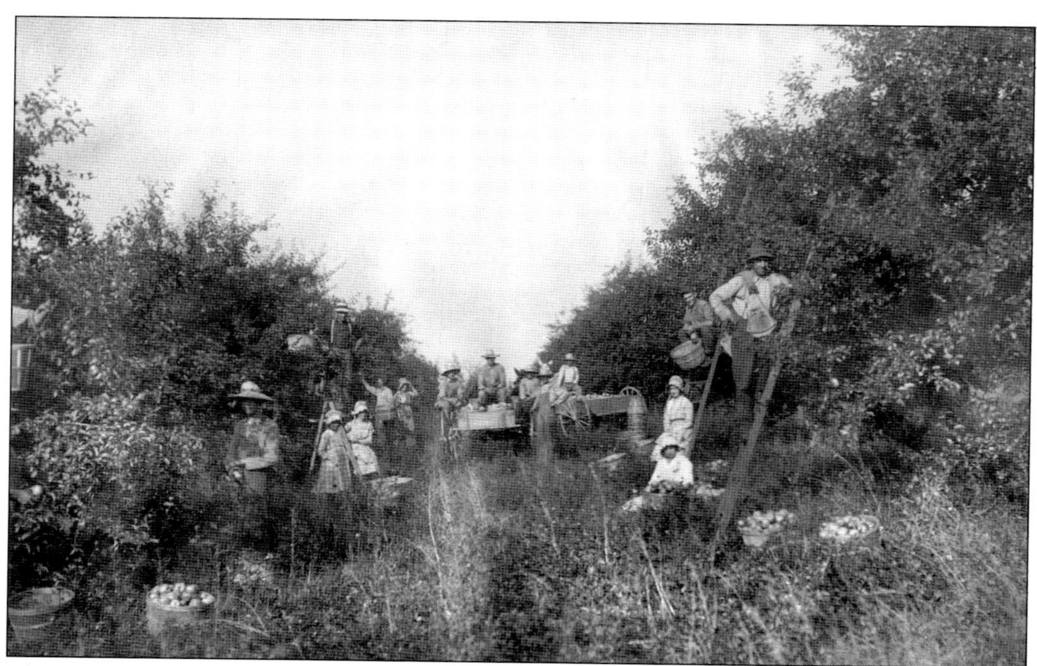

These workers are picking apples in the Myers and Bickers orchards in Westminster. (Courtesy of the University of Maryland Extension, Carroll County.)

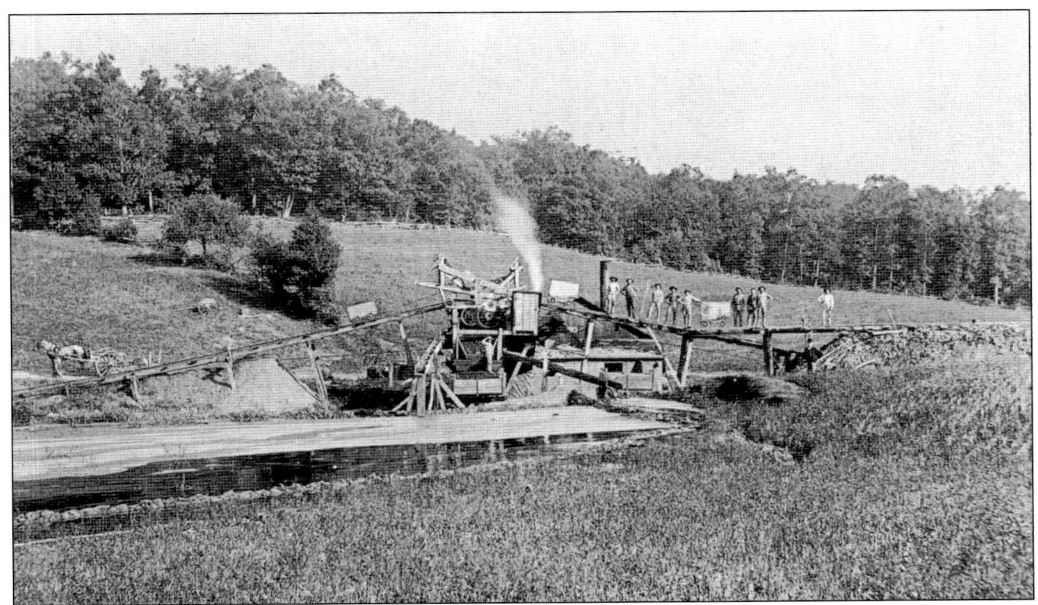

These men are mining iron ore on the Schaeffer farm. A contract was made in 1872 between Jacob Schaeffer and the Cameron Furnace Company for a minimum of 1,000 tons of ore per year at 50¢ per ton. In 1916, John D. Schaeffer had a contract for ore with the Mason Dixon Mining Company. Ore was transported by the Bachman Valley Railroad. (Courtesy of Helen Totura Schaeffer.)

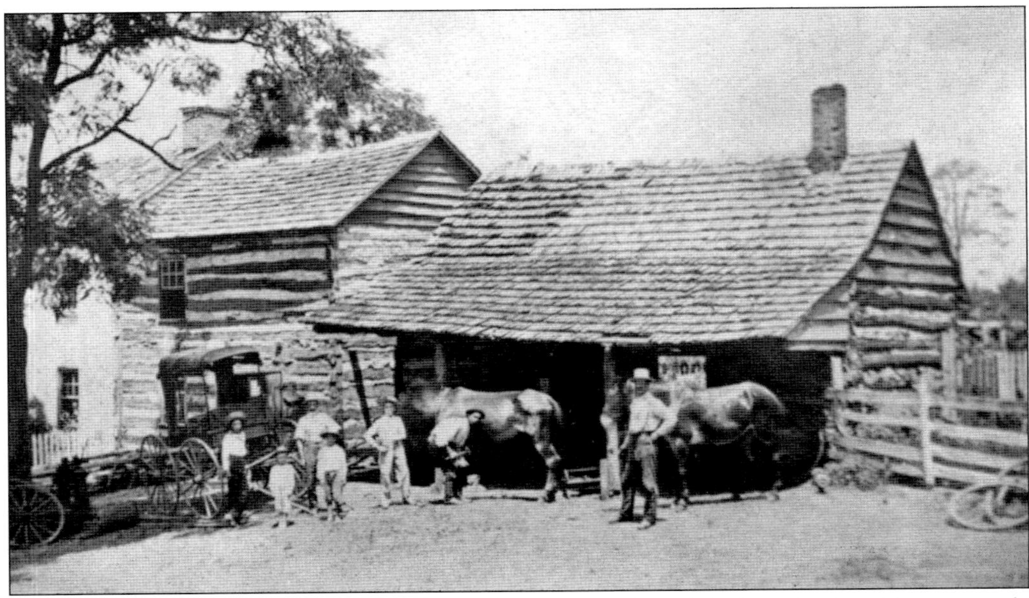

This is a *c.* 1876 photograph of a blacksmith's shop in Finksburg. Blacksmiths shoed horses, made kitchen utensils and harness hooks, repaired farm equipment, and even made parts. (Courtesy of the Historical Society of Carroll County.)

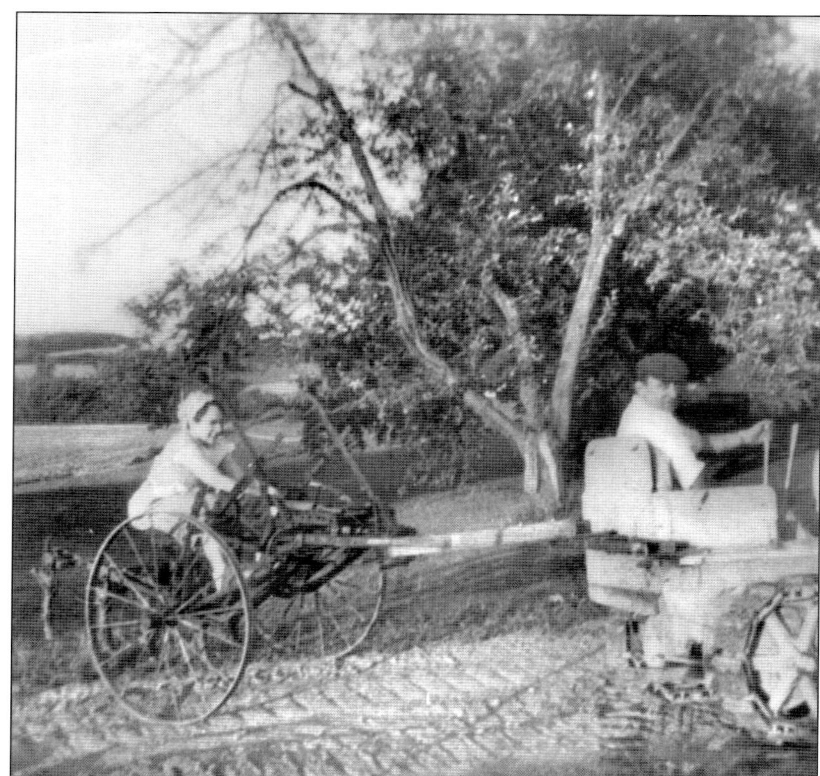

Edward Baugher is driving a tractor with Romaine, his wife, operating the cultivator in their truck patch in the 1940s. They peddled produce in town door to door. Romaine baked pies and cakes that she sold in town for a quarter. Her son Allen said that was too cheap, so her cakes went up to 50¢ the next week. (Courtesy of the Baugher family.)

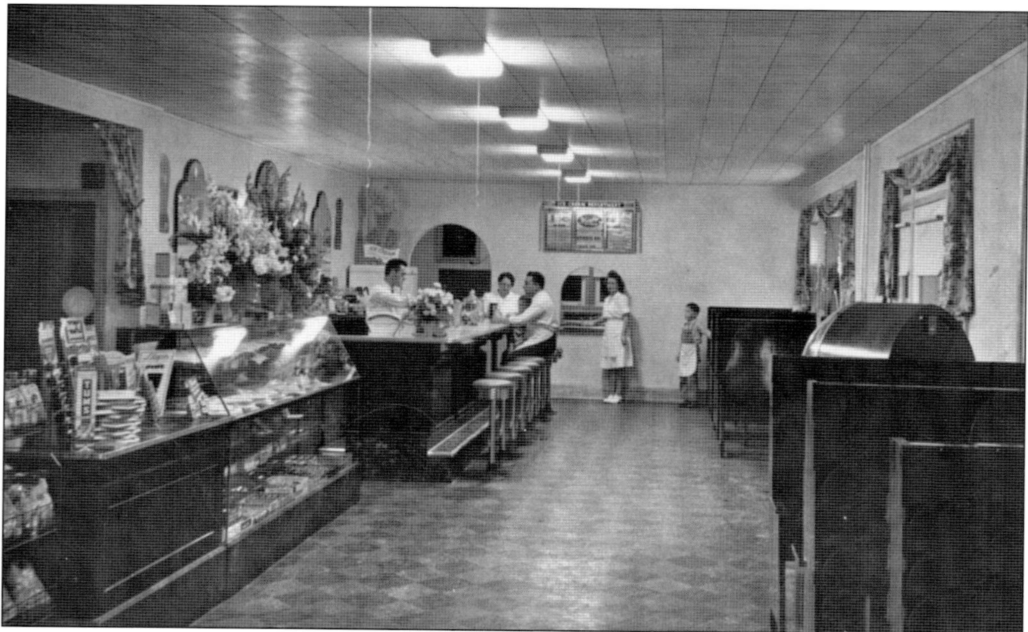

In 1948, when Baugher's restaurant opened in Westminster, Edward Baugher catered to college students with hot dogs, hamburgers, and a soda fountain, and he sold farm produce. Less than a year later, it was so popular with everyone that he made the kitchen bigger and served platters. When the restaurant opened, Romaine Baugher baked pies and cakes in her basement from 2:00 to 3:00 a.m. on weekends. Addie Leppo, her mother, peeled fruit. (Courtesy of the Baugher family.)

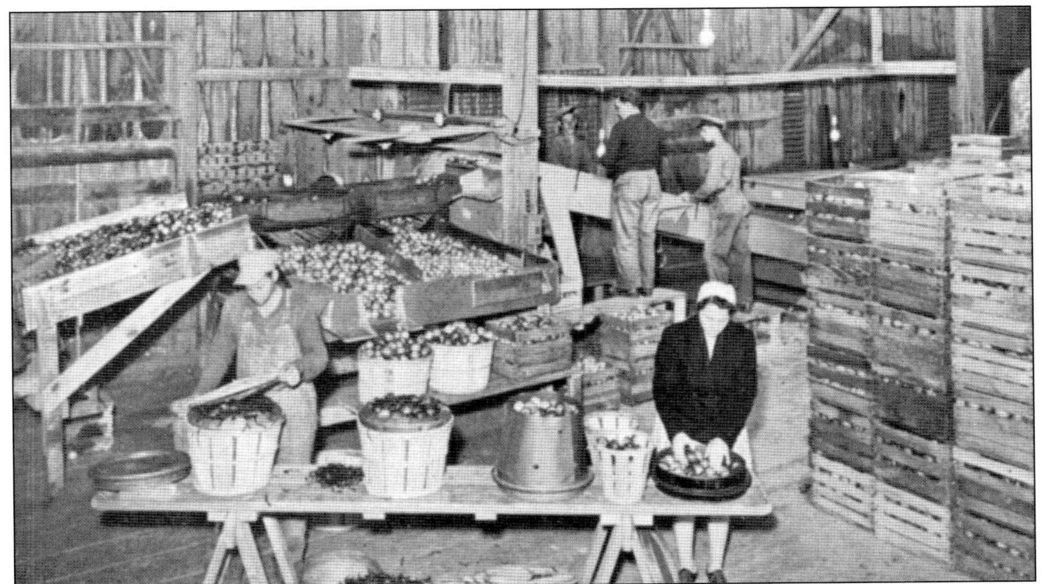

Romaine Baugher (front, right), along with other farm workers, is sorting and packing peaches at Baugher's Orchard in Westminster. When Allen Baugher was 16, he drove the fruit to Baltimore and later Pittsburg. They started picking fruit early in the morning, packed it in the afternoon, and left by 7:00 p.m. to get to Pittsburg by midnight. Baugher's was one of the first farms in Carroll County to install electricity in the barn to improve work production. (Courtesy of the Baugher family.)

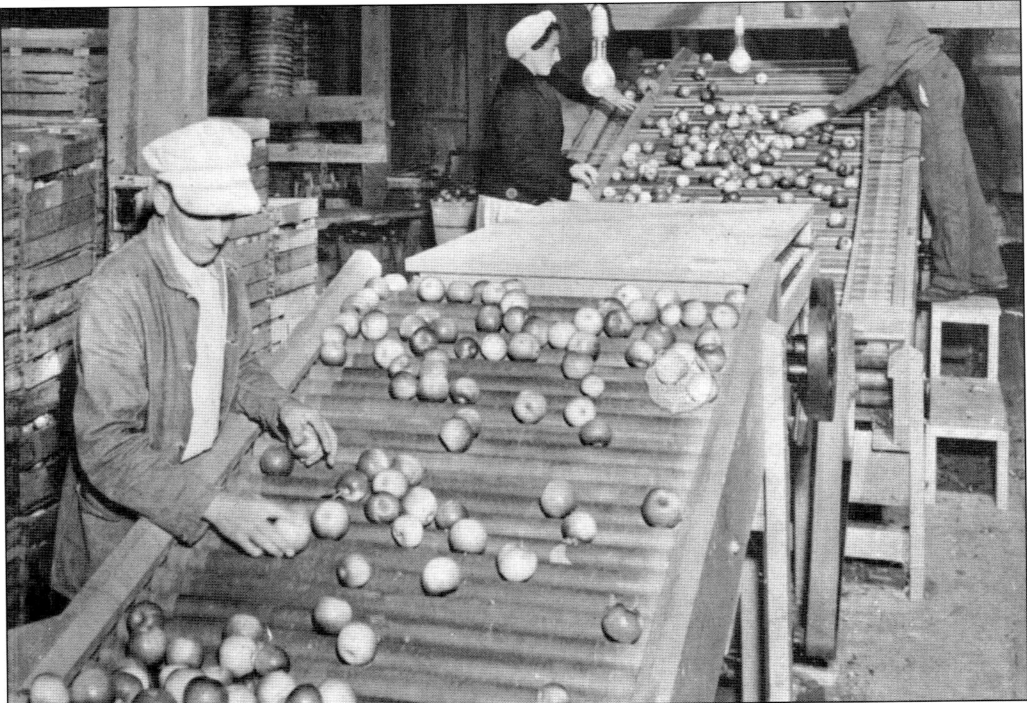

These workers are sorting apples at Baugher's Orchard and Farm in Westminster. Romaine Baugher is standing second from left. (Photograph from the *Rural Power Pictorial* magazine, September 1948; courtesy of the Baugher family.)

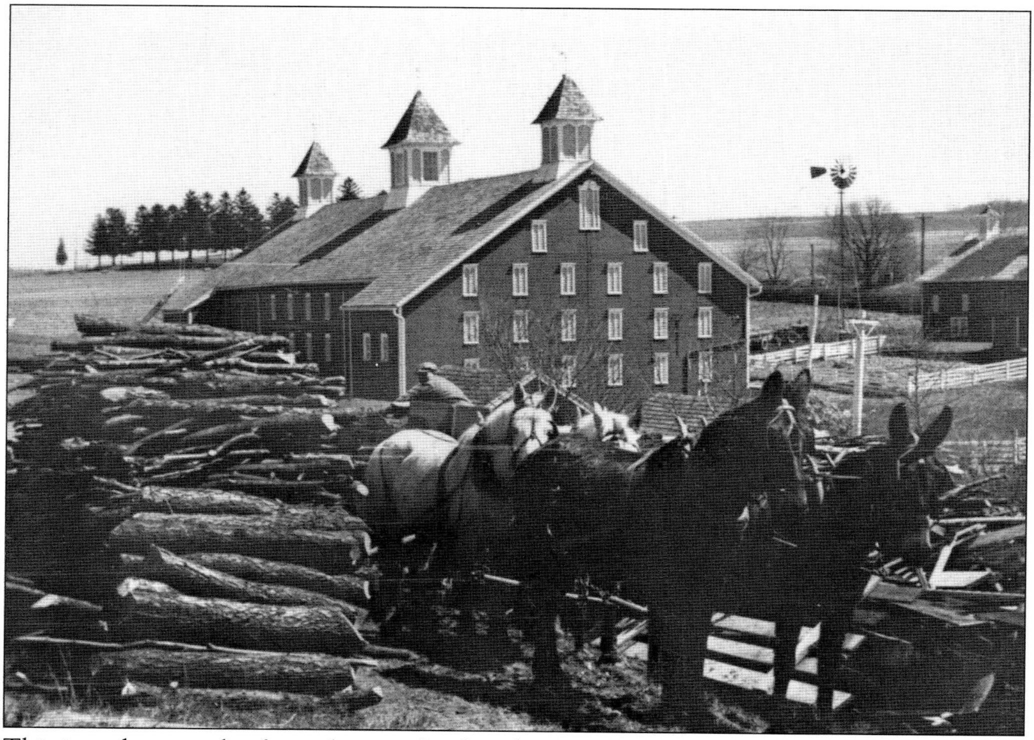

This is a photograph of a mule team hauling logs on a farm on Old Bachman Valley Road. (Courtesy of the Historical Society of Carroll County.)

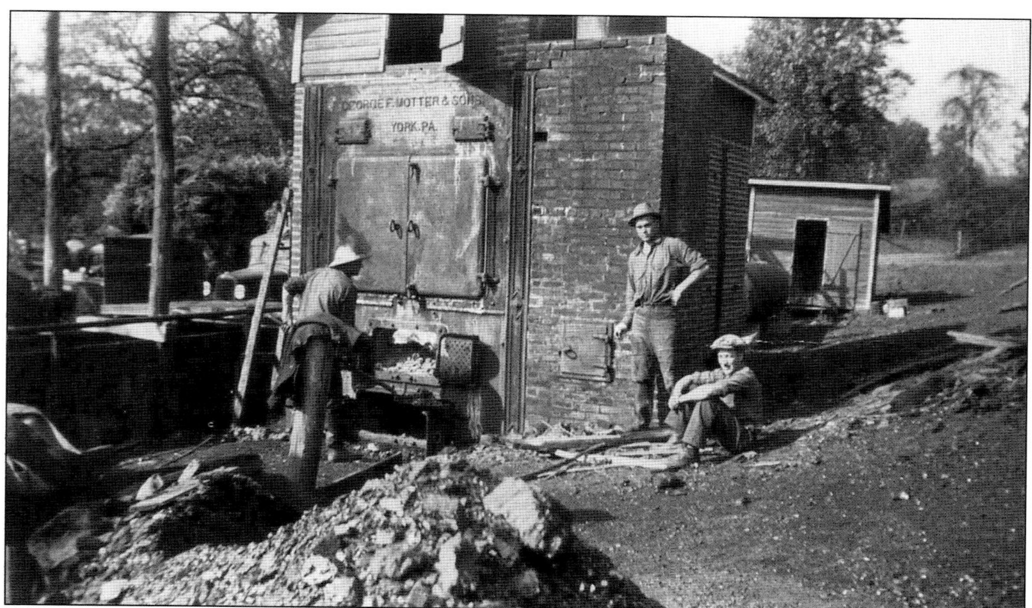

In 1940, this wormseed still on Bollinger Road was owned by Edward Bollinger Sr. Wormseed was distilled in October because the dew held heavy on the plants, which kept the seeds on the plant. When the boiler reached the correct temperature, the whistle blew. Local farmers who grew wormseed plants knew when the whistle blew they should line up their wagons. Wormseed was used as a hookworm remedy and as a wood preservative. (Courtesy of Edna Bollinger.)

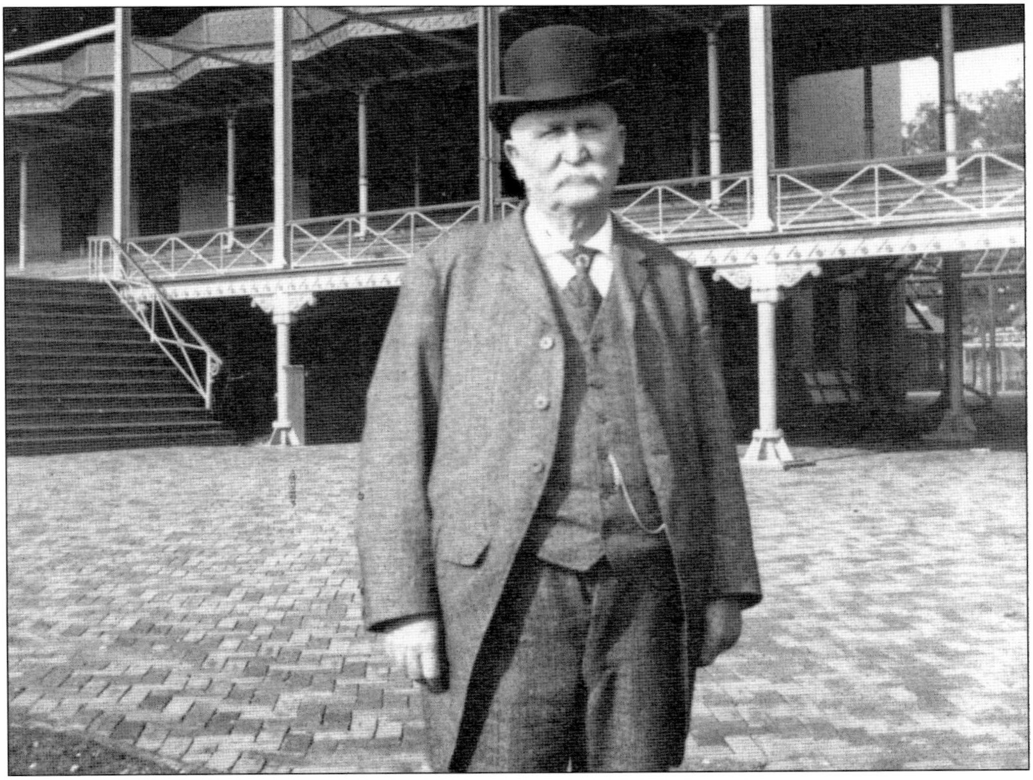

A member of the National Museum of Racing Hall of Fame, R. Wyndham Walden (pictured at Pimlico) was one of the most famous Thoroughbred horse trainers of the 19th century. On his farm, Bowling Brook in Middleburg, established in 1872, he bred and trained seven Preakness winners and four Belmont Stake winners. His son, Robert J. Wyndham, trained a Kentucky Derby winner. Wyndham won more than 1,000 races. (Courtesy of the Historical Society of Carroll County.)

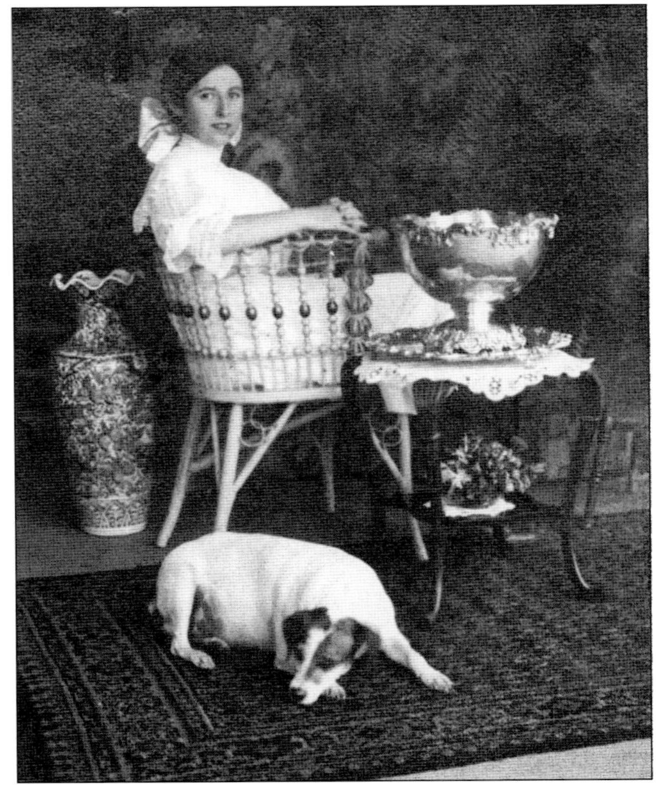

Thelma Littlefield Walden (Shriner) sits with her dog Jack beside a 1905 trophy won at Pimlico by her grandfather R. Wyndham Walden and given to her as a gift. Her father, Frederick Littlefield, was a jockey at Bowling Brook. (Courtesy of the Historical Society of Carroll County.)

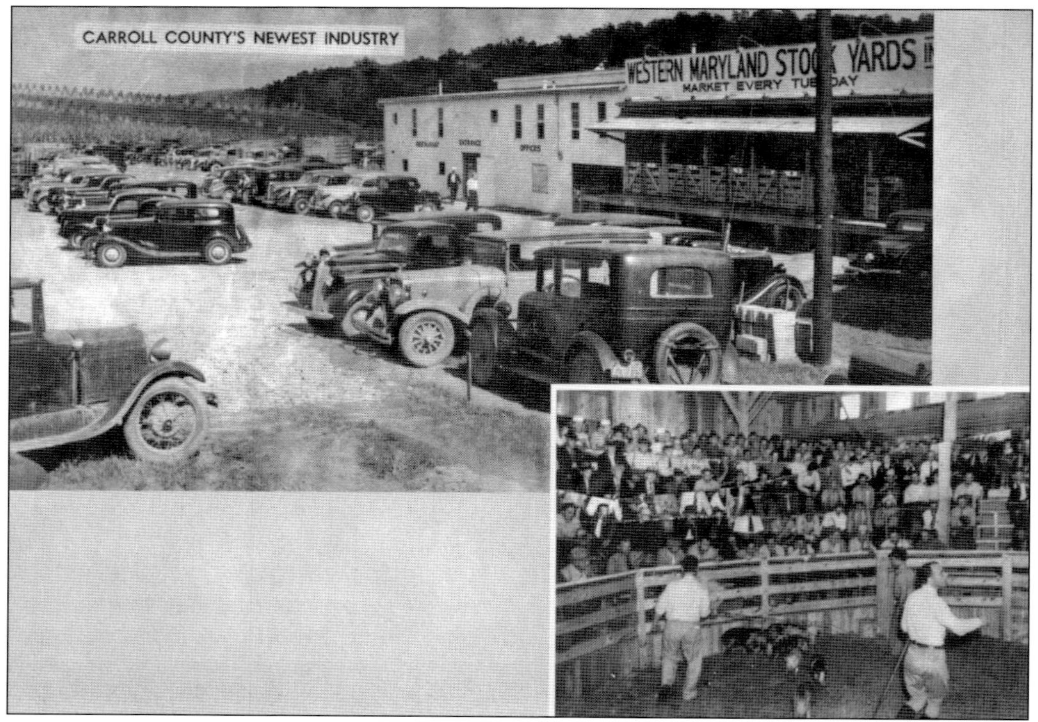

This is a 1939 photograph of the Western Maryland Stockyards on John Street in Westminster. Farmers gathered there to buy and sell livestock, eggs, and produce. (Courtesy of Bonnie Fold.)

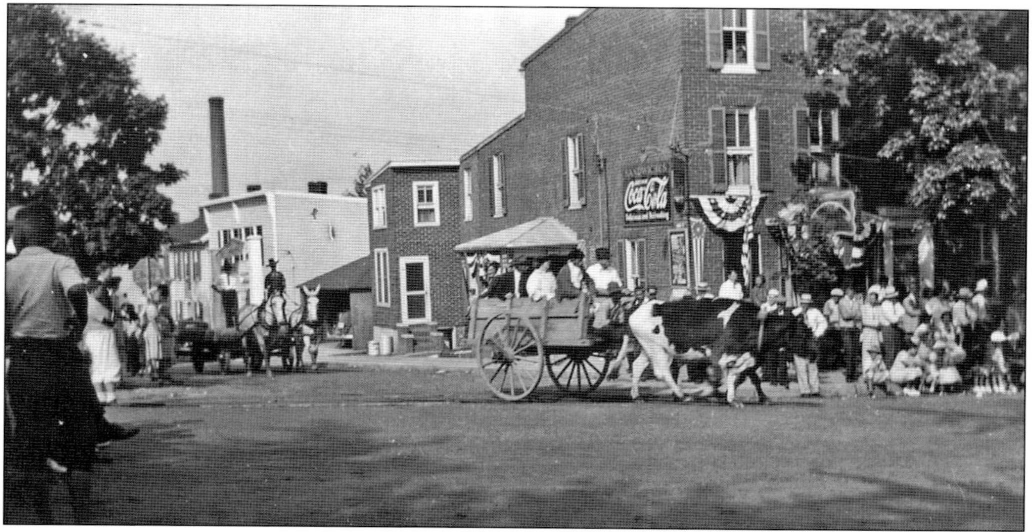

This photograph was taken at the intersection of West Main and Union Streets, adjacent to what was then Western Maryland College. A cart drawn by oxen turns down Main Street in Westminster in the Centennial Parade of 1937. (Courtesy of the Historical Society of Carroll County.)

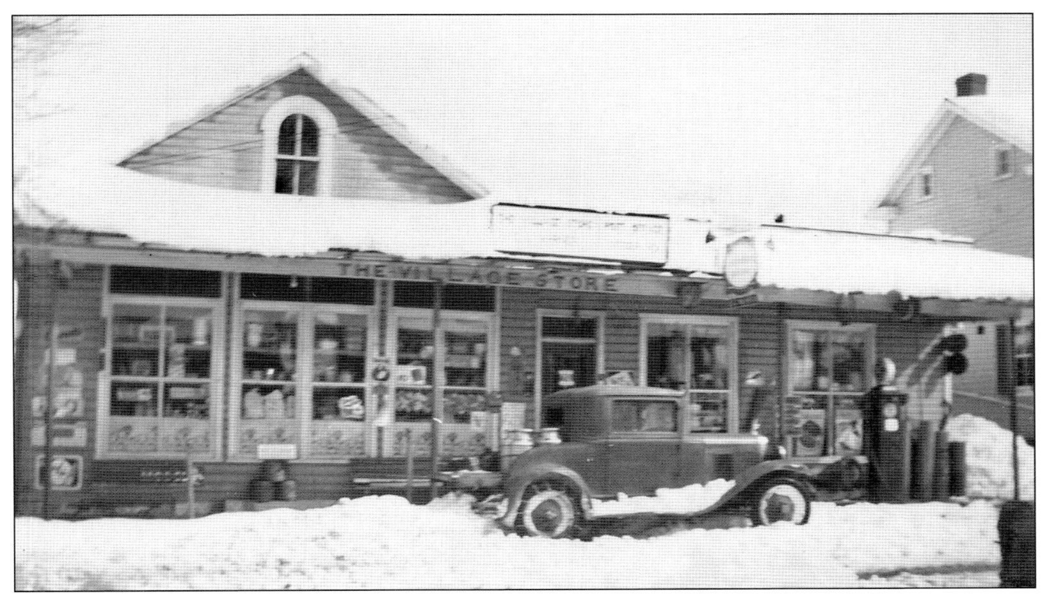

The Wilhides in Keymar delivered milk to the cooling station near Detour in the 1930s. Then they went to the Village Store and post office with their car still filled with the empty milk cans from the day before. They made a truck out of a car by cutting out the trunk and building a wooden platform in the back. (Courtesy of the Wilhide family.)

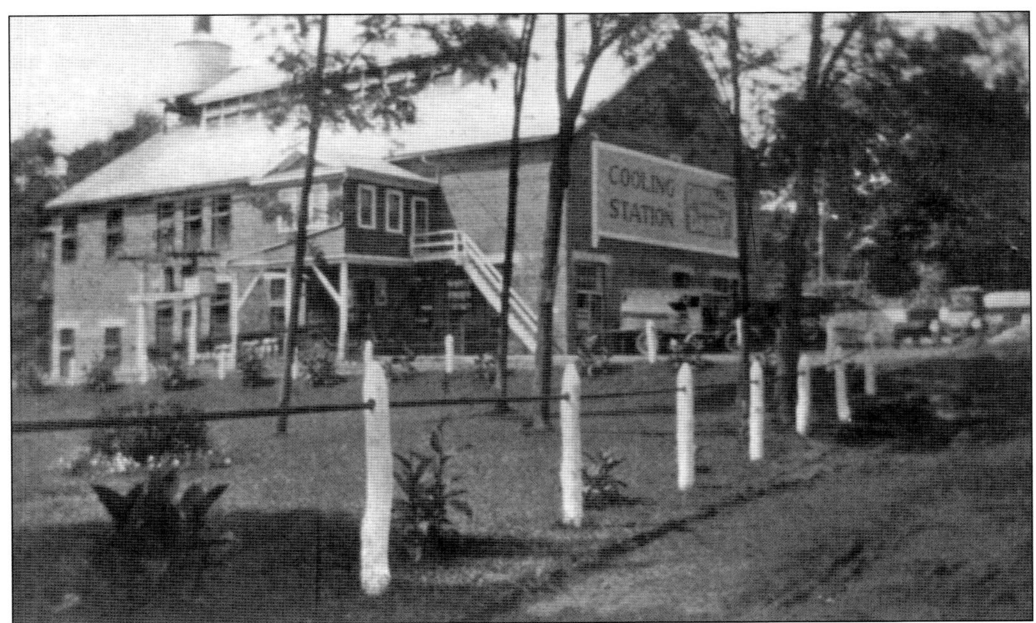

The Fairfield Western Maryland Dairy and Cooling station in Detour is pictured in 1922. Milk was stored here until it could be put on the train or transported by truck. Later the company manufactured powdered milk. (Courtesy of the Wilhide family.)

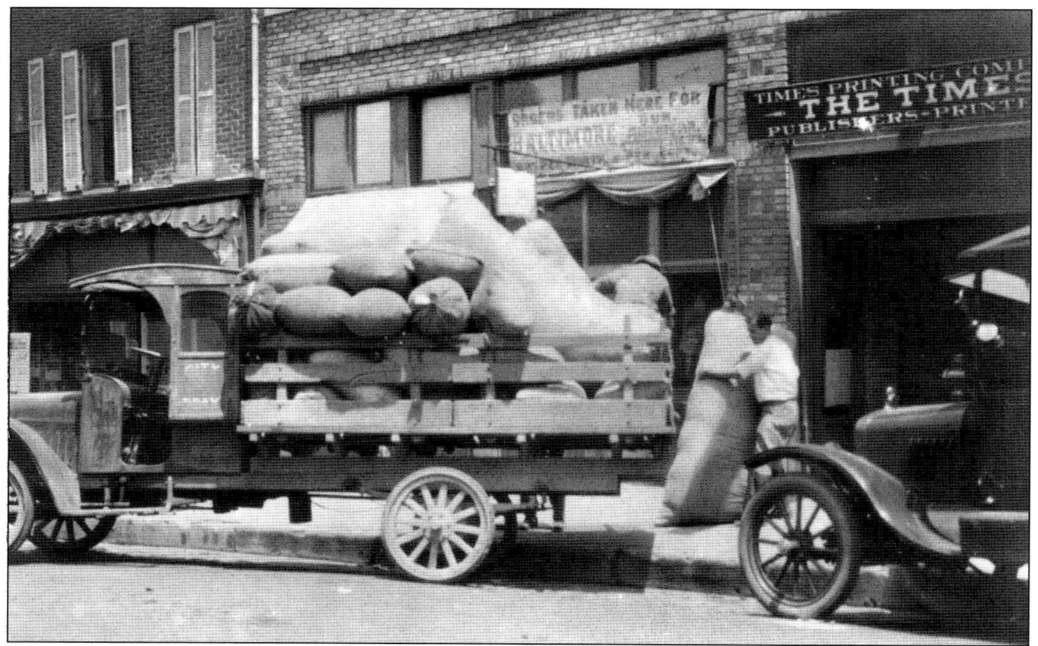

This is a wool shipment in Westminster in 1921. According to the county agent, the sheep men sent 3,000 pounds of wool to a Southern blanket manufacturing company to be made into blankets and robes. They saved $1,000 by shipping together. Sheep were not raised to any extent in Carroll County. (Courtesy of the University of Maryland Cooperative, Carroll County.)

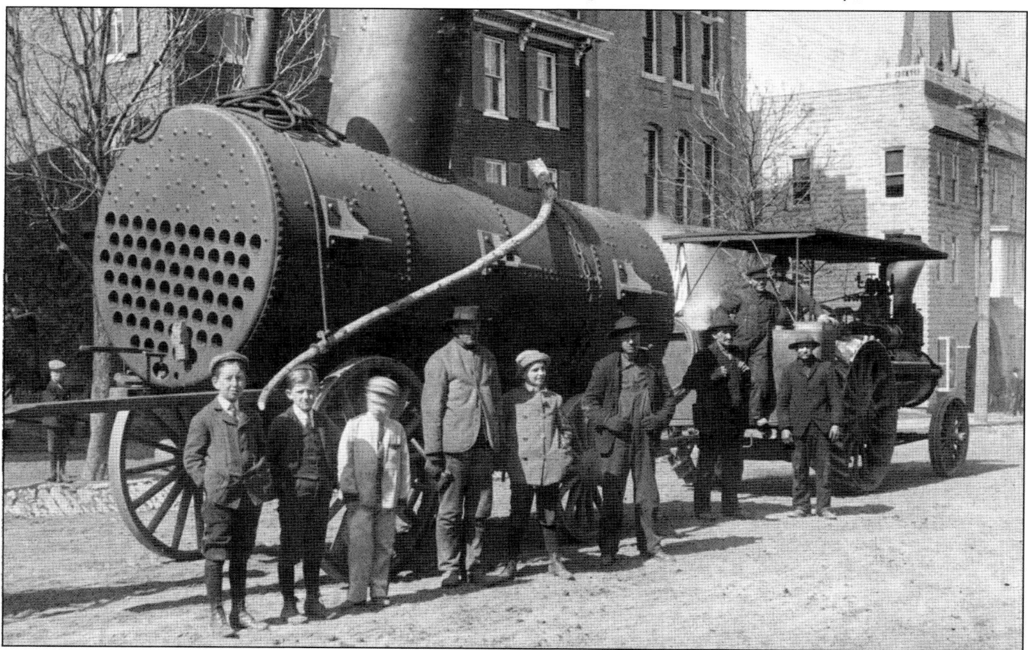

In this 1904 photograph, a steam engine boiler is being pulled by a steam tractor when Main Street was still dirt. The photograph was taken in front of the fire department. The second man from the right standing is Jacob Holmes. In 1872, the Taylor Manufacturing Company, previously the Union Agricultural Works, made steam engines and farm equipment near Court Street in Westminster. (Photograph by James D. Mitchell; courtesy of Virginia Ecker Hierstetter.)

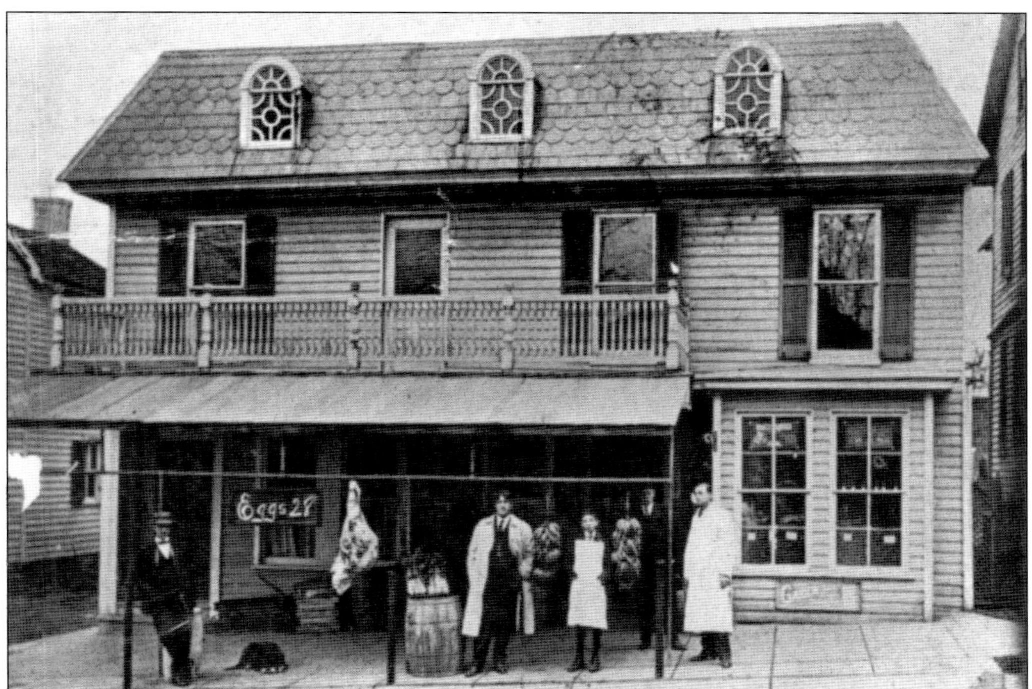

This was originally the Harry F. Mitten Meat Market in New Windsor. In 1920, it became the William O. Barnes Meat Market. (Courtesy of the New Windsor Heritage Committee.)

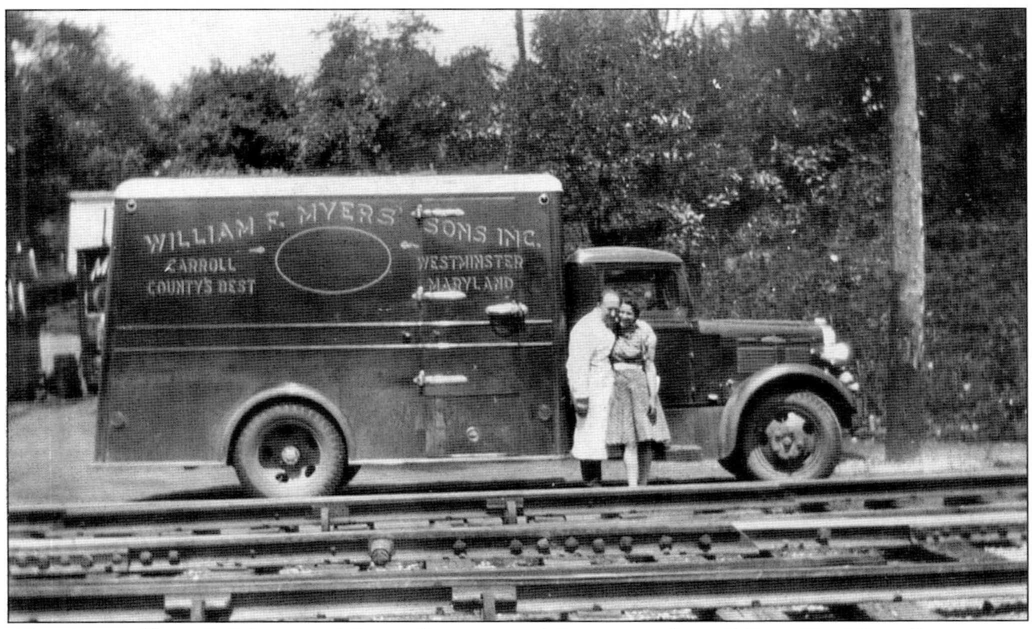

This is a William F. Myers and Sons, Inc., meat delivery truck in Sykesville. Myers began as a huckster. In 1896, when his customers in Baltimore asked him for country sausages and hams, he decided to deliver meat, increasing his business. About 1912, he opened his own business on the corner of Liberty and Green Streets in Westminster, processing 1,000 pounds of meat per week and 60 barrels of cider per day. (Courtesy of the Sykesville Gate House Museum.)

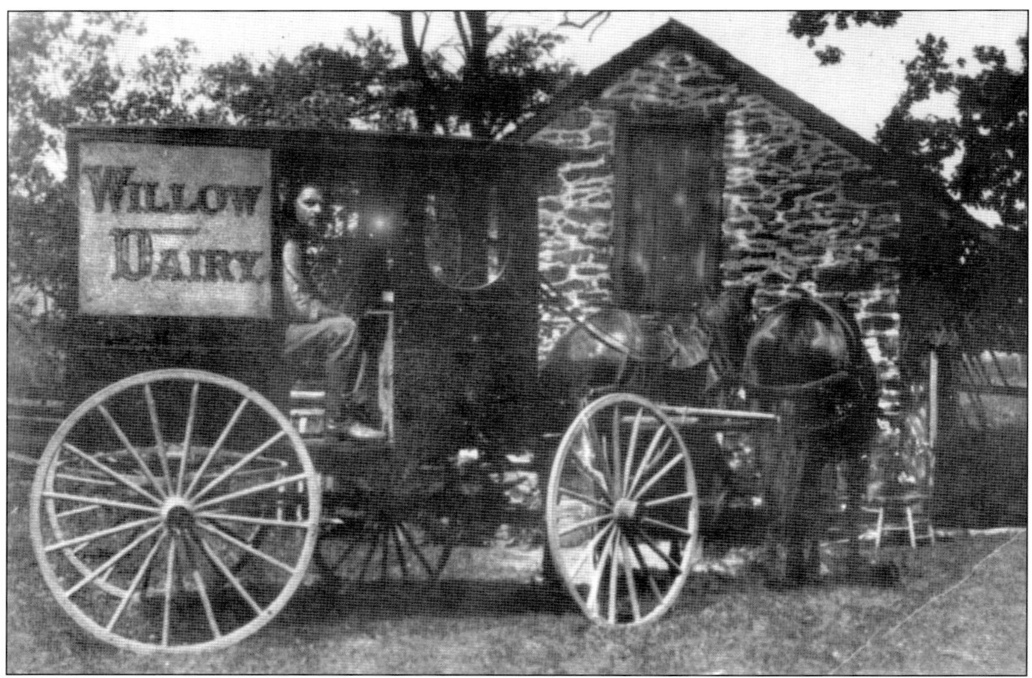

This is an early Willow Farm Dairy delivery wagon. The dairy was later called Warner's Willow Farm Dairy. Amos Oliver Warner and Minnie May Lease Warner bought the dairy in the 1920s. Farmers brought milk to the dairy in cans, where it was bottled. The farmers caught up on news in the early morning hours while the cans were steam cleaned and returned to them. (Courtesy of the Mathias family.)

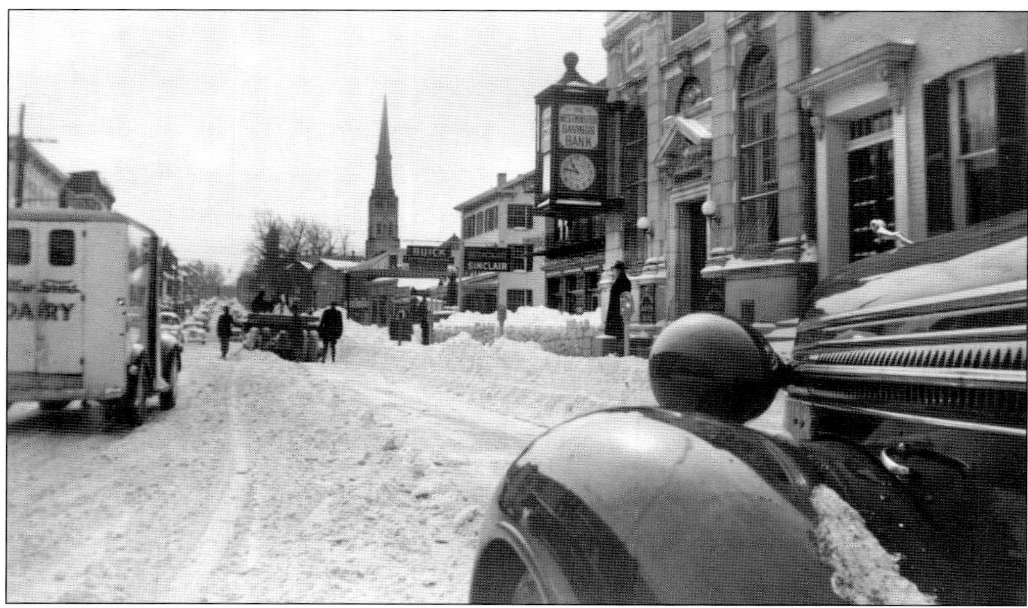

A Willow Farm Dairy truck is pictured driving through Westminster in a February 1947 snowstorm. Milk was delivered in glass bottles and put in aluminum boxes on the front porch of homes as late the 1960s. The photograph was taken facing east and shows the original St. John's Catholic Church steeple. (Courtesy of Virginia Ecker Hierstetter.)

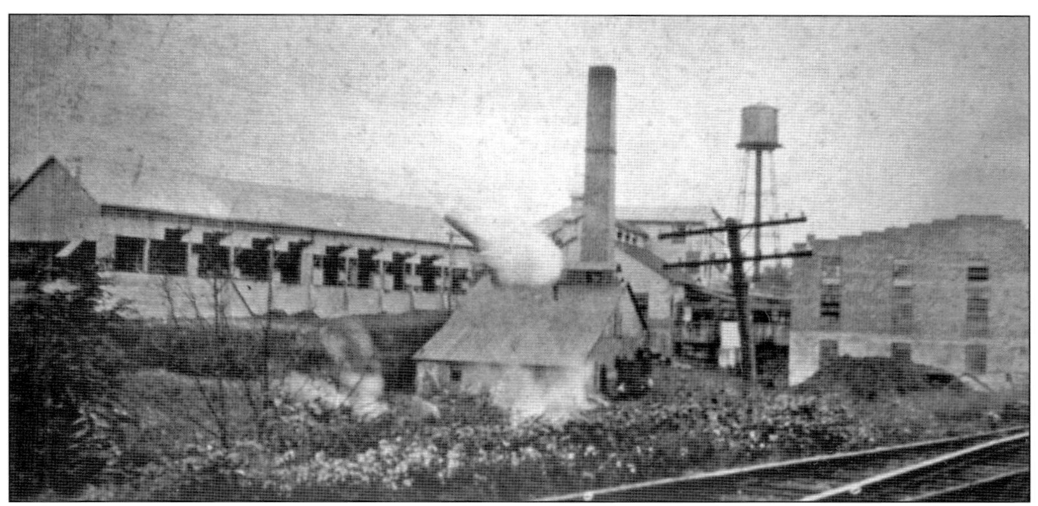

Above, this is a 1939 view of the Mount Airy Canning Factory, established in 1915. At one time, the factory had 1,000 acres of corn, 250 acres of peas, 229 acres of beans, and 125 acres of tomatoes put out for it. Some 250 employees worked during the busy season. The factory grew its own seed corn, "The Evergreen," tested by the University of Maryland. The farmers were paid for their peas in August, beans in October, and corn and tomatoes in December. In the husking shed, 18 shuckers husked 60 ears of corn per minute. They also had cold storage available for farm families. Below is a photograph of an unidentified cannery with wagons of corn waiting in line at the factory. (Above, courtesy of the Historical Society of Mount Airy, Maryland; below, courtesy of the Sykesville Gate House Museum.)

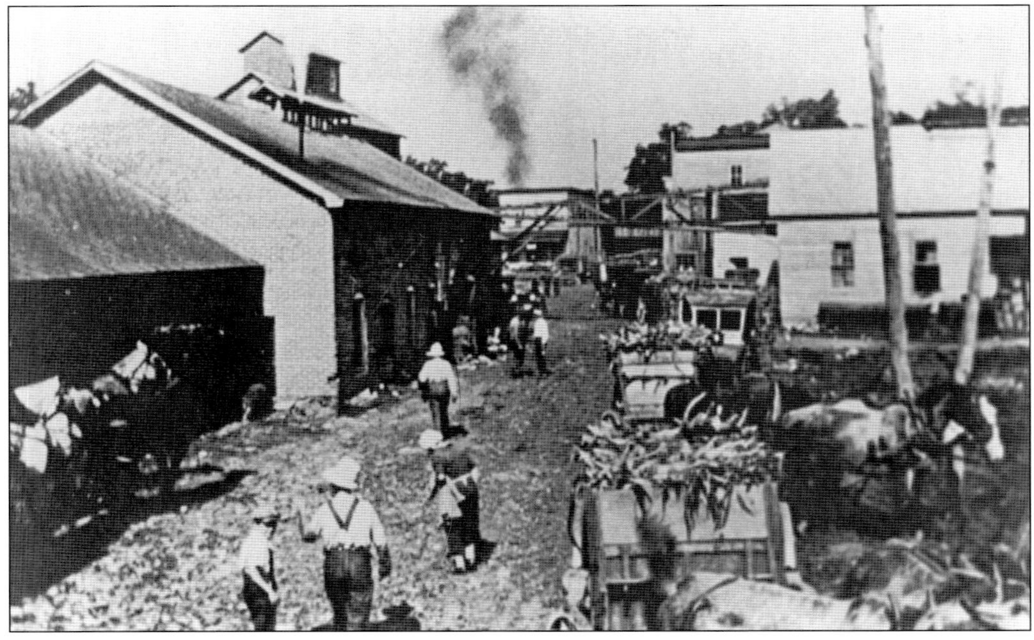

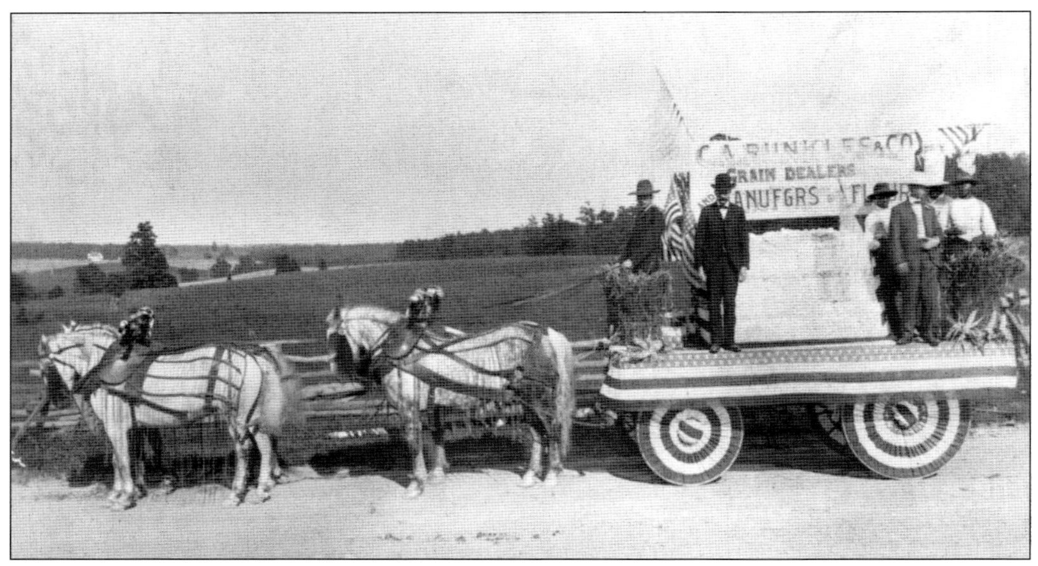

Grain dealers stand proudly on their float in the Farmers Parade in Mount Airy at Park Avenue and Dorsey Street. Four horses wearing fly nets pull a wagon for C. A. Runkles and Company Grain Dealers. In 1919, C. A. Runkles built a successful grain elevator with a capacity of 12,000 bushels on the northern side of the Baltimore and Ohio (B&O) Railroad in Mount Airy. (Courtesy of the Historical Society of Mount Airy, Maryland.)

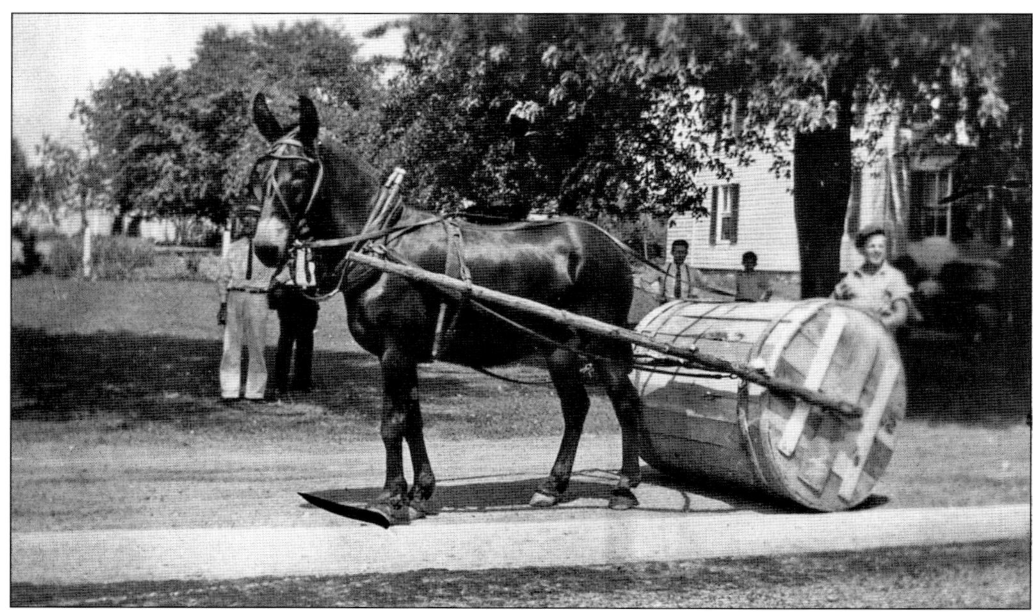

In 1937, the Carroll County Centennial Parade exhibited a horse-drawn cart with a tobacco container. From the 1700s to the early 1800s, tobacco was packed in a wooden hogshead to transport it. In 1880, there were 88 tobacco growers in the county, mostly in Winfield, Woodbine, and Mount Airy, producing 1,000 pounds a year. Manchester was a center for cigar making even though tobacco was not grown there. (Courtesy of the Historical Society of Carroll County.)

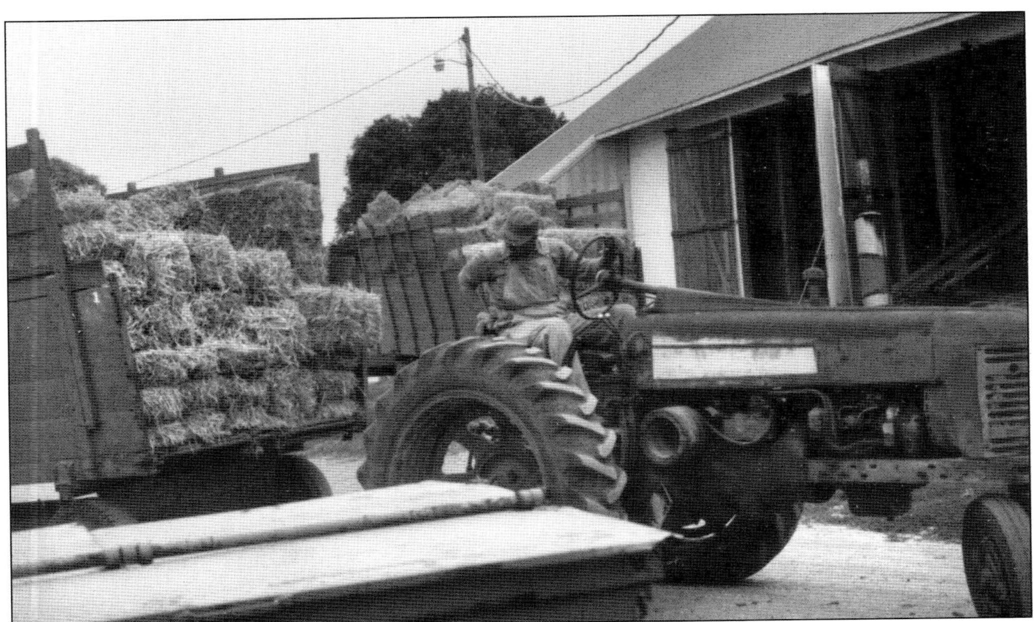

Earl Beard is driving the tractor with a load of straw bales on his farm on Sullivan Road near Westminster in the 1960s. Christian Royer Jr., the original owner of the property, built a gold mine on the farm, but his mining operation proved unsuccessful. (Courtesy of Ed Beard.)

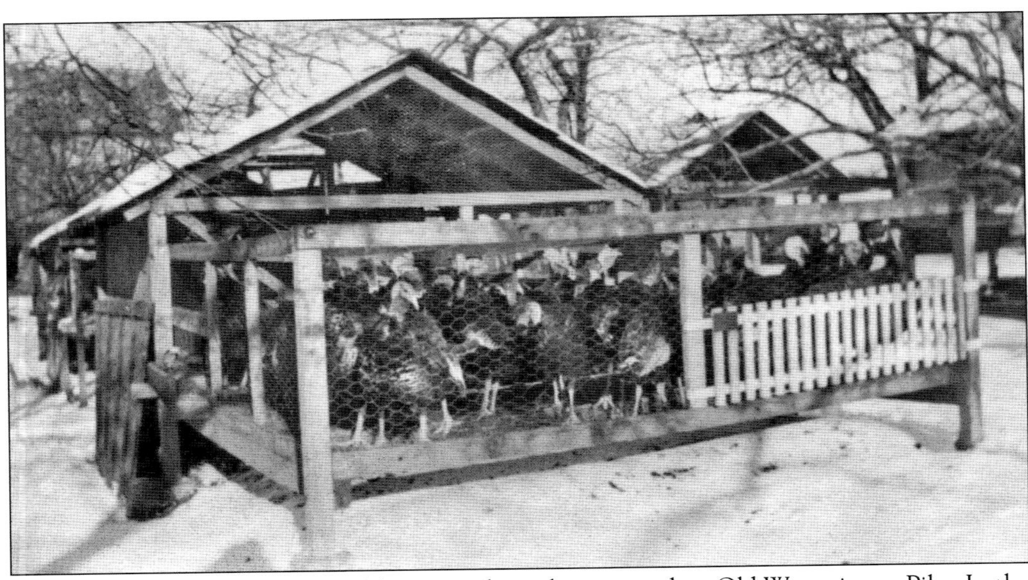

Clyde Ecker raised broad-breasted bronze turkeys aboveground on Old Westminster Pike. In the 1940s, Ecker raised 2,000 turkeys. Eckers sold turkeys to the fire company for its annual supper. People came from Baltimore to buy the dressed turkeys at the holidays. He also raised pheasants, minks, chickens, bantam hens, hogs, and rabbits. (Courtesy of Virginia Ecker Hierstetter.)

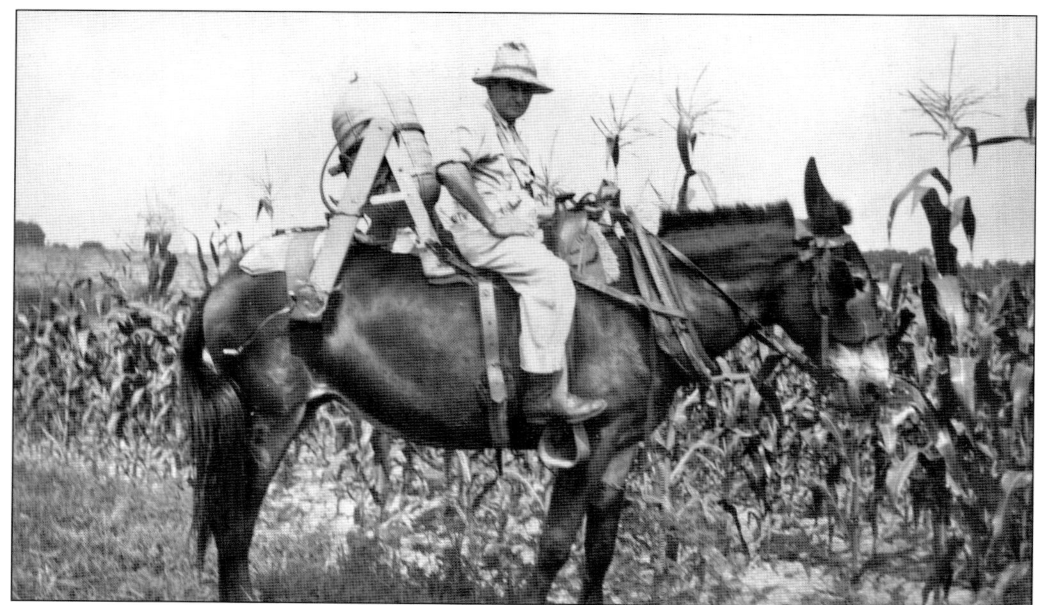

Vernon Mathias is spraying corn while riding a mule around 1930 on the Hillcrest Farm near Westminster. (Courtesy of the Mathias family.)

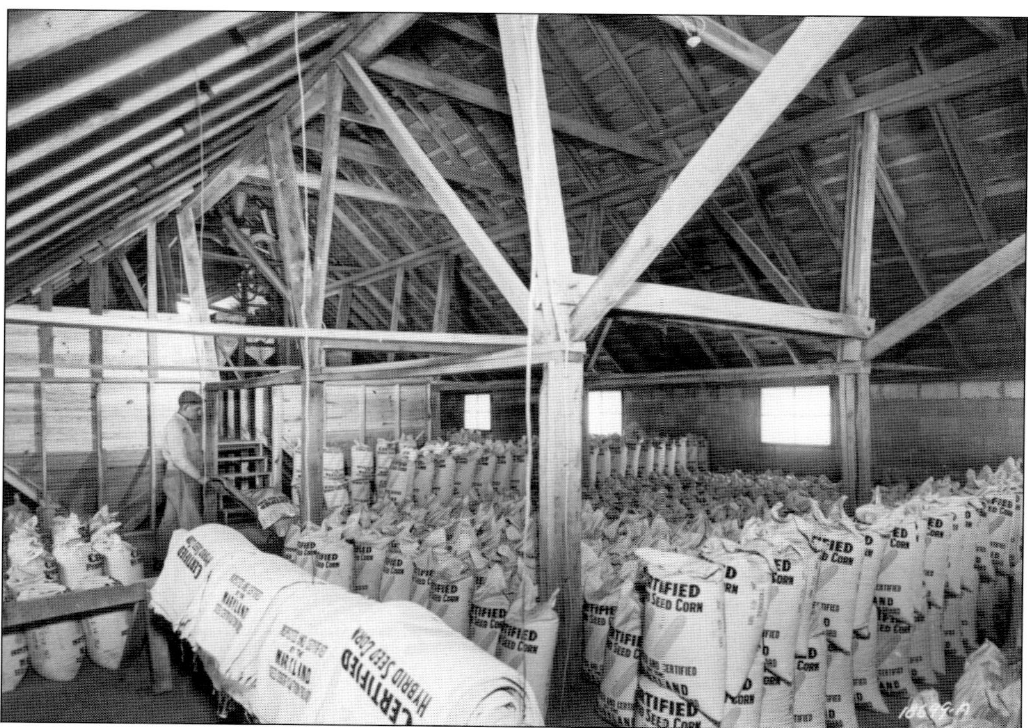

Rows of Maryland certified seed corn, lined up by type, are stored on the second floor of the Vernon Mathias corn building near Westminster. Good corn seed was so important to increase yields both for field corn and for canning that, as early as 1924, a group of six banks got together to give free seed corn to the local farmers. (Courtesy of the Mathias family.)

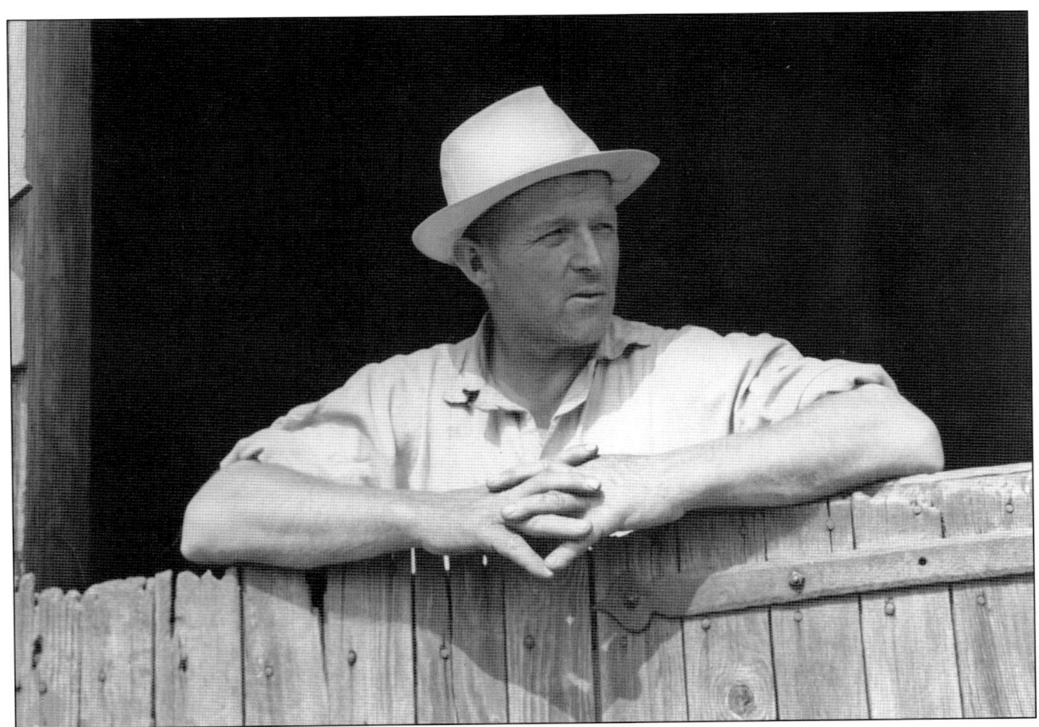

Solomon Hoke Sr. raised beef feeder cattle, hay, wheat, and corn on his 100-acre farm in Bachmans Valley, purchased in 1928. Hoke was president of the Greenbelt Consumer Cooperative, which bought wholesale groceries and sold retail. He brought the Southern States Cooperative to Carroll County and was president of the Penn-Carroll Canner's Cooperative, a tomato and sweet corn canning factory located in Melrose. (Courtesy of the Hoke family.)

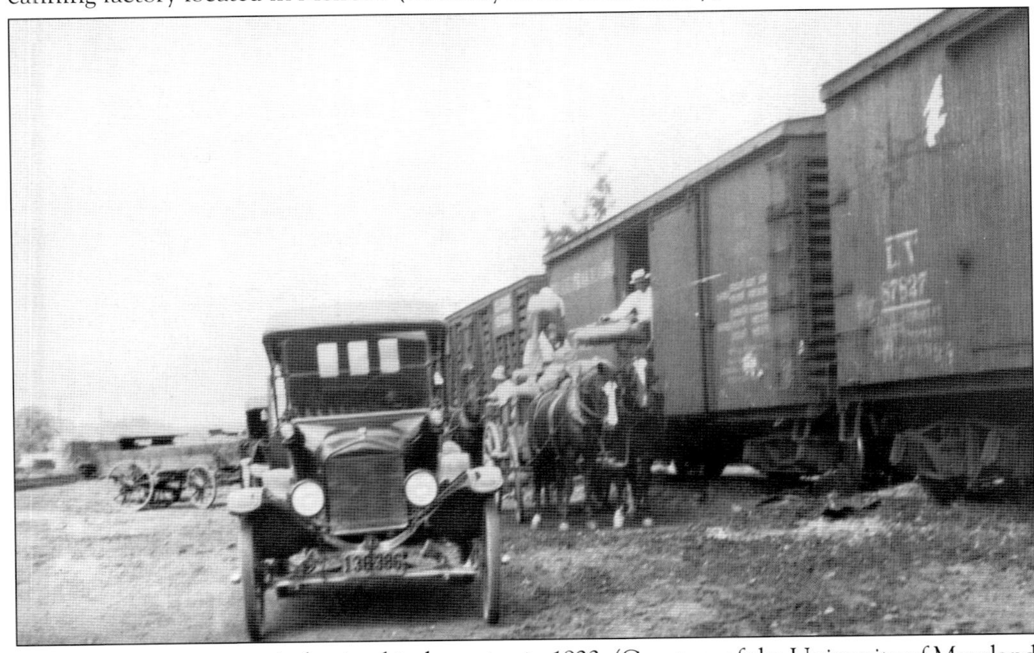

Farmers are cooperating in buying binder twine in 1923. (Courtesy of the University of Maryland Cooperative Extension, Carroll County.)

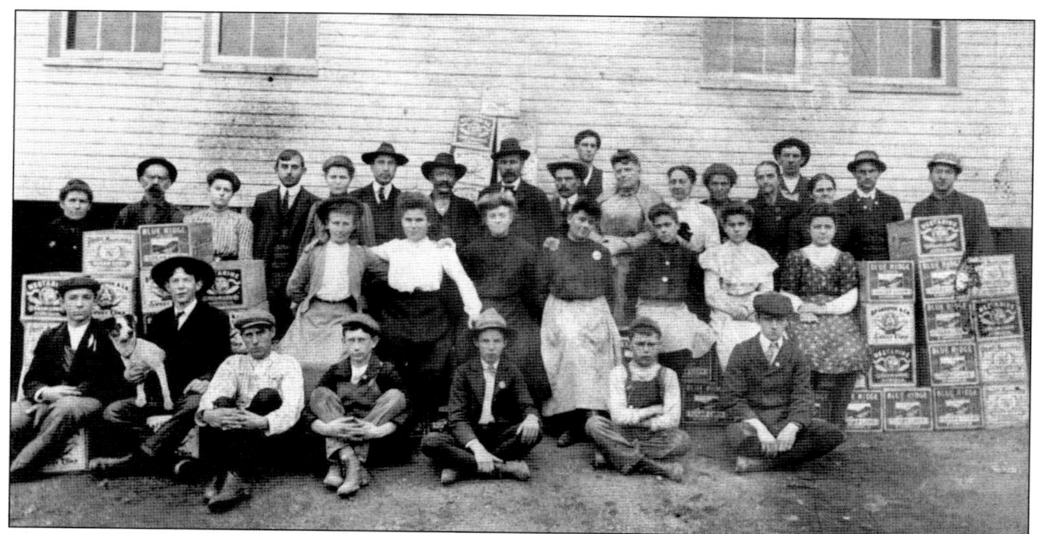

These are the employees of the B. F. Shriver Canning Company. The company raised tomatoes, corn, peas, and wheat. B. F. Shriver went around to each farmer in the spring and asked them to plant for him. That was popular because he met with them in person. The farmers had contracts for their crops and got bonuses if they had a good season. (Courtesy of the Historical Society of Carroll County.)

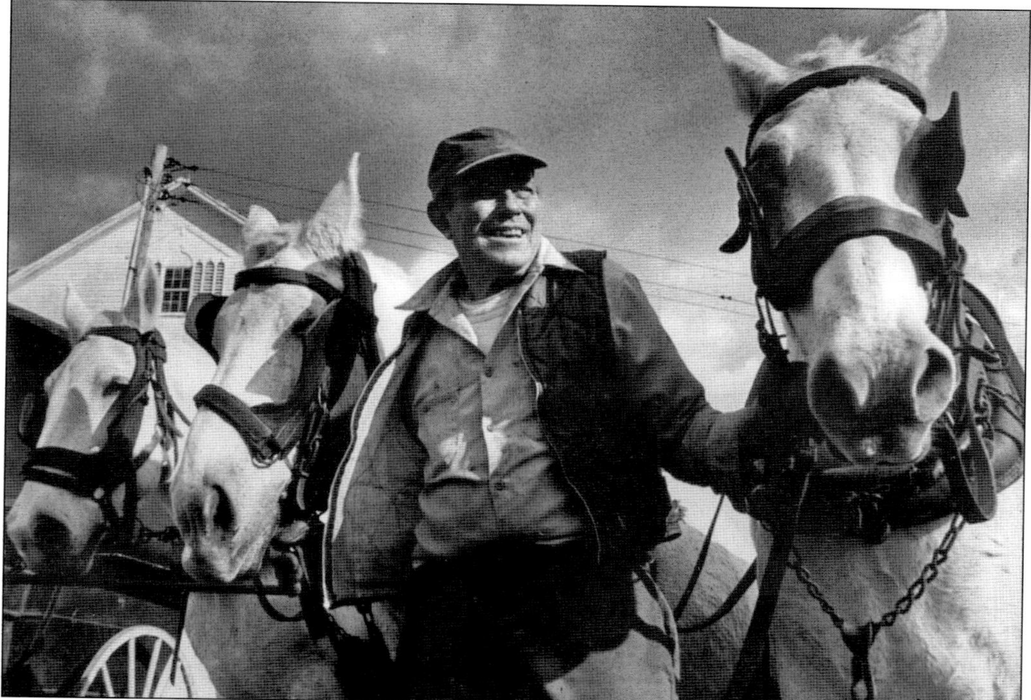

This is a photograph of Charles Shriver on his farm, purchased in 1958, on Ruth Shriver Road. He is pictured in the 1970s with his work horses. Shriver sill uses his grandfather's horse-drawn corn planter from the 1930s. Until 2004, he was a dairy farmer and had 27 cows under one roof. He is a strong believer that the government should stay out of his business and was an independent dairyman. Shriver still farms with horses. (Photograph by Phil Grout; courtesy of Charles Shriver.)

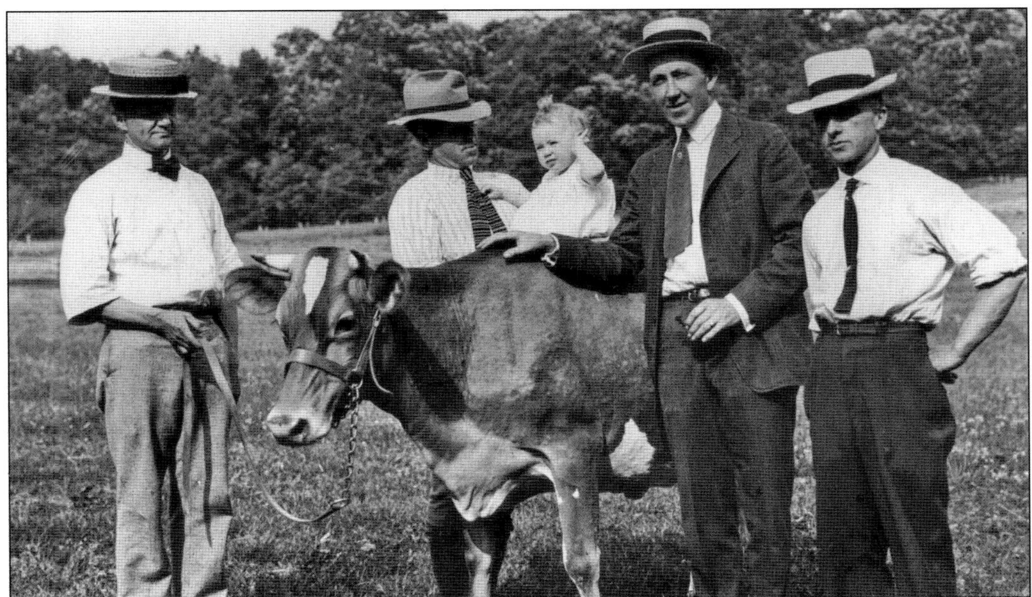

In 1860, J. Frank Getty bought this farm. Herbert Getty owned Overbrook Farm from 1915 until 1943 and raised 50 pure registered Guernsey cattle. Getty also had his own dairy, made ice cream, and opened an ice cream parlor at the end of the road. He sold to the college students at Blue Ridge College. Pictured at a 1919 Guernsey cattle show are, from left to right, John Baile, Herbert Getty holding his daughter Nancy Getty (Haifley), Granville Hibberd, and Charles Harmon. (Courtesy of Nellie Getty Hoke.)

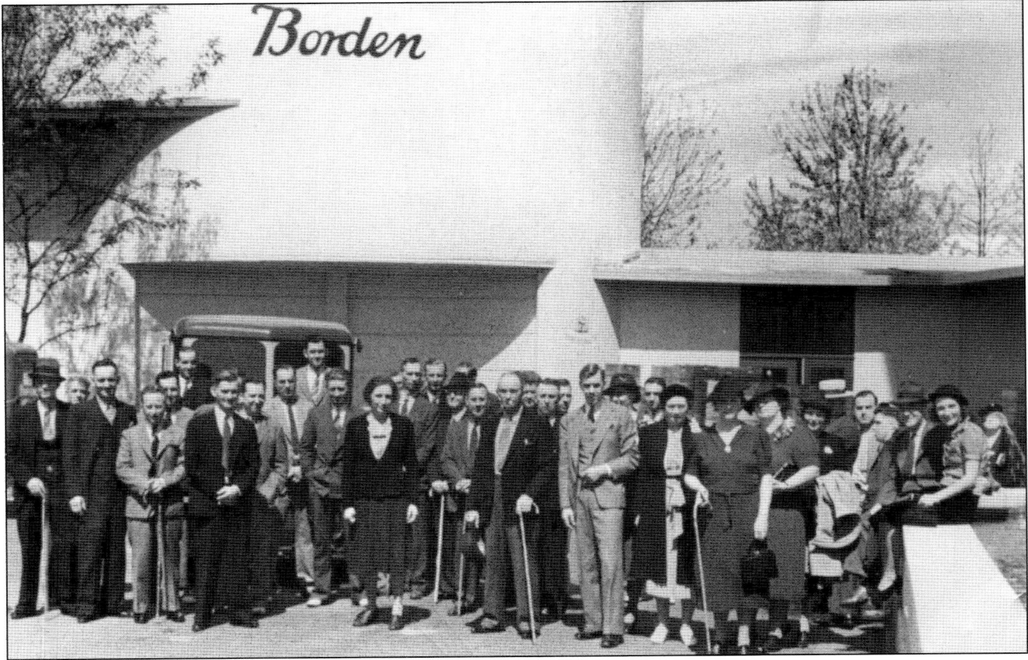

The Borden Ice Cream Plant on Chase Street in Westminster is pictured here. Tenth from right is Mrs. Earle (Jane T.) Eichelberger of Union Bridge. This group took a tour to the World's Fair in 1939. The tour was given by Borden's to the dealers that sold the most ice cream in the area. (Courtesy of the Historical Society of Carroll County.)

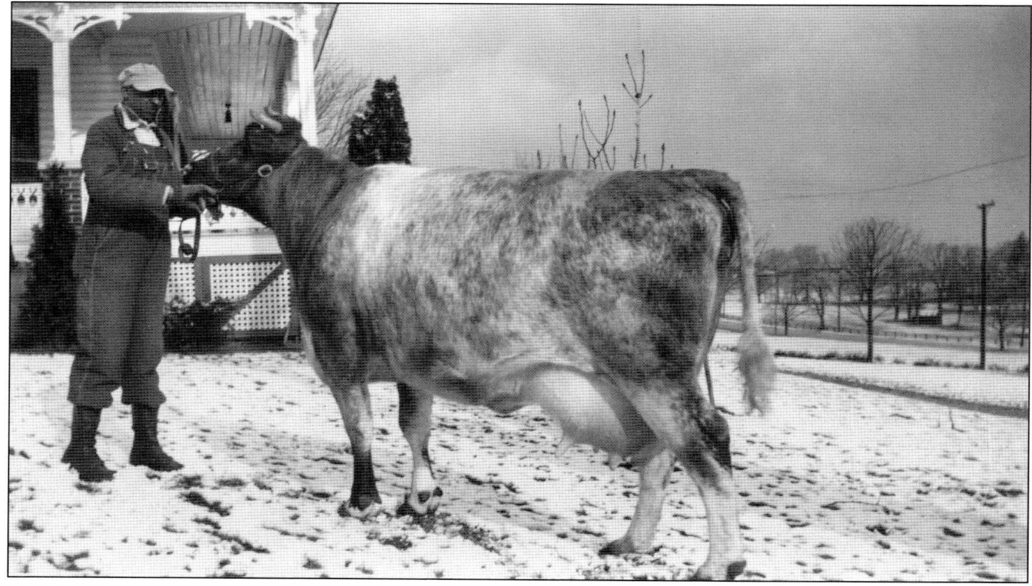

Ralph Morrison is pictured here with a milking shorthorn on the Hillcrest Farm near Westminster in the 1940s. Vernon Mathias raised milking shorthorns, going to fairs as far away as the National Dairy Exposition in Indianapolis. All the breeding was done naturally. Then they marketed the bull calves and shipped them in crates out of Westminster by railroad. Malcolm Mathias traveled in the train cars with the show cows. (Courtesy of the Mathias family.)

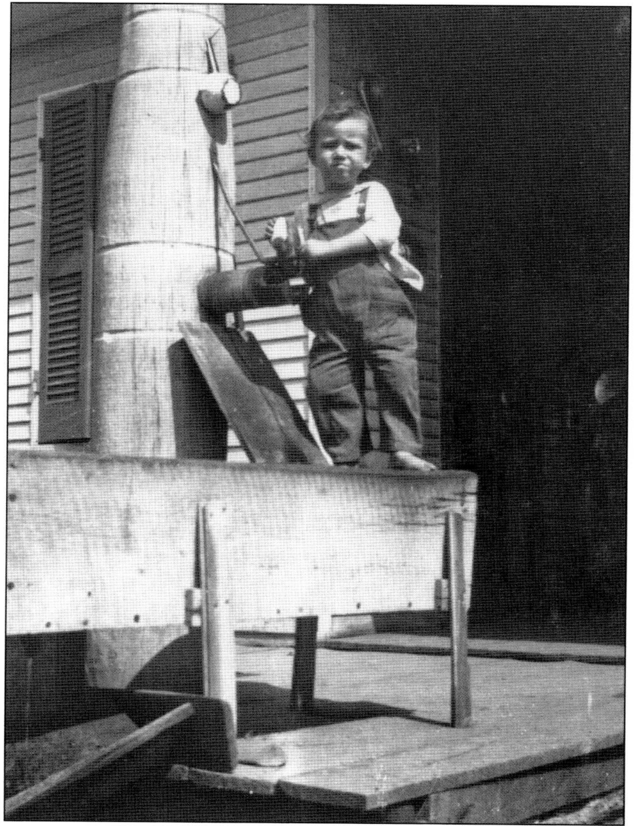

In 1921, Jesse Hollingsworth Jr. is standing by a Palmer pump on the family farm in Finksburg. The pump was invented by James Palmer of Hampstead in the late 1800s. Each pump had an octagon-shaped top, making it unique. They were made so that they were easy to repair. Each one was made of 20-foot logs joined together and could last 100 years. (Courtesy of Ann Horvath.)

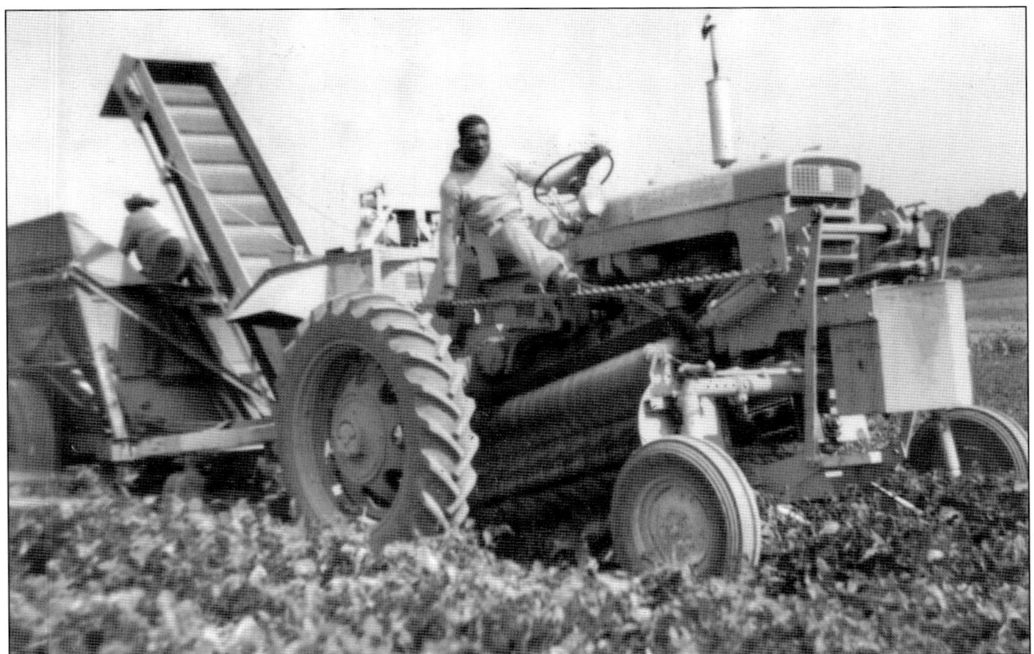

Workers for the B. F. Shriver Canning Company are pictured harvesting string beans with an International tractor on the Mathias farm in the 1950s. It was common for the canning company to supply the seed. The farmer planted and cultivated it, and hoped to grow a good crop. (Courtesy of the Mathias family.)

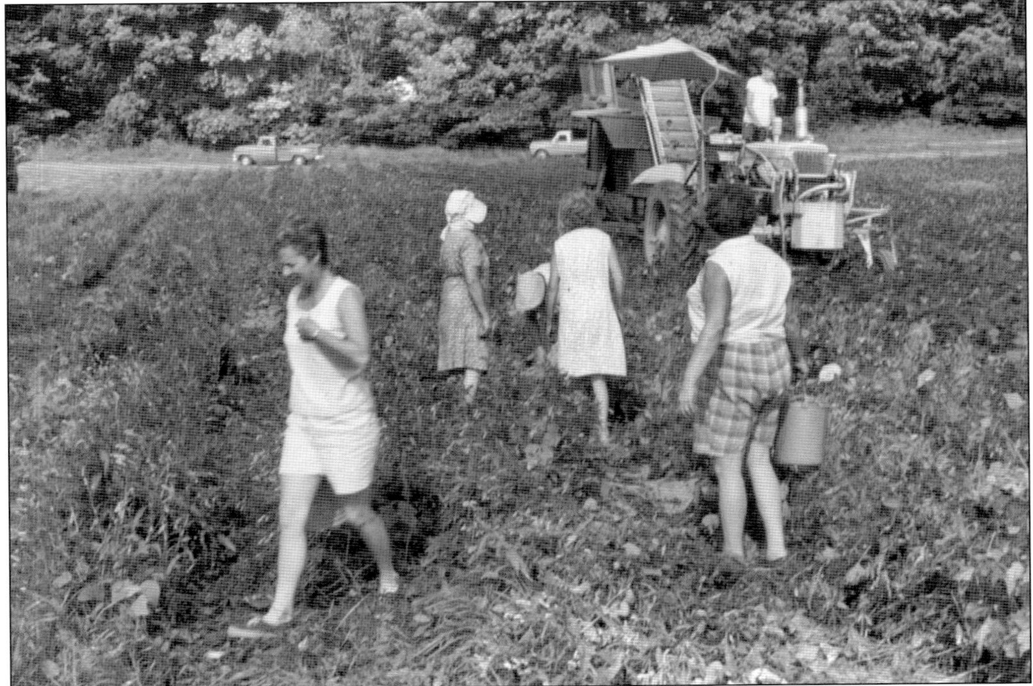

In this photograph, women are gleaning peas after the harvester has gone through. There are always plenty of peas left that the machine misses for the industrious who are willing to work for them. (Courtesy of Lippy Brothers, Inc.)

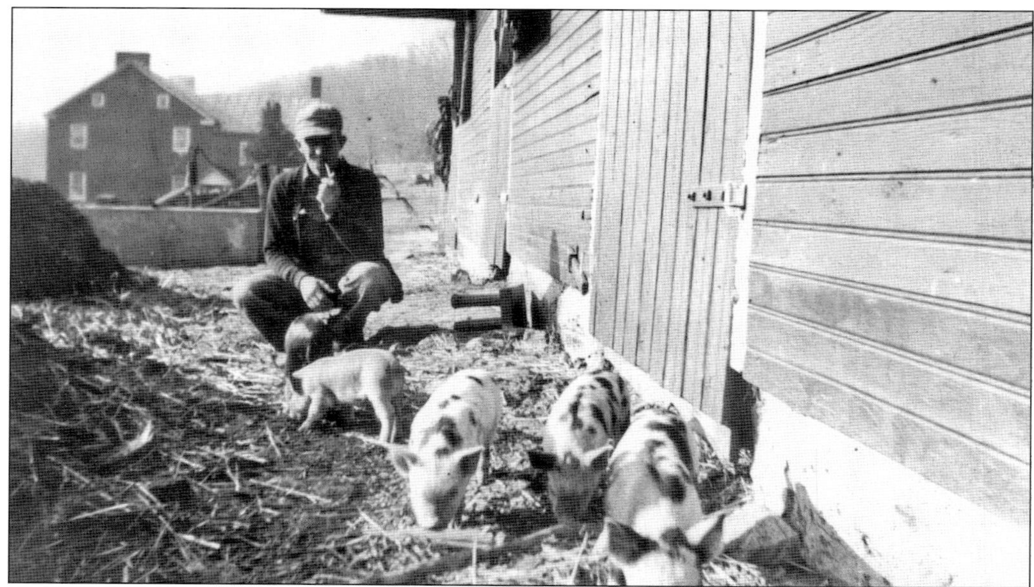

Vince Nevius, pictured here in the 1950s, watched his piglets on his dairy farm on Fridinger Mill Road near Manchester. Vince and Carrie Nevius purchased the farm in the 1940s. (Courtesy of the Nevius/Maurer families.)

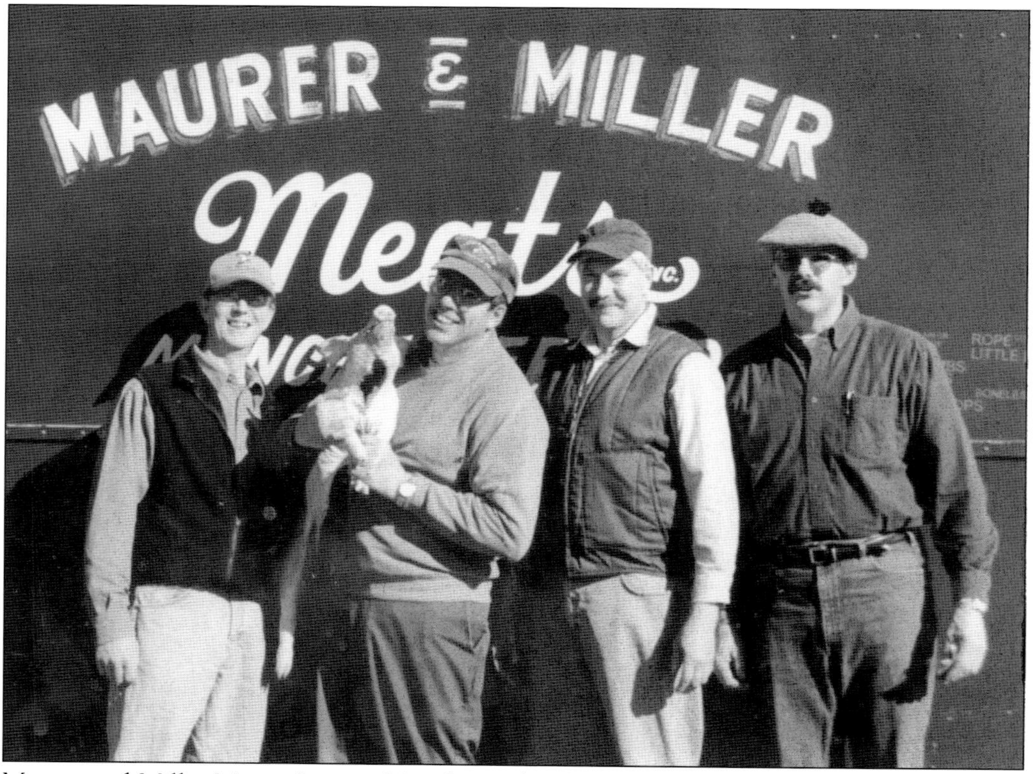

Maurer and Miller Meats, Inc., in Manchester has been in business since 1962. It is a family business that delivers meat to restaurants and homes. Pictured from left to right are Tom Richards, Steve Maurer, Stanley Maring, and George Maurer. (Photograph by Pricilla Dy; courtesy of the Maurer family.)

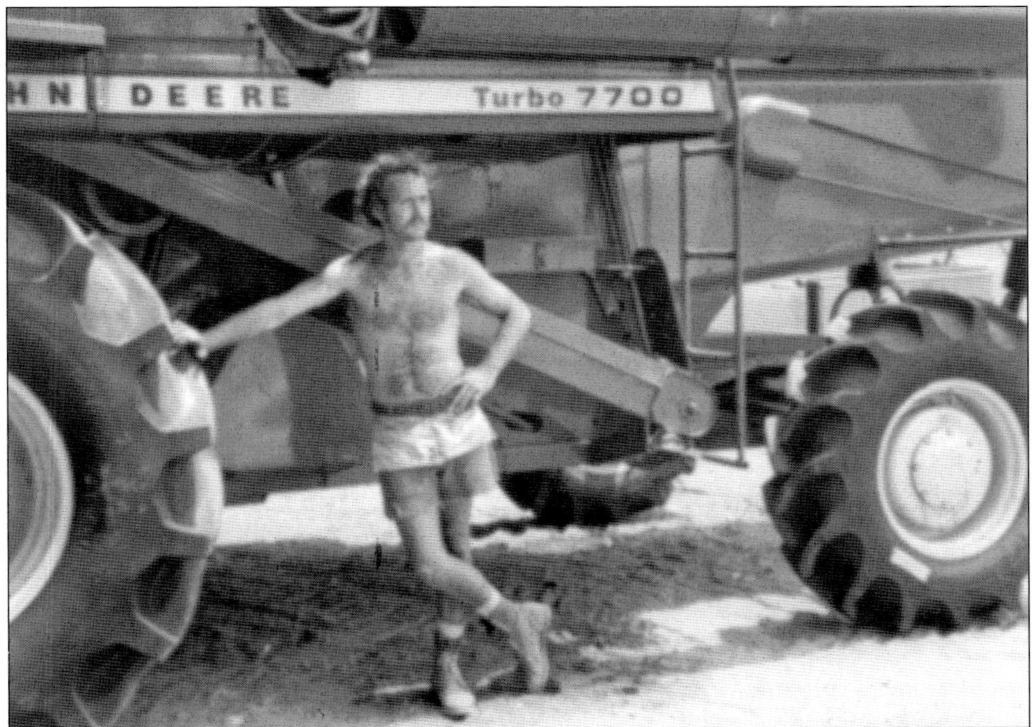

John Kable is pictured in front of a combine in 1973. He and William Finch Jr. were flown around the United States to put together farm equipment. Shop owners and employees took bets on how long it would take the boys put a combine or other equipment together. It took them six hours versus 40 hours for shop employees. (Courtesy of John Kable.)

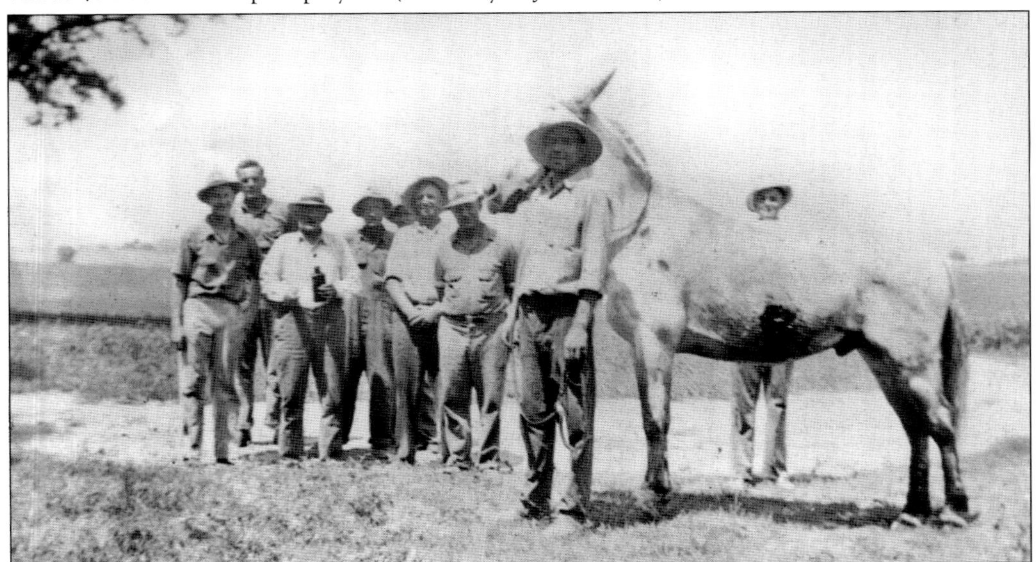

A farmer and his large animal restraint crew are pictured around 1940 after Charles ("Doc") Kable removed a tumor from the work mule. Charles H. Kable started his veterinary practice in 1933. Since there were no antibiotics, Kable bought stock chemicals and made his own medicines. The average cost of a visit was $5. His son John, also a veterinarian, often got eggs and corn as payment in his early years. (Courtesy of John Kable.)

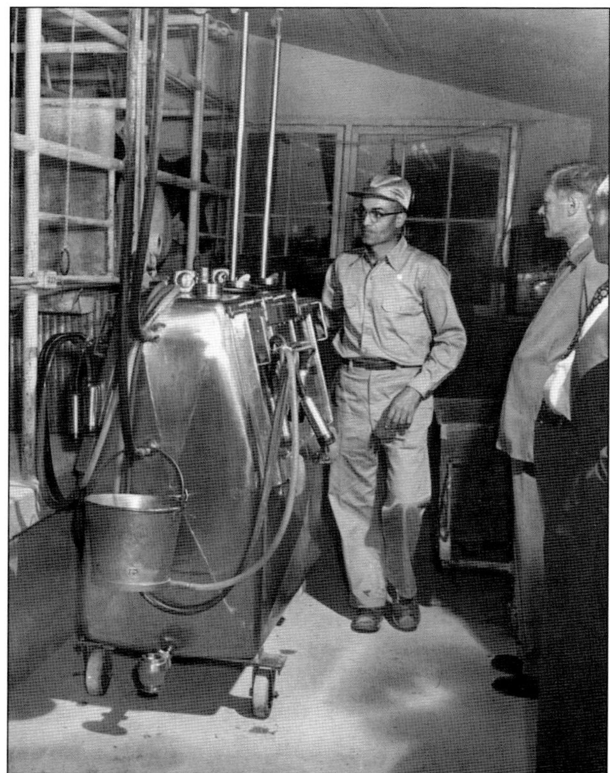

W. Roger Roop is pictured here demonstrating the milking machine he invented and manufactured, called the Miracle Milker. He patented it in the 1950s. It was manufactured in Lancaster, Pennsylvania, by the Mellinger Manufacturing Company. Although it never achieved commercial success, one of the machines is in the National Dairy Farm Museum in Olathe, Kansas. Roop was respected for his innovative genius. (Courtesy of Patricia Roop Robinson.)

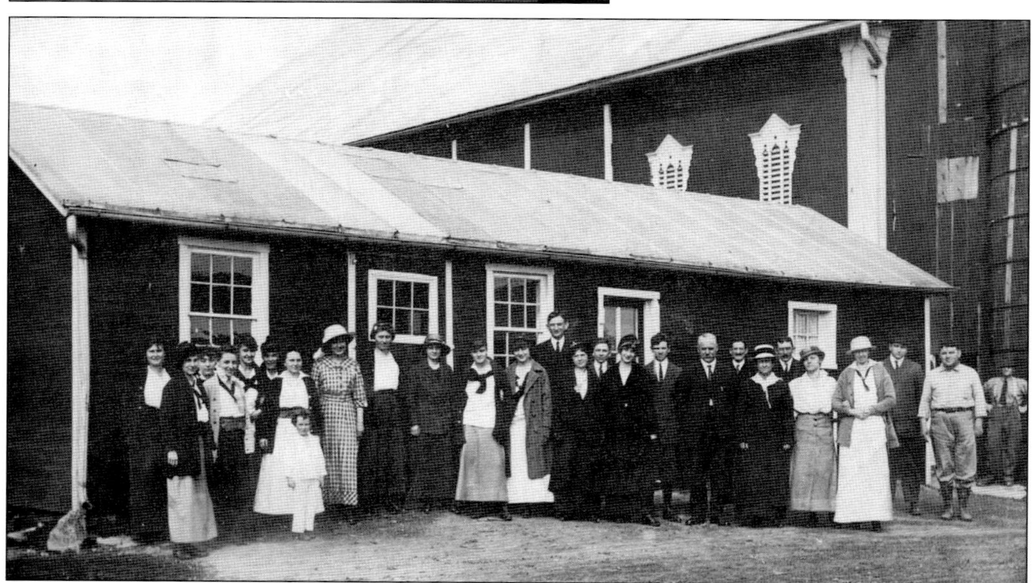

In 1915, Mrs. ? Troy's 11th-grade domestic science class of Westminster High School visited the Herr Dairy Farm near Westminster, where they were shown the latest milking demonstration. Visitors included Sarah Brown, Mary Snader, Derma Yeiser, Elizabeth Reaver, Margaret Gehr, Emily Zepp, Mildred Royer, Ella Lee, Mary Schaeffer, Nena Roses, Gertrude Gehr, Louise Miller, Grace Devilbiss, Charles Zahn, Earl Young, ? Kolb, ? Morelock, Dr. ? Rose, ? and ? Dinst, ? and ? Kimmey, Henry Kimmey, Mary Billingslea, ? Shaeffer, ? Wolf, and ? Troy. (Courtesy of the Historical Society of Carroll County.)

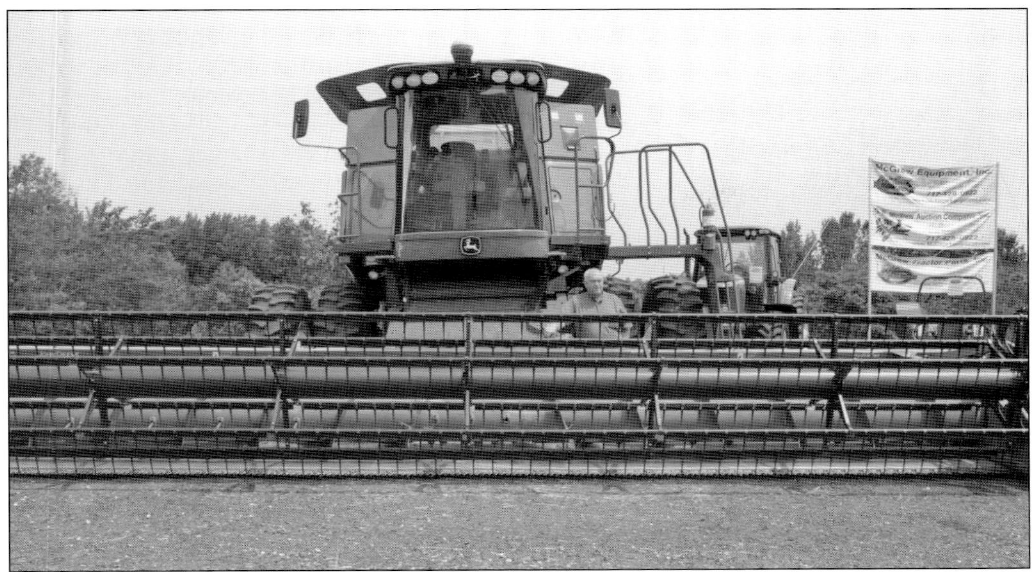

Donald Lippy of Lippy Brothers, Inc., stands in front of his John Deere 9870 STS combine, priced at $365,000 ($105,000 extra for the 30-foot, 12-row corn head). It is equipped with a yield monitor that is linked to a global positioning system (GPS) to collect site-specific yield data for use in future management decisions. Lippy Brothers farms 8,500 acres in Carroll and surrounding counties. Edward, Donald, Wilson, and Joseph Lippy started the business in 1951. (Photograph by and courtesy of Pamela Zappardino.)

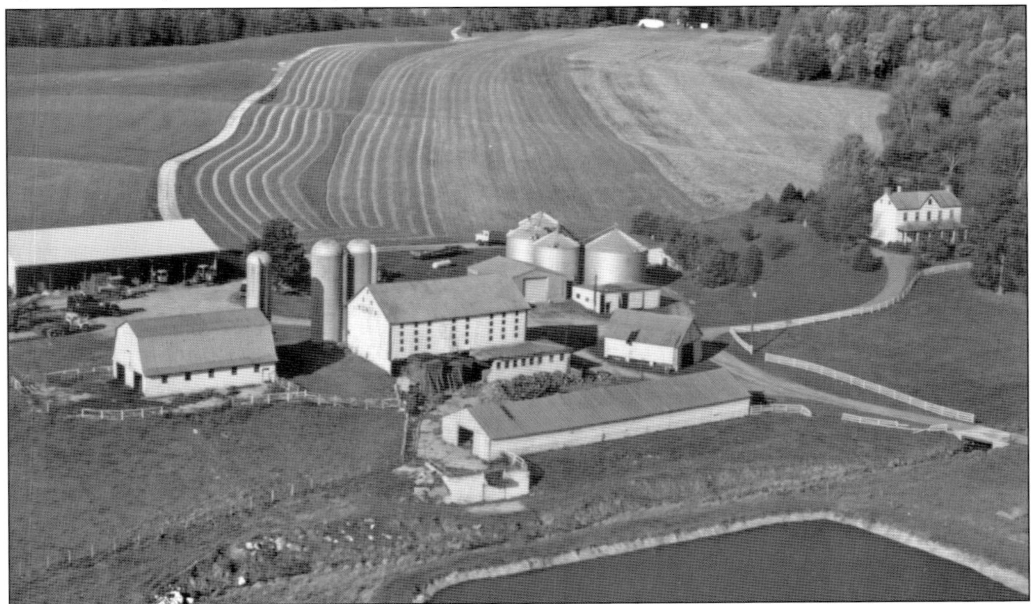

In 1928, Curtis E. and Alice Bossom Rash purchased the Oakhill Farm on Eden Mill Road and Route 97. Beginning in the 1950s, the Rash brothers, Glenn, Claude, and Edwin, continued the dairy operation, milking 100 head of cows. From the 1970s until 1988, they raised grain on 3,000 acres. Large grain bins on the farm stored the soybeans, wheat, and corn until the price was favorable instead of being forced to sell it at prevailing prices when it was harvested. They sold to granaries and also sold hay for horses and cattle. Their grain was sometimes put on ships in Baltimore and shipped overseas. (Courtesy of the Rash family.)

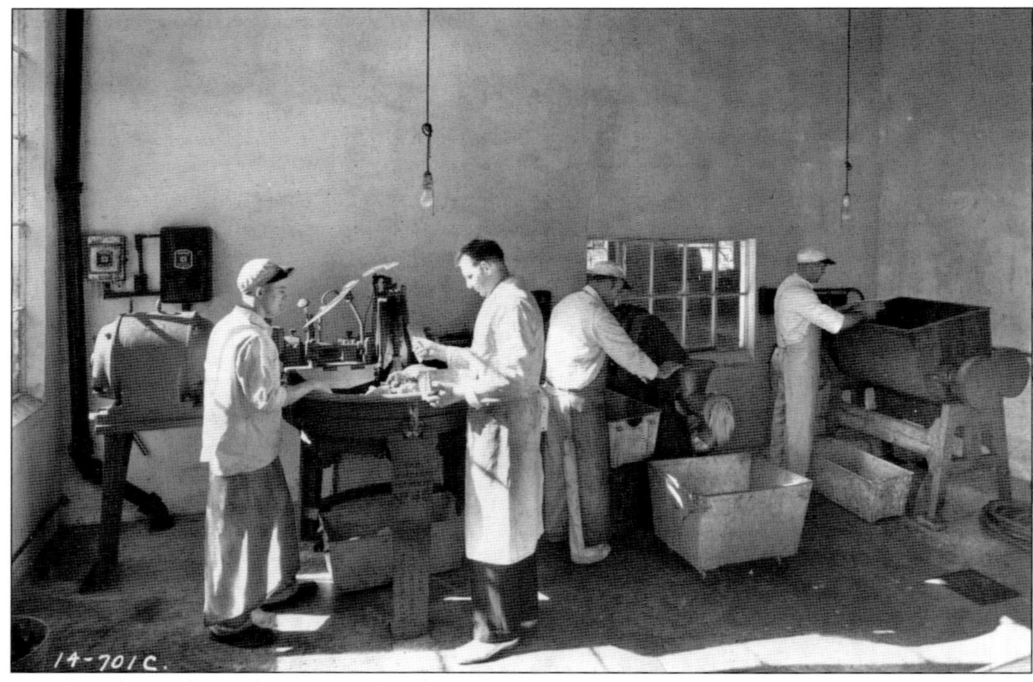

Joseph Hahn Jr. (center) is pictured at the Hahn meat plant on Manchester Road in Westminster. Hahn's meat-packing business was founded in 1919 by Joseph H. Hahn Sr. and his wife, Claire. The train came in behind the plant, and Hahn went down to unload the hogs. The Hahn store on East Main Street is pictured below. (Both courtesy of Trudy Jo Hahn Snader.)

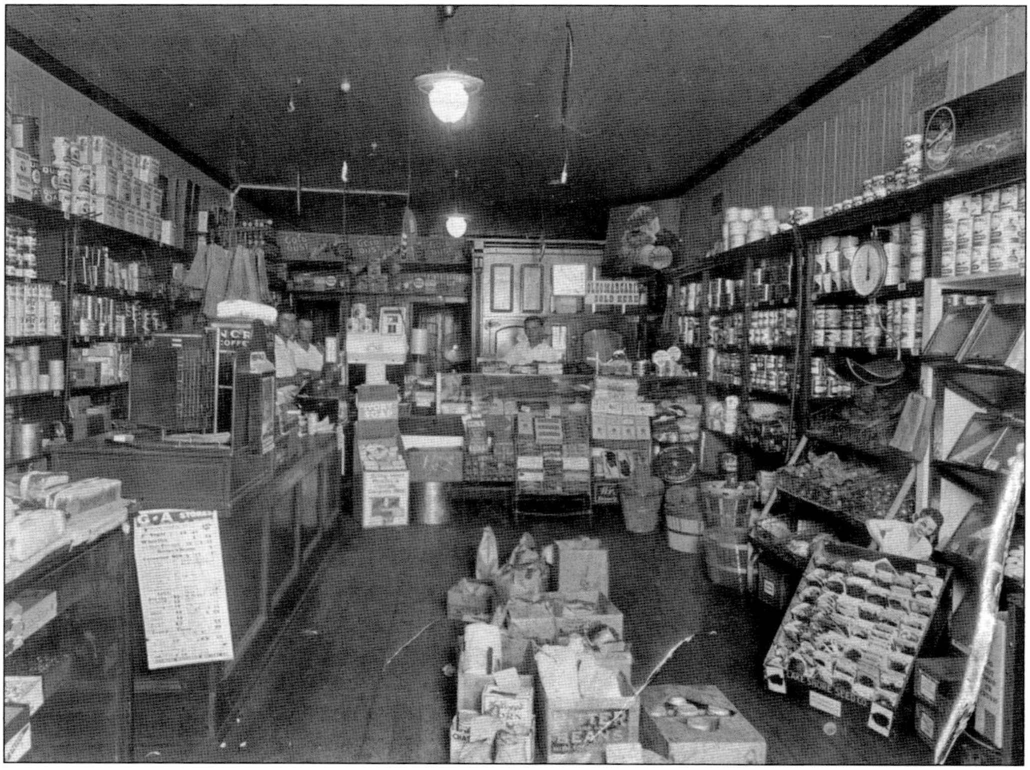

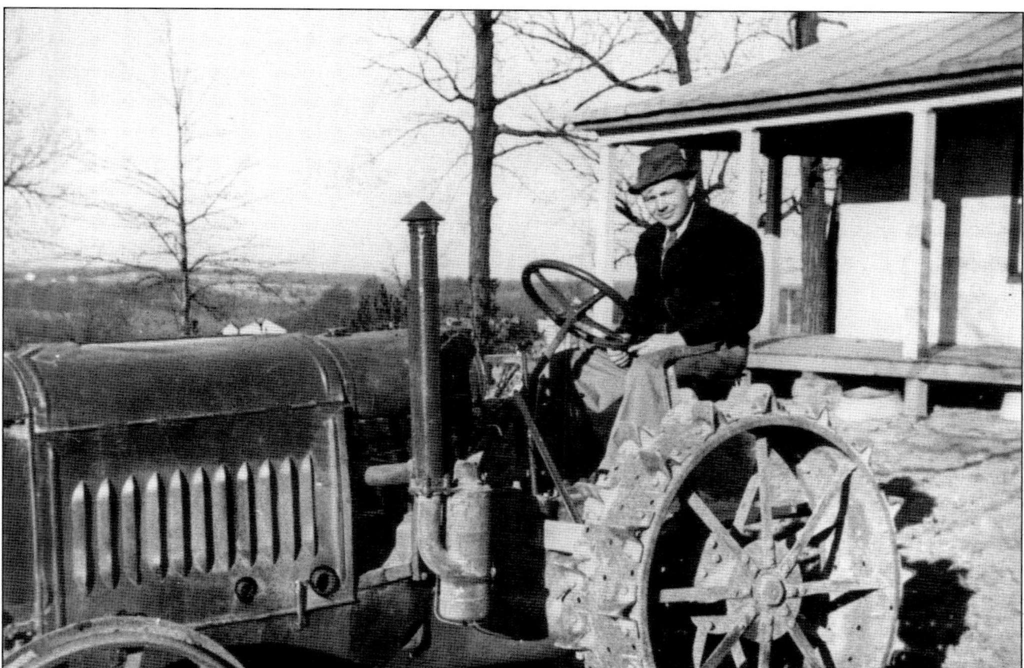

G. Winston Bullock, pictured here in the 1940s, works on his 10-acre farm and market near Smallwood. G. Winston and Ruth Bullock started an abattoir and market in 1937 near Smallwood. Bullock went to the farms, killed the hogs, and brought them to the butcher shop for processing. Farmers brought their pigs and cattle in for custom processing. (Courtesy of the Bullock family.)

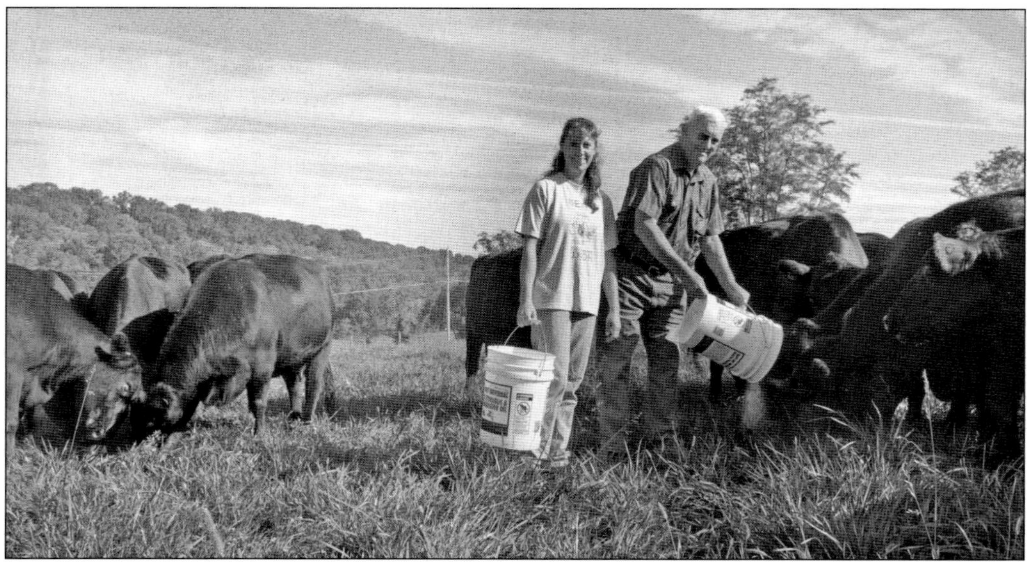

Paula Putman and her father, Herman Steffen, are pictured feeding cattle on their beef farm between Keysville and Detour in 2008. Steffen designed a cattle handling facility that allows them to do work on the cattle. This is important because cattle are not the friendliest creatures, according to Putman. Their heifers are first bred to Texas Longhorns so the calves will be smaller and will make an easier birth. After their first calf, the cows are bred to registered Angus bulls. (Photograph by and courtesy of Desirée Myers/Stover.)

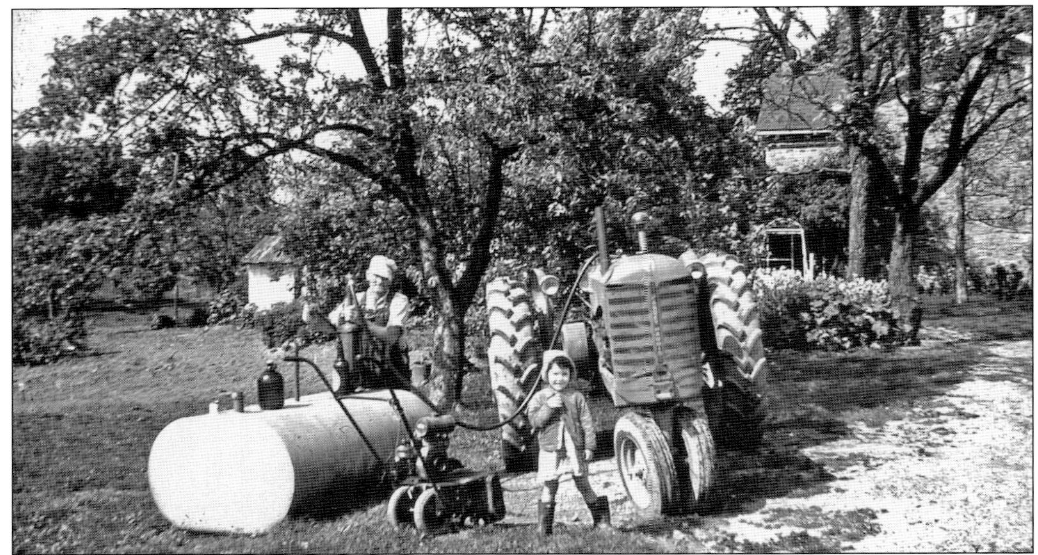

In the mid-1950s, Hubert Null is pumping gas into a Massey Harris 44-6, which he bought new in 1947 from the local Massey Harris dealer, Hoke Ommert. His granddaughter, Virginia Lee Null (Mullican), is in front of the tractor. (Courtesy of the Null family.)

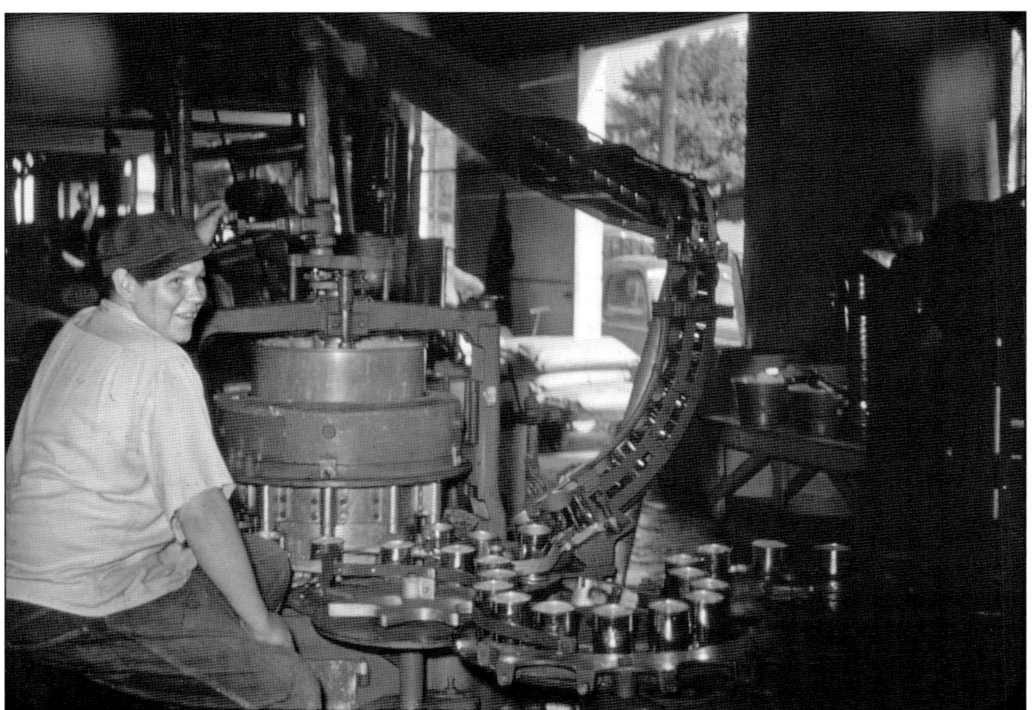

Corn cans are being filled with corn before they go to the capper in this 1952 photograph of the cannery owned by the Bankert Brothers Cannery in Hampstead. (Photograph by and courtesy of Robert O. Bond.)

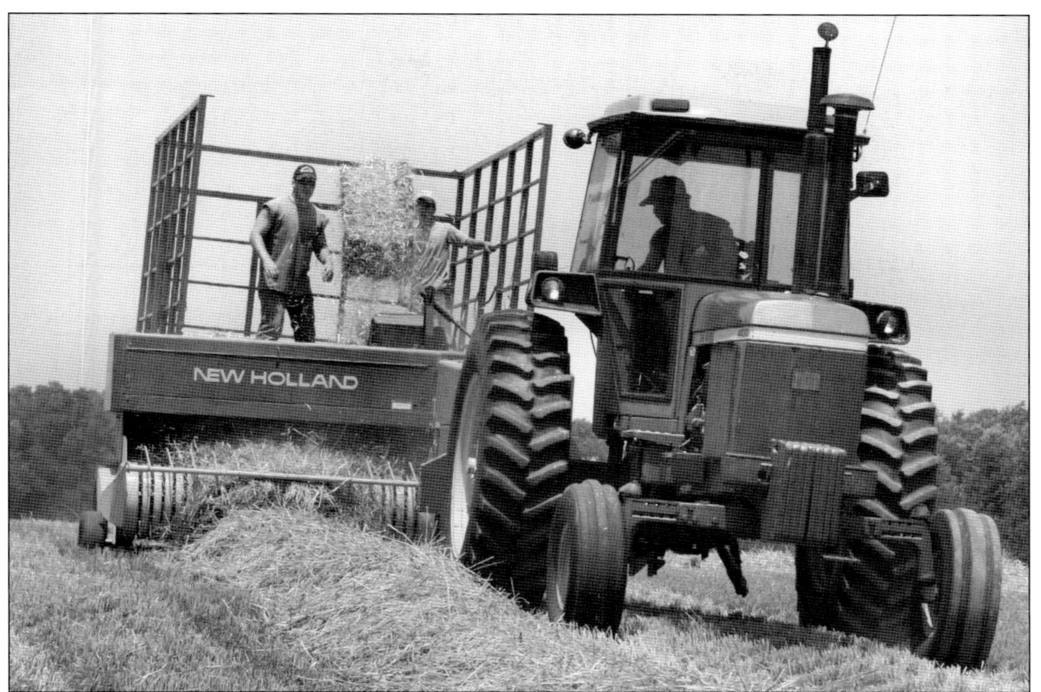

From left to right, Jeff Krumrine, Matt Talbert, and Robert L. Uhler (on tractor) are bailing wheat straw on Arnold Road in Westminster in July 2007. (Photograph by and courtesy of Diana F. Stager.)

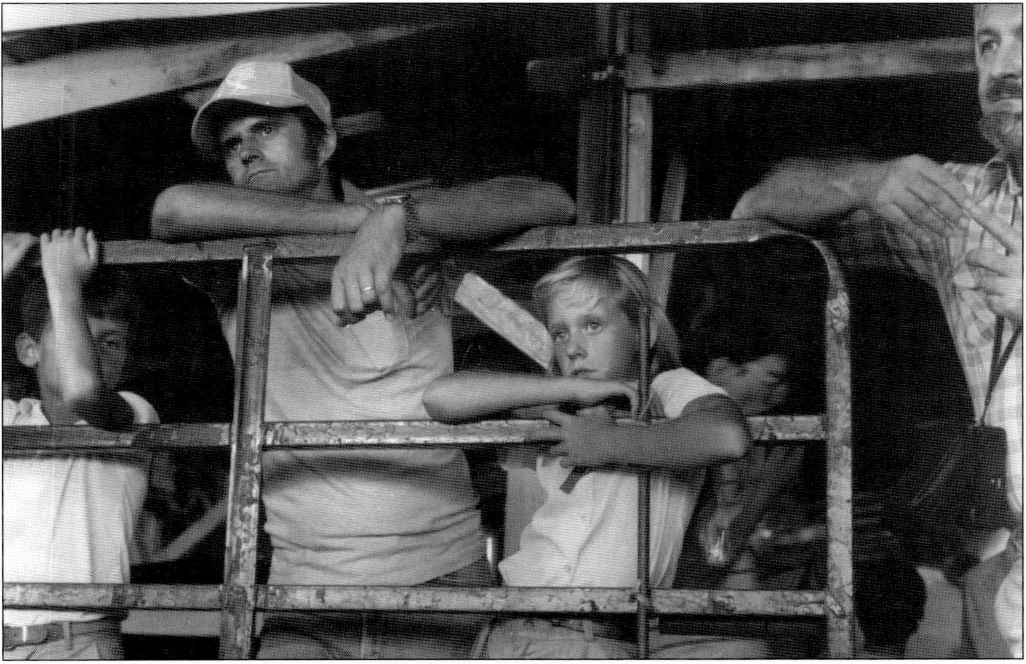

Watching the judging at the 4-H Fair are, from left to right, Brett Fogle (arms up), Dave Brummitt, and Brandy Brummitt. Some of the children at the fair every year will learn to be the future of farming in Carroll County. They are also lucky enough to have grown up on a farm. (Courtesy of Peggy Soper.)

www.arcadiapublishing.com

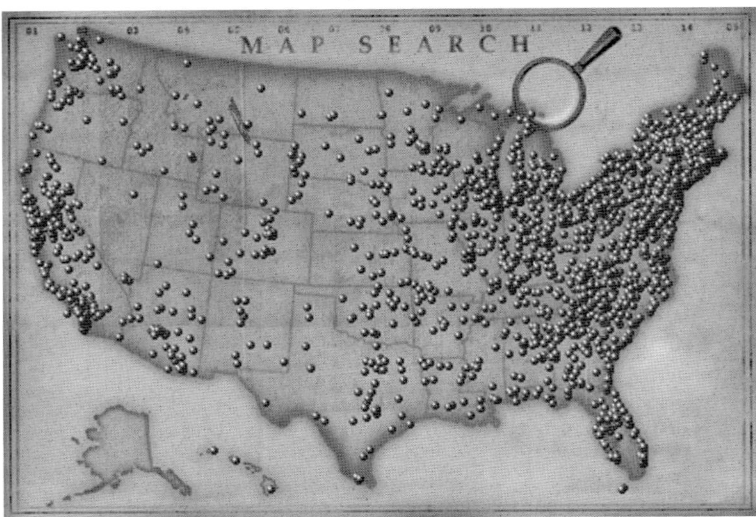

Discover books about the town where you grew up, the cities where your friends and families live, the town where your parents met, or even that retirement spot you've been dreaming about. Our Web site provides history lovers with exclusive deals, advanced notification about new titles, e-mail alerts of author events, and much more.

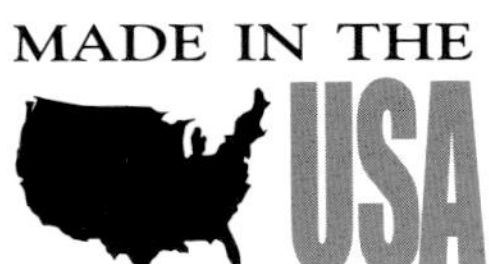

Arcadia Publishing, the leading local history publisher in the United States, is committed to making history accessible and meaningful through publishing books that celebrate and preserve the heritage of America's people and places. Consistent with our mission to preserve history on a local level, this book was printed in South Carolina on American-made paper and manufactured entirely in the United States.

This book carries the accredited Forest Stewardship Council (FSC) label and is printed on 100 percent FSC-certified paper. Products carrying the FSC label are independently certified to assure consumers that they come from forests that are managed to meet the social, economic, and ecological needs of present and future generations.

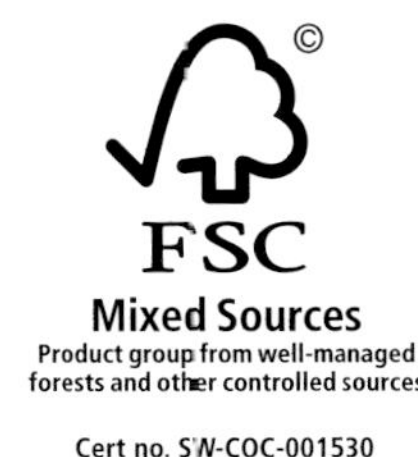

Mixed Sources
Product group from well-managed forests and other controlled sources

Cert no. SW-COC-001530
www.fsc.org

Find *Your* Place in History.